Acting: The First Six Lessons

Acting: The First Six Lessons is a key text for drama students today. These dramatic dialogues between the teacher and "the Creature"—an idealistic student—explore the "craft" of acting according to one of the godfathers of method acting. The book also features Boleslavsky's lectures to The Creative Theatre and American Laboratory Theatre, as well as "Acting with Maria Ouspenskaya," four short essays on the work of Ouspenskaya, his colleague and fellow actor trainer. This new edition is edited with an introduction and bibliography by Rhonda Blair, author of *The Actor, Image, and Action.*

Richard Boleslavsky (1889–1937) (born Ryszard Boleslawski) was a Polish actor and director. He was a member of the Moscow Art Theatre and director of its First Studio. He emigrated to New York in the 1920s and was the first teacher of the Stanislavski system of acting in the West. He went on to produce plays on Broadway and was a leading Hollywood director in the 1930s.

Rhonda Blair is Professor of Theatre at Southern Methodist University. She is a leading voice on the applications of cognitive science on the acting process and the author of *The Actor, Image, and Action: Acting and Cognitive Neuroscience.* She is currently the President of the American Society for Theatre Research (ASTR).

Acting: The First Six Lessons

Documents from the American Laboratory Theatre

Richard Boleslavsky

Edited and introduced by Rhonda Blair

LONDON AND NEW YORK

First published 2010
by Routledge
2 Park Square, Milton Park, Abingdon, Oxon OX14 4RN

Simultaneously published in the USA and Canada
by Routledge
270 Madison Avenue, New York, NY 10016

*Routledge is an imprint of the Taylor & Francis Group,
an informa business*

Originally published 1933 by Theatre Arts Books, Inc.
This edition © 2010 Routledge
Selection and editorial material © 2010 Rhonda Blair

Typeset in Sabon by Taylor & Francis Books
Printed and bound in the United States of America by
Edwards Brothers, Inc.

British Library Cataloguing in Publication Data
A catalogue record for this book is available from the British Library

Library of Congress Cataloging in Publication Data
Boleslavsky, Richard, 1889-1937.
  Acting : the first six lessons / by Richard Boleslavsky ; edited by
Rhonda Blair.
      p. cm.
  Includes bibliographical references.
  1. Acting. I. Blair, Rhonda, 1951- II. Title.
  PN2061.B55 2010
  792.02′8–dc22
                    2010002843

ISBN 13: 978-0-415-56385-7 (hbk)
ISBN 13: 978-0-415-56386-4 (pbk)
ISBN 13: 978-0-203-84723-7 (ebk)

Contents

Acknowledgments

My deep thanks must go first to Talia Rodgers for suggesting this project to me; this provided an excuse to return to material that I had long ago left behind—only to discover I had so much more to learn and appreciate about Boleslavsky's heritage. Many thanks to Sharon Carnicke and Laurence Senelick for directing me to a range of useful background sources and materials for Boleslavsky. My sincere appreciation to Robert Ellerman for corresponding and meeting with me about Boleslavsky, Stanislavsky, and Strasberg, and for providing a copy of the 1924–25 American Laboratory Theatre lectures, among other materials. Once again my former professor Ronald Willis has deeply informed my work; besides providing me with valuable insights on Boleslavsky and the American Laboratory Theatre, he also loaned me a wonderful and rather ancient copy of the Creative Theatre lectures. My thanks to our Meadows School of the Arts librarian, Amy Turner, for assistance in copyright research, and to my graduate assistant, Jamie Rezanour, for diligently typing and proofing the Boleslavsky lectures and Ouspenskaya essays. Niall Slater has been a patient and gracious shepherd; I am happily indebted to him for his effective facilitation of this project. As always, I am joyfully thankful to my partner Bill Beach for his support.

Editor's introduction
Boleslavsky and *Acting:*
The First Six Lessons

More than any other person, Polish actor, director, and teacher Richard Boleslavsky (February 4, 1889—January 17, 1937) is responsible for the initial dissemination of the teachings of Stanislavsky in the United States. As founder and central teacher at the American Laboratory Theatre (1923–29), he taught Stanislavsky's basic principles to hundreds of actors; here he had a profound influence on those who would become leading figures of the theatre over the next decade and who would teach Stanislavsky-based approaches to acting into the late twentieth century. His book, *Acting: The First Six Lessons*, made it possible for theatre practitioners across the country to have a primer in Stanislavsky. Published in 1933, it preceded the publication of Stanislavsky's *An Actor Prepares* by three years, and it has remained in print ever since. The basic materials in *Acting* in fact appeared even earlier: in his lectures at the Princess Theatre in 1923 (under the title "The Creative Theatre"); in lectures he gave at the Lab; and in a series of articles in *Theatre Arts Magazine* and *Theatre Arts Monthly* from 1923 to 1932. The book you hold was a crucial "first-wave" component in the dissemination of Stanislavsky-influenced principles among American actors. It is the first in any language ever to describe basic principles of Stanislavsky-based approaches to actor training, and it has remained in widespread use since its publication. *Acting* continues to be on the bookshelves of many actors and acting teachers.

Boleslavsky's credentials as an acolyte of Stanislavsky are impeccable. Admitted provisionally to the Moscow Art Theatre as a 17-year-old student actor in fall 1906, he joined the company in summer 1908 and was immediately cast in a wide range of roles, including that of Laertes in the infamous Gordon Craig production of *Hamlet*. His first role was that of Belyayev in Turgenev's *A Month in the Country*; here Boleslavsky was in on the ground floor of the earliest work on the System, for this production was Stanislavsky's "first coordinated effort to prove his new system of acting" (Roberts 1981: 18). In 1912 he was propitiously chosen to be an original member of MAT's First Studio; there he fell under the influence of Sulerzhitsky's Tolstoyan spirituality and developed a close relationship with Yevgeny Vakhtangov, both of whom would have a significant impact on his approach to theatre. Maria Ouspenskaya, who would work with Boleslavsky at the American Laboratory Theatre as the primary acting studio teacher, was also a member of the Studio, and it was during this time that the foundation for their relationship was laid. While continuing to act, Boleslavsky also quickly became a much-admired Studio director, and in 1916 he was invited to share leadership responsibilities at the Studio; his work with actors was marked by a "sharpening of the actor's expression, his 'stripping bare' of the characters" (Roberts 1981: 73), which Boleslavsky's biographer J. W. Roberts argues was in fact a precursor to Yevgeny Vakhtangov's "fantastic realism" – theatricality in support of emotional truthfulness (ibid.: 76). After serving in the cavalry in World War I and following the 1917 October Revolution, Boleslavsky managed to avoid arrest, unlike many other actors (even though he did not support the new communist regime). However, due to increasing government repression, Boleslavsky left Russia by early 1920, passing through Minsk, Warsaw, and Prague to direct and act with a number of companies, before arriving in New York in September 1922 with the *Revue Russe* (Willis 1968: 29).

When the Moscow Art Theatre arrived in New York on January 3, 1923 for its US tour, Boleslavsky rejoined the company as an actor and assistant to Stanislavsky. He was given Stanislavsky's blessing to deliver a series of lectures, beginning on January 18, at the Princess Theatre. These lectures, typically known as the Princess Theatre Lectures, were "the first enunciation of Stanislavsky's ideas publicly presented to an American audience" (Roberts 1981: 106); there is little doubt that these lectures are those recorded by Michael Barroy in "Creative Theatre" (Willis 1968: 31) and which are included here. These lectures describe the vision that guided Boleslavsky, first in his formulation of the American Laboratory Theatre, a theatre and school inspired by the work of the MAT that was formally established on June 29, 1923 (ibid.: 40), and then in writing *Acting*, published a decade later; the fundamental principles remain the same.

The American Laboratory Theatre, founded by Boleslavsky with the invaluable moral and financial support of a number of well-placed New Yorkers, most particularly Miriam and Herbert Stockton, was central to the course of twentieth-century American acting. The curriculum was multifaceted, addressing all aspects of actor training—mental, emotional, physical, and spiritual. The heart of the curriculum were lectures given by Boleslavsky and acting classes taught by him and by Ouspenskaya. Other components included voice, singing, eurythmics, fencing, ballet, art history, theatre design, and culture, sometimes taught by leading lights such as Norman Bel Geddes, Robert Edmond Jones, and Mortimer Adler. The Lab also regularly hosted guest speakers such as Jacques Copeau and George Pierce Baker. What Boleslavsky called the spiritual and creative components of the work were the most important for him; these encompassed the actor's work on sensitivity, imagination, and general cultural education. However, he believed that this aspect would be of limited efficacy unless it was supported by training in technique; students who were regularly enrolled followed a rigorous two-year regimen. In this regard he mirrored Stanislavsky, who was adamant about training the whole actor.

Among the Lab's students was Lee Strasberg, who attended classes consistently only in fall 1924; because he was unsure about the future prospects of the Lab, he soon left to work with the Theatre Guild, though two years later he returned for five months to attend Boleslavsky's special course for directors. Two of the other students on this course were Harold Clurman and Francis Ferguson (Roberts 1981: 27; Garfield 1980: 17). Stella Adler, already a well-established actor, began her studies at the Lab in fall 1925 and became a member of the Lab acting group in May 1926 (Roberts 1981: 153–54); other students who went on to substantial careers in theatre and film included the great film actor John Garfield (ibid.: 236). Throughout its existence the Lab was plagued by problems of finances and real estate; it moved almost every year and its patrons, particularly Miriam Stockton, often underwrote its debt. Beginning in 1927, Boleslavsky began taking on an increasing number of activities outside the Lab, directing in both theatre and film (ibid.: 189–93); from this time on he primarily lectured and rarely taught acting at the Lab. He left the Lab in early April 1929 (Willis 1968: 285), and the Lab ceased operations in summer 1930 as the Depression took hold. Boleslavsky continued directing and had some success in Hollywood, including directing the MGM film version of the Group Theatre's Broadway success, *Men in White*, in 1934 (Garfield 1980: 31). He died on January 17, 1937; it is believed the cause was a heart attack.

Acting: The First Six Lessons

Acting: The First Six Lessons is a primer on key principles of Stanislavsky-based approaches to acting. It is boiled down to six brief with Boleslavsky over what he (and by extension Stanislavsky) thought was most central to the actor's work: emotion or action. Reading these men's books and essays is a bit like reading the Bible: the writing is a product of its time and context is crucial. Quotations and passages from writing and talks, as well as statements from students, can be used to support a myriad of positions, but the texts support the position that both believed that action—the through-action or spine or desire— was the heart of acting ... and that it could not exist without emotion, a vital driver of action and of "artistic truth"—whether this be engaged through affective memory or by some other means. To use yet another "book" analogy, applying the principles in practice is like using a cookbook: one might have a list of all of the ingredients (rather like chapter titles), but the test is in the chemistry of their particular combination in the cooking—and *all* of the ingredients are essential. There is no evidence that Boleslavsky or Stanislavsky ever completely rejected an attachment either to action or to affective memory. What some might see as "mixed messages" (Gordon 2002: 38) can also be seen as variant articulations of how to address problems in acting, thereby acknowledging acting's contingent nature and the subjectivity involved in the process. One point on which Boleslavsky and Stanislavsky did differ was in the importance they gave to the playwright's text; though Stanislavsky's valuing of the playwright's contribution grew over time, from early on Boleslavsky regularly directed the actor to the value of a close engagement with the text (see Gordon 2002: 35–38).

There is little major scholarly critical writing on Boleslavsky, apart from the Roberts and Willis works cited and Jonathan Pitches' useful chapter on Boleslavsky and Lee Strasberg in his book on the Stanislavskian tradition and science (2006). This latter takes up in some detail the known influences of behaviorism (or reflexology, an early French and Russian incarnation of behaviorism), and succinctly considers the behavioral psychology that informed Boleslavsky. Pitches' discussion of possible influences of Freud is potentially useful as a way of opening up parts of Boleslavsky's work, but much of this is indeed hypothetical and runs counter to some of what is known about Boleslavsky and his thinking. Pitches' linkage of Boleslavsky and Strasberg in this chapter is understandable, but requires some caveats and contextualization. His discussion of the way Boleslavsky's view of action and feeling moved back and forth between emphasizing "emotion-driven action" versus "action-based emotion" (Pitches 2006: 96), depending upon which perspective would best solve the particular acting problem of the moment, nicely lays out how this might have created the ground for arguments between acting teachers more comfortable with objective (i.e., behaviorist) theories of emotion and those more comfortable with subjective (i.e., Freudian) views. What these binaristic views miss—a flaw that is reflected in the arguments of some of Boleslavsky's students who became our leading acting teachers—is that Boleslavsky's view was adamantly holistic in its recognition that action and emotion are inseparable. And, in spite of their fights with each other, the great teachers and students of Boleslavsky, Stella Adler and Lee Strasberg, ultimately held holistic views.

Boleslavsky's influence on US actors and acting teachers

Boleslavsky influenced a great many people, including myself, who are the spokesmen for Stanislavsky in this country, who have influenced the whole of the theatre and all of the movie industry. And it was Boleslavsky who did it. [...] My whole career I really owe to the Laboratory Theatre. I think that's true of everybody who studied there.

> (Stella Adler, interview with J. W. Roberts,
> October 21, 1975, quoted in Roberts 1981: 230)

The work that was being done [at the Lab] was, of course, decisive to my own career and has affected everything that I have done, so that Boleslavsky actually represents for me a major post in the history of the American theater in terms of the way in which the ideas of Stanislavsky got into the American stage. Without him I don't know what would have happened.

> (Lee Strasberg, interview with J. W. Roberts, October 11, 1975,
> quoted in Roberts 1981: 127)

I would say the whole atmosphere of the Group [Theatre] was so theoretical, and [the Lab] was totally the opposite of my experience with Boleslavsky, which was total love. [...] for me at any rate, you learn best with love. And in Boleslavsky there was tremendous love.

> (Ruth Nelson, interview with J. W. Roberts,
> quoted in Roberts 1981: 235)

During much of his time at the Lab, Boleslavsky's work with students was primarily in masterclasses and lectures, in which he took up key principles and tenets. Ouspenskaya was the one in the "trenches" teaching acting every year. "Boley," as he was nicknamed, is generally

1 The First Lesson

Concentration

Morning. My room. A knock at the door.

I: Come in. *(The door opens, slowly and timidly. Enter a Pretty Creature of eighteen. She looks at me with wide-open, frightened eyes and crushes her handbag violently.)*

THE CREATURE: I ... I ... I hear that you teach dramatic art.

I: No! I am sorry. Art cannot be taught. To possess an art means to possess talent. That is something one has or has not. You can develop it by hard work, but to create a talent is impossible. What I do is to help those who have decided to work on the stage, to develop and to educate themselves for honest and conscientious work in the theatre.

THE CREATURE: Yes, of course. Please help me. I simply love the theatre.

I: Loving the theatre is not enough. Who does not love it? To consecrate oneself to the theatre, to devote one's entire life to it, give it all one's thought, all one's emotions! For the sake of the theatre to give up everything, to suffer everything! And more important than all, to be ready to give the theatre everything—your entire being—expecting the theatre to give you nothing in return, not the least grain of what seemed to you so beautiful in it and so alluring.

THE CREATURE: I know. I played a great deal at school. I understand that the theatre brings suffering. I am not afraid of it. I am ready for anything if I can only play, play, play.

I: And suppose the theatre does not want you to play and play and play?

THE CREATURE: Why shouldn't it?

I: Because it might not find you talented.

THE CREATURE: But when I played at school ...

I: What did you play?

THE CREATURE: *King Lear.*

ground for arguments between acting teachers more comfortable with objective (i.e., behaviorist) theories of emotion and those more comfortable with subjective (i.e., Freudian) views. What these binaristic views miss—a flaw that is reflected in the arguments of some of Boleslavsky's students who became our leading acting teachers—is that Boleslavsky's view was adamantly holistic in its recognition that action and emotion are inseparable. And, in spite of their fights with each other, the great teachers and students of Boleslavsky, Stella Adler and Lee Strasberg, ultimately held holistic views.

Boleslavsky's influence on US actors and acting teachers

Boleslavsky influenced a great many people, including myself, who are the spokesmen for Stanislavsky in this country, who have influenced the whole of the theatre and all of the movie industry. And it was Boleslavsky who did it. [...] My whole career I really owe to the Laboratory Theatre. I think that's true of everybody who studied there.

> (Stella Adler, interview with J. W. Roberts,
> October 21, 1975, quoted in Roberts 1981: 230)

The work that was being done [at the Lab] was, of course, decisive to my own career and has affected everything that I have done, so that Boleslavsky actually represents for me a major post in the history of the American theater in terms of the way in which the ideas of Stanislavsky got into the American stage. Without him I don't know what would have happened.

> (Lee Strasberg, interview with J. W. Roberts, October 11, 1975,
> quoted in Roberts 1981: 127)

I would say the whole atmosphere of the Group [Theatre] was so theoretical, and [the Lab] was totally the opposite of my experience with Boleslavsky, which was total love. [...] for me at any rate, you learn best with love. And in Boleslavsky there was tremendous love.

> (Ruth Nelson, interview with J. W. Roberts,
> quoted in Roberts 1981: 235)

During much of his time at the Lab, Boleslavsky's work with students was primarily in masterclasses and lectures, in which he took up key principles and tenets. Ouspenskaya was the one in the "trenches" teaching acting every year. "Boley," as he was nicknamed, is generally described by his students as being warm and approachable; actress Blanche Tancock Hogg said of her first encounter with him,

> What I remember most about Boley was the wonderful way in which he set you at ease. [...] the predominant quality which seemed to flow from him was of kindness, great gentleness. I never knew him rough. He had a wonderful capacity for unlocking the person with whom he was talking, of relaxing their nervousness. And you found yourself speaking happily, sort of an outflowing – something that came from you, communicating with him.
> (Blanche Tancock Hogg, interview quoted in Willis 1968: 2)

Ouspenskaya, on the other hand, seems to have been almost the polar opposite. Hogg's comments are representative of what is typically heard from her students:

> [...] there was a sort of fierce, demanding quality in her relation to you when she was working with you. [...] I know I for one, and I think most people, were really terrified of her. Her classes were both a delight and a torture. [...] And once she had kind of broken you on the rack of this kind of horrible experience, from then on you had much more freedom, much less fear of showing emotion.
> (ibid.: 3–4)

While there is no doubt that the two artists worked in tandem to revolutionize American approaches to acting by passing on the fundamental principles of Stanislavsky, a number of factors affected students' understanding of what Boleslavsky and Ouspenskaya were imparting, not the least of which were language and culture. English was Boleslavsky's third language, after his native Polish and then Russian; according to reports, Ouspenskaya's English was even weaker (for example, the two teachers' accented use of the word "bit" to describe a piece of a play text was heard as "beat," and a new, mystifying term was born). Also, students received what was given through their own personal filters; as Sharon Carnicke has written, how students such as Strasberg and Adler received what Boleslavsky said "depended as much upon what [the] students expected to hear, as it did upon what Boleslavsky himself actually had to say. [...] Boleslavsky's students turned the oral transmission of knowledge into an art itself" (Carnicke 1998: 64). Ultimately, because we are talking about acting—an intensely subjective and ephemeral process—my sense is that all of the voices likely hold some truth.

Some may disagree about Boleslavsky's and Ouspenskaya's gifts and about what they stressed in their teaching, but there is no doubt that many who studied at the Lab and went on to significant careers in US theatre were profoundly influenced by them.

When the Group Theatre, arguably the most influential theatre in US history to date, was founded in 1929 by Strasberg, Clurman, and Cheryl Crawford, a good number of Lab students, including Stella Adler, became part of the company; inescapably, the atmosphere of the Group was permeated by the teachings and philosophy of Boleslavsky. But, because of the different backgrounds and proclivities of some of the key players, passionate disagreement arose quickly about what the teachings were, what was intended, and what—to put it quite simply—worked. A virtual cacophony of voices claimed to know the truth about Boleslavsky's teaching and sometimes, by extension, Stanislavsky, and the artistic and spiritual "Truth" of what they meant. The disagreement can be distilled as follows: "Affective memory is the core," "No, action is the core." "No, emotion!" "No, action!" This is embodied nowhere more clearly than in the arguments between (and about) Lee Strasberg and Stella Adler, who are traditionally aligned with emotion and action respectively. However, when one reads the record closely and reviews a range of responses not just about Boleslavsky, but also about the two Americans, it becomes evident that the perception of a polarized opposition between action and feeling is a deeply reductive one.

There is no doubt that intense conflict and antipathy existed between Adler and Strasberg. Drawing on her studies with Boleslavsky and Ouspenskaya, as well as on her weeks with Stanislavsky in Paris in 1936, Adler emphasized given circumstances, observation, and imagination in the service of action; she struggled with sense memory and emotion memory at the Group Theatre and was in great conflict with Strasberg about it, for whom it was central. While Strasberg was genuinely much taken by the Lab's system overall and the methodical and holistic approach it provided, he was particularly focused on relaxation, concentration, and affective memory (which Strasberg—problematically, I believe—broke into categories of sense and emotion memory); these were to remain central to his work throughout his career. Regardless of their differences, both Americans were heavily influenced by Boleslavsky's basic principles of relaxation, concentration, action, affective memory and/or imagination, and observation, and by Ouspenskaya's teaching of these principles.

Perhaps because of both the great emphasis Strasberg placed on affective memory and the myth that has grown up around him in this regard, it is easy to overlook the centrality of action to his Method, though he in fact foregrounds it in his writing. In his chapter on the Lab in *A Dream of Passion*, he is extremely clear that an understanding and appreciation of action, in the sense of motivated engagement, was a key part of what he took away from Boleslavsky and that he viewed action as "*the* essential element in the theatre":

> Action is not a literal paraphrase of [Boleslavsky's] words, nor a synonym for what transpires on the stage, nor a logical analysis of the scene. Action has always been *the* essential element in the theatre. The very word *actor* implies that. Every actor makes use of one or another kind of action.
>
> (Strasberg 1987: 75)

One way of understanding the difference between Strasberg and Adler is in their approach to action. Adler approached it through imagination and an extremely close engagement with the given circumstances (i.e. imaginary world) of the text; this is right in line with Boleslavsky's respect for the playwright's work. Strasberg approached action through an intense psychophysical engagement with memory and sensory experience in support of the play.

Ultimately both Strasberg and Adler are deeply indebted to Boleslavsky, and they have the same goal. At the center of their work is the actor's engagement of the senses through imagination for the purpose of the effective, active embodiment of the character. For both, the senses had to be trained to respond to imaginary stimuli for the purpose of embodiment and enactment; one key difference between their techniques lay in whether, simply put, the emphasis was on a remembered past or a fictive present. But this core of sense, feeling, and action is precisely what the first three chapters of *Acting* are about: concentration, memory of emotion, and dramatic action.

A note on Sanford Meisner: While Meisner never studied with Boleslavsky, as a member of the Group Theatre he learned the basic principles taught to Strasberg, Adler, and others at the Lab. In fact, his assertion that "The most important single element to me [...] is the reality of doing" (Meisner, in Soloviova et al. 1964: 155) strongly echoes both Boleslavsky's primacy of action and Maria Ouspenskaya's focus on doing: Boleslavsky—"The action – that means doings, achievements – is the foundation of dramatic art" (Boleslavsky Lectures 10–11 [57]); Ouspenskaya—"At the beginning of your work, do not do any characterization that will lead you away from the five senses. *Really* see, instead of *acting* seeing. *Don't act, do*" (Pratt 1954). Meisner, with his focus on concentration, doing, and observation, is part of the Boleslavsky "family."

Boleslavsky and cognitive science

Boleslavsky urged his students to understand acting within a holistic context, in which action, affective memory, emotion, and imagination are ultimately inseparable. In this regard, he and those who were influenced by him are direct heirs of Stanislavsky, who was both intensely spiritual and yet highly pragmatic in his use of the psychology of his day, particularly the work of Theodule Ribot. Ribot and his colleagues operated from a materialistic perspective that envisioned all aspects of the person as being organic—of the organism—unlike earlier views that separated mind from body or feeling from reason. This holistic view of the actor connects all Stanislavsky-based acting methods to research in the cognitive sciences of the past quarter century.

Cognitive science supports much of the basic structure of Stanislavsky-based teaching, particularly in the connections it makes among attention (which, for our purposes here, includes concentration), action, imagination, memory, and feeling. There is a strong congruence between Boleslavsky's and Stanislavsky's key terms and cognitive linguist Stephen Pinker's description of the main features of consciousness *"sensory awareness, focal attention, emotional coloring, and the will"* (Pinker 1997: 136, italics in original). These traits are also aligned with Stanislavsky's three inner motive forces—mind, will, and feeling (Stanislavsky 2002: 271–77), which are also echoed in Boleslavsky. In his Creative Theatre lecture entitled "What is an Actor?" Boleslavsky describes the actor as containing two entities: the "artist creator," which is the individual's innate talent (to use Boleslavsky's term) and the "creative material," which itself has two parts, the external and the inner, each requiring "thorough study and training." The inner part consists of

> the *intellect*, the *will* and the *emotions* – three separate parts which allow the actor to attain the chief essential in his art, the ability to *"live* through his role". Only the actor who is able to *"live"* his part can expect to create a bit of "better life". Only by developing his intellect, his will and his emotions can he learn how to "live" his parts.
> (Boleslavsky "The Creative Theatre": "4. What is an actor?")

This reflects inherent features of the way we function neurocognitively and which are the basis for a technique that allows self-manipulation to trigger things to happen in the body. The actor basically manipulates herself or, in acting school parlance, she engages in self-use to construct a character and, e.g., to access the unconscious by conscious means. This self-use is founded on the way in which the self is constructed.

Our sense of self develops as we become aware of ourselves in relationship to something and responding to it—i.e., *doing* something to maximize survival. *Doing* in reaction to something is the ground of consciousness. Neuroscientist Antonio Damasio and others posit a kind of proto-narrative as the beginning of consciousness: the organism imagines a rudimentary "story" in which it (the self) encounters something (an object, external or internal) that causes it to react, thereby causing changes in the organism. This begins with something as simple as moving toward pleasure or nourishment and away from pain or danger. This should sound familiar to anyone who has studied Stanislavsky-based acting, and possibly especially Meisner. It also parallels theatre's very being as embodied narrative:

> Consciousness begins when brains acquire the power [...] of telling a story without words, the story that there is life ticking away in an organism, and that the states of the living organism, within body bounds, are continuously being altered by encounters with objects or events in its environment, or for that matter, by thoughts and by internal adjustments of the life process. Consciousness emerges when this primordial story – the story of an object causally changing the state of the body – can be told using the universal nonverbal vocabulary of [neural and chemical] body signals. The apparent self emerges as the feeling of a feeling.
>
> (Damasio 1999: 30–31)

A preconscious narrative provides the organism with an elemental story about its basic condition; the story arises when the organism begins glimmeringly to become aware of and then registers the feelings of the neural and chemical events of the body, which it uses to define itself—a self—in relationship to objects and events. Stanislavsky-based principles such as "throughgoing action" or Boleslavsky's "spine" are all about helping the actor devise an image-based narrative to carry her effectively through the play. (An interesting side note: the Russian word for "consciousness" is *samochuvstvo*—literally "self[*sam*]-feeling[*chuvstvo*]," i.e., the feeling, or experiencing, of a self.)

Actors are involved in creating fictional selves. This is in essence what any human being does every waking moment; the mind basically creates a fictional self out of the very small portion of the brain's activities that actually reach consciousness. One neuroscientist asserts with good evidence that "98% of what the brain does is outside of consciousness awareness" (Gazzaniga 1998: 21). Our conscious sense of self is necessarily selective and filtered, i.e., "fictional," depending on what story we're trying to tell ourselves at any given moment. This conscious self, a culmination of our biology, developed as a survival tool that maximized human evolutionary potential by making it possible for us to become *aware* of being a self, an entity, in a particular situation. The ability of the brain to portray "the living organism in the act of relating to an object" leads to, among other things, the ability of the organism to imagine its self in potential—not just actual—situations. Stanislavsky-based systems fundamentally mirror this, for they ask the actor to imagine and experience a fictive self engaged with issues of survival or thriving that ultimately involve, affect, and change the body. The actor plays out a variation on the organism–object relationship in order to embody a character: she engages internal (mental) and external objects of the text and its given circumstances, integrates these with her own mental objects that are derived from memory and personal history, and devises a pattern of behavior—typically a course of action related to the character's desire to acquire or avoid something. This sketch of what the actor does is reductive, but generally accurate: what characters do is engage with issues of survival and prosperity in one form or another, whether they be physical, economic, emotional, sexual, or spiritual.

Key attributes of consciousness, which grows out of the sense of a self, have correlatives in the vocabulary of Stanislavsky-based systems to connect the science directly to elements in approaches to acting and character. Among the key terms are self (as described above), consciousness, reason, environment, behavior, attention, emotion, feeling, memory, and imagination. The following thumbnail descriptions lay out parallels in principles and terminology between Boleslavsky and some of the recent science:

Consciousness and *reason* can be connected to points at which a character registers *given circumstances* in a play. Consciousness has to do with the organism's awareness of and ability to respond to the *environment*—another word for given circumstances; these include anything the actor has to take into consideration, including the play's story, the conditions and history of the play's setting, the particular interpretations being used, and all physical elements of the production. In short—the entirety of all the conditions affecting the actor-character in her immediate and extended environment, especially in relationship to her history and agency. More particularly, this can be connected to Boleslavsky's emphasis on concentration, the topic of his first lesson.

He is adamant that the actor must be closely—or, in his words, spiritually—attuned to her environment, and she must be able to take in and experience her surroundings fully and in specific detail.

Behavior is a correlative for *action*, i.e., the organism/character does or attempts certain things out of necessity or desire, in order to negotiate her environment; "behavior" is, of course, also a word commonly used in film-oriented approaches to acting to describe the actor's successful replication of naturalistic, non-"theatrical" (even anti-theatrical) activities. All of these refer to a person, character, or organism engaging in some activity that the organism generally experiences as moving itself toward pleasure or comfort and away from pain or discomfort. In Boleslavsky, as in biology, things ultimately come down to the organism taking action—engaging in tasks—to solve problems.

Attention is resonant with concentration and point of focus—being present and able to respond as fully as possible to one's environment. In formal neuroscientific terms, attention is what allows the organism to prioritize and engage elements in its environment, sorting through stimuli and focusing on what might affect it positively or negatively in the most immediate way. Being able to direct our attention allows us to take care of what matters most, by allowing us to focus our imagination and actions: I may be intently involved in making love, but the smell of smoke or the sound of a gunshot nearby might (and would, I hope) draw my attention and cause me to get out of bed and leave immediately. This parallels Stanislavsky's *point of attention* and *circle of attention* and Boleslavsky's emphasis on concentration and observation: the actor manipulates the direction of her concentration, aided by imagination, in order to pursue the character's task successfully.

Emotion and *feeling*, terms fundamental to consciousness and to acting, are similar in both cognitive science and in acting, though they are parsed somewhat differently. In the science, "emotion" is the preconscious physiological response to an internal or external situation, i.e., it is a body-state, while "feeling" is the conscious registration of that body-state. Feeling is emotion made conscious—"*the perception of a certain state of the body along with the perception of a certain mode of thinking and of thoughts with certain themes*" (Damasio 1999: 86). To use Damasio's apt metaphor, "Emotions play out in the theater of the body. Feelings play out in the theater of the mind" (ibid.: 28). Feelings may in fact be the beginning of what it means to be human, for they could be an essential link between being and knowing, i.e., between mere existence and consciousness (ibid.: 43). Put another way, feeling is how we register and interpret emotions; thus, consciousness begins with the "*feeling of a feeling.*" This is crucial in understanding the nature of feeling in the actor's work. The movement from emotion to conscious feeling is an *enchained* process: the inducer of the emotion (the internal or external object perceived by the organism) produces an automated emotion in neural sites, which leads to a feeling, which leads to the organism *knowing* the feeling, i.e., becoming aware of the feeling in a second-order processing of the encounter with the object (ibid.: 291). Being aware of feelings—i.e., consciously registering emotions—allows us to be innovative and creative in our responses to the thing causing the emotion. The great degree of interpretation involved in translating emotional and body states into feeling reinforces the idea that the actor must think creatively and adventurously in imagining a role, and in responding to and using emotion and feeling. Stanislavsky-based systems have, as a substantial component, techniques that allow for the manipulation and mastery of processes of affective and imaginative enchainment.

Memory, a way of processing and using experience to maximize survival, can be viewed as a kind of learning. In the most basic terms, a memory is a neurochemical event—the activation of a neural pattern, the firing of a set of neuronal connections. Memory is intensely fluid and dynamic, and it is crucial for the actor to come to terms with this in using the activation of memory as part of her process. Neural reconsolidation is involved in memory retrieval, regardless of the kind of memory. For any memory, a synaptic pattern needs to be reactivated through a neurochemical process, i.e., "if you take a memory out of storage you have to make new proteins (you have to restore, or reconsolidate, it) in order for the memory to remain a memory." Possibly the most radical corollary of this is that "the brain that does the remembering is not the brain that formed the initial memory" (LeDoux 2002: 161). That is, memory is "an imaginative reconstruction, or construction, built out of the relation of our attitude toward a whole active mass of past experience" (ibid: 177).

This makes concepts such as affective memory and sense memory not necessarily false, but more complex than they might initially seem; in some ways, *any* memory is an affective memory, because it causes a change in the body. Actors regularly use past emotional and kinesthetic experiences to connect ourselves more immediately to a character's situation; in much standard actor training this is seen as reliving an experience or reconstructing an emotional or sensory state to reach a kind of truthfulness and authenticity. However, we are not in fact reliving anything; we are having a new experience in the moment, drawing on experiences of the past, shaped by our current condition and imagination. Memory is not a completely accurately retrievable truth, nor is it an object, in the sense of being a "fact." Rather, it is a reconstruction whose nature is affected by the context in which the retrieval occurs. A view of memories as processes, not objects, can allow us to manipulate memory more effectively as a tool for acting. There is a richer and more productive interpenetration of the biological, psychological, and imaginative than was ever imagined by the master acting teachers.

In some ways, Boleslavsky's vision of memory is understandably problematic, in that, given his era, he viewed memories as something to be retrieved, rather than as neural reconstructions. However, his view is productive in that it does *not* separate out the physical from the emotional. He specifically uses the term "affective memory"; it is Strasberg who generally separates this into "sense memory" and "emotion memory." Affective memory seems more apt because it reinforces the truth of our holistic natures, of "feeling" being a word that operates in a multifaceted way—even along a continuum—and that can be applied to physical, emotional, and intellectual experiences, among others.

Even *imagination* is part of our evolutionary survival kit; it has an organic source and serves a pragmatic function. The evolutionary development of the brain links the "world of homeostasis" and the "world of imagination." The former world is that of the biological maintenance of the organism within the narrow parameters required for survival and organic balance. The latter is that of image-making, in which the organism envisions or projects possible conditions and outcomes that allow it to adjust its behavior to maximize homeostasis. What this means is that the autonomic drive for homeostasis, i.e., the automatic ways in which our bodies regulate themselves, is fundamental to the biology of consciousness; without the body's homeostatic functions, there would be no source of—or need for—imagination. Imagination is the result the brain's evolutionary development and is essential to the fact of our physicality, not just our psyches. Actors get at imagination and attention by engaging the senses—the visual, aural, olfactory, and kinesthetic—i.e., through the body. Our direct experience of the link between the imagination and the body is perhaps most obviously evident in basic responses such as blushing, blanching, palpitations, or trembling, which can occur in response to embarrassing or frightening situations, whether real or merely imagined. Imagination, in not just its psychological, but also its physical dimensions, is a basic component of consciousness. For Boleslavsky, it is the very essence of our art: "The theatre is all imagination" (Boleslavsky Lab Lectures, 7–6 in ms.).

The cultivation and manipulation of imagination—the process of seeing and being in a story that is simultaneously fictive and real—in the service of the actor's embodiment of an inner life is the heart of Boleslavsky's teaching. In this he is precisely in line with his mentor, Stanislavsky, and with much of what the mind and brain sciences of the last few decades have discovered about how we work and live and dream. Given the cross-cultural, political, and linguistic challenges related to the dissemination of Stanislavsky's work, we are indebted to Boleslavsky's choice to come to the US to teach actors here. As Lee Strasberg said, "Without him I don't know what would have happened."

Resources

Boleslavsky, Richard (1923). "The Creative Theatre." Ms. New York: New York Public Library, Lincoln Center.

——(1932). "A Fifth Lesson in Acting: A Pseudo-Morality." *Theatre Arts Magazine* 16, 4 (April 1932), 294–98.

——(1923). "The First Lesson in Acting: A Pseudo-Morality." *Theatre Arts Magazine* 7 (October 1923), 284–92.

——(1932). "A Fourth Lesson in Acting: A Pseudo-Morality." *Theatre Arts Monthly* 16, 2 (Feb. 1932), 121–28.

——(1924–25?). Lectures at the American Laboratory Theatre. Ms.

——(1929). "A Second Lesson in Acting: A Pseudo-Morality." *Theatre Arts Monthly* 13, 7 (July 1929), 498–505.

——(1932). "A Sixth Lesson in Acting: A Pseudo-Morality." *Theatre Arts Monthly* 16, 6 (June 1932), 477–83.

——(1931). "A Third Lesson in Acting: A Pseudo-Morality." *Theatre Arts Monthly* 15, 7 (July 1931), 608–12.

Boleslavski, Richard and Helen Woodward (1932). *Lances Down.* Indianapolis: Bobbs-Merrill.

—— (1932). *The Way of the Lancer.* Indianapolis: Bobbs-Merrill.

Carnicke, Sharon M. (1998). *Stanislavsky in Focus: an Acting Master for the Twenty-first Century*, 2nd ed. London and New York: Routledge.

Damasio, Antonio (1999). *The Feeling of What Happens: Body and Emotion in the Making of Consciousness.* New York: Harcourt Brace.

Garfield, David (1980). *A Player's Place: the Story of the Actors Studio.* New York: Macmillan.

Gazzaniga, Michael (1998). *The Mind's Past.* Berkeley: University of California Press.

Gordon, Marc (2002). *Stanislavsky in America: Russian Émigré Teachers of Acting.* Medford, MA: Tufts University dissertation.

LeDoux, Joseph (2002). *Synaptic Self: How Our Brains Become Who We Are.* New York: Viking.

Pinker, Steven (1997). *How the Mind Works.* New York: Norton.

Pitches, Jonathan (2006). *Science and the Stanislavsky Tradition of Acting.* London and New York: Routledge.

Pratt, Harriet (1954–55). "Notes on Acting with Maria Ouspenskaya." *American Repertory Theater: The Art Magazine*. Los Angeles: American Repertory Theatre, October 1954, November 1954, December 1954, January 1955.

Roberts, J. W. (1981). *Richard Boleslavsky, His Life and Work in the Theatre*. Ann Arbor: UMI Research Press.

Soloviova, Vera, Stella Adler, and Sanford Meisner. "The reality of doing." *Tulane Drama Review*, Vol. 9, Number 1 (Fall 1964), 136–55.

Stanislavsky, Konstantin (2002). *An Actor's Work: a Student's Diary*. Ed. Jean Benedetti. London and New York: Routledge.

Strasberg, Lee (1987). *A Dream of Passion: the Development of the Method*. Ed. Evangeline Morphos. Boston: Little, Brown.

Willis, Ronald A. (1964). "The American Lab Theatre." *Tulane Drama Review* 9, 1 (Fall), 112–16.

Willis, Ronald Arthur (1968). *The American Laboratory Theatre, 1923–1930*. Ames: University of Iowa dissertation.

Acting: The First Six Lessons

Richard Boleslavsky

Introduction

The *Way of the Lancer* brought immediate literary acclaim to Richard Boleslavski, spelled with an "i" after the manner of his Polish ancestors. The book was variously called a work of genius, the best human document of the events preceding the Russian Revolution, a masterly narrative biography, a new writing of history. But no matter what else critics said of it, they almost invariably added that it was intensely dramatic, obviously the work of a mind trained in the theatre. As rightly they might say, for the uniform of an officer of the Polish Lancers and the change from "y" to "i" was no disguise for Richard Boleslavsky, an actor of the Moscow Art Theatre, Director of the Moscow Art Theatre Studio and, in America, Director of the Laboratory Theatre, of many successful plays on Broadway, of films in Hollywood.

What many of the critics seemed to miss, however, in this splendid book and its sequel, *Lances Down*, was the fact that Boleslavsky's style and point of view, dramatic as it undoubtedly was, had little to do with the art of the writer of plays. *Way of the Lancer* was not the product of a dramatist's mind, turned narrator, but of an actor's mind. One is almost the converse of the other. The actor is usually word-shy and inarticulate. Often he does not know what it is he does or how he does it, that makes him an actor. Even when he knows, it is difficult for him to say it or write it. He can only express it in action. His language is a language of movement, of gesture, of voice, of the creation and projection of character by things done or left undone. The dramatist, on the other hand, works easily with words, writes fluently, interprets character, situation, and events, manner and method in his own terms. So far as the art and the craft of acting have been written of at all, it is usually the dramatist or the critic who has written of them. That is why there is so little in print really to explain the actor to himself and to his fellows.

Talma, Fanny Kemble, Coquelin and, among the moderns, Louis Calvert and Stanislavsky stand out as actors who have tried to interpret acting. But Stanislavsky's fine contribution is welded into the text of his autobiography, *My Life in Art*, and all the rest are, generally speaking, an effort to create a philosophy of acting rather than to analyze the elements of the art of acting or to establish a technique for the player. Must an actor have experienced an emotion to portray it; will he portray it better if he actually renews the feeling every time he assumes it; shall acting be far removed from life, or as close to it as possible? Such are the problems these actor-philosophers set themselves to solve. And with the illustrations drawn from high experience, their writings have greatly illumined the field. They have clarified the fundamental laws of the art for many artists. But they do not help an actor to learn the elements of his craft.

So that, in a way, these essays of Boleslavsky's, these *First Lessons in Acting*, in dialogue form, stand alone in their field. Gayly as they are told, there is not a word in any of them that is not seriously to the point, that is not calculated, out of long years of work and study as an actor and as a director in the professional and in the art theatre, to help a young actor on his way. They actually select his tools for him and show him how to use them. And that is a grateful task. For while an actor's tools are all within his own body and mind and spirit, they are by their very nearness harder to isolate and put to special use than tools of wood and iron. Concentration and observation, experience and memory, movement and poise, creation and projection—an actor must make them all the servants of his talent.

In an article he wrote some years ago on the *Fundamentals of Acting*, Boleslavsky himself defined the field he covers here. "The actor's art," he said, "cannot be taught. He must be born with ability; but the technique, through which his talent can find expression—that can and must be taught. An appreciation of this fact is of the utmost importance, not only to students of acting but to every actor who is interested in the perfection of his art. For, after all, technique is something which is perfectly realistic and quite possible to make one's own."

The basis of this technique, the mere development of the actor's physical resources, although he recognizes and stresses its importance, is not what Boleslavsky calls "technique". The training of the body he likens rather to the tuning up of an instrument. "Even the most perfectly tuned violin," he goes on to say, "will not play by itself, without the musician to make it sing. The equipment of the ideal actor ... is not complete unless he has ... the technique of an 'emotion maker' or creator; unless he can follow the advice of Joseph Jefferson to 'Keep your heart warm and your head cool'. Can it be done? Most certainly! It is merely necessary to think of life as an unbroken sequence of two different kinds of steps. ... Problem steps and Action steps. ... The first step is for the actor to understand what the problem is that confronts him. Then the spark of the will pushes him toward dynamic action. ... When an actor realizes that the solution of a certain part may consist merely in being able first, to stand on the stage for perhaps no more than one-five-hundredth of a second, cool-headed and firm of purpose, aware of the problem before him; and then in the next one-five-hundredth of a second or, it may be, five or ten seconds, to precipitate himself intensely into the action which the situation requires, he will have achieved the perfect technique of acting."

First to know rightly what to do, and then to do it rightly. That is all. It seems little enough. But it is not by chance that Boleslavsky puts the visits of *The Creature*, who is the subject of these lessons, months, sometimes years, apart. He is thinking practically, not wishfully. He knows the length of the road she will need to travel between lessons. He knows that in acting more than in any other art a little less than good is worlds away from good. An actor cannot be made between luncheon and dinner. He accepts the fact that the profession may take a lifetime of work and that it is a profession well worth the work of a lifetime.

Edith J. R. Isaacs

1   The First Lesson

Concentration

Morning. My room. A knock at the door.

I: Come in. *(The door opens, slowly and timidly. Enter a Pretty Creature of eighteen. She looks at me with wide-open, frightened eyes and crushes her handbag violently.)*

THE CREATURE: I ... I ... I hear that you teach dramatic art.

I: No! I am sorry. Art cannot be taught. To possess an art means to possess talent. That is something one has or has not. You can develop it by hard work, but to create a talent is impossible. What I do is to help those who have decided to work on the stage, to develop and to educate themselves for honest and conscientious work in the theatre.

THE CREATURE: Yes, of course. Please help me. I simply love the theatre.

I: Loving the theatre is not enough. Who does not love it? To consecrate oneself to the theatre, to devote one's entire life to it, give it all one's thought, all one's emotions! For the sake of the theatre to give up everything, to suffer everything! And more important than all, to be ready to give the theatre everything—your entire being—expecting the theatre to give you nothing in return, not the least grain of what seemed to you so beautiful in it and so alluring.

THE CREATURE: I know. I played a great deal at school. I understand that the theatre brings suffering. I am not afraid of it. I am ready for anything if I can only play, play, play.

I: And suppose the theatre does not want you to play and play and play?

THE CREATURE: Why shouldn't it?

I: Because it might not find you talented.

THE CREATURE: But when I played at school ...

I: What did you play?

THE CREATURE: *King Lear.*

I: What part did you play in this trifle?

THE CREATURE: King Lear himself. And all my friends and our professor of literature and even Aunt Mary told me I played wonderfully and that I certainly had talent.

I: Pardon me, I don't mean to criticize the nice people whom you name, but are you sure that they are connoisseurs of talent?

THE CREATURE: Our professor is very strict. He himself worked with me on King Lear. He is a great authority.

I: I see, I see. And Aunt Mary?

THE CREATURE: She met Mr. Belasco personally.

I: So far, so good. But can you tell me how your professor, when working on King Lear, wanted you to play these lines, for instance: "Blow winds, and crack your cheeks! Rage! Blow!"

THE CREATURE: Do you want me to play it for you?

I: No. Just tell me how you learned to read those lines. What were you trying to attain?

THE CREATURE: I had to stand this way, my feet well together, incline my body forward a little, lift my head like this, stretch out my arms to heaven and shake my fists. Then I had to take a deep breath and burst into sarcastic laughter—ha! ha! ha! (*She laughs, a charming, childish laugh. Only at happy eighteen can one laugh that way.*) Then, as though cursing heaven, as loud as possible pronounce the words: "Blow winds and crack your cheeks! Rage! Blow!"

I: Thank you, that is quite enough for a clear understanding of the part of King Lear, as well as for a definition of your talent. May I ask you one more thing? Will you, if you please, say this sentence, first cursing the heavens and then without cursing them. Just keep the sense of the phrase—only its thought. (*She doesn't think long, she is accustomed to curse heaven.*)

THE CREATURE: When you curse the heavens, you say it this way: "Blooooow wiiiiinds, and Craaaaack your cheeks, Raaaaage Blooooow." (THE CREATURE *tries very hard to curse the heavens but through the window I see the azure heavens laughing at the curse. I do the same.*) And without cursing them, I must do it some other way. Well ... I don't know how. ... Isn't it funny? Well, this way: (THE CREATURE *becomes confused and, with a charming smile, swallowing the words, hurriedly pronounces them all on one note.*) "Blowwindsandcrackyourcheeksrageblow." (*She becomes completely confused and tries to destroy her handbag. A pause.*)

I: How strange! You are so young; you do not hesitate a second before cursing heaven. Yet you are unable to speak these words simply and plainly, to show their inner meaning. You want to play a Chopin

Nocturne without knowing where the notes are. You grimace, you mutilate the words of the poet and eternal emotion, and at the same time you do not possess the most elemental quality of a literate man—an ability to transmit the thoughts, feelings, and words of another logically. What right have you to say that you have worked in the theatre? You have destroyed the very conception of the word Theatre. *(A pause; the Creature looks at me with the eyes of one innocently condemned to death. The little handbag lies on the floor.)*

THE CREATURE: So I must never play?

I: And if I say *Never? (Pause. The eyes of the Creature change their expression. She looks straight into my soul with a sharp scrutinizing look, and seeing that I am not joking, clenches her teeth, and tries in vain to hide what is happening in her soul. But it is no use. One enormous real tear rolls out of her eye, and the Creature at that moment becomes dear to me. It spoils my intentions completely. She controls herself, clenches her teeth, and says in a low voice—)*

THE CREATURE: But I am going to play. I have nothing else in my life. *(At eighteen they always talk that way. But just the same I am deeply touched.)*

I: All right then. I must tell you that this very moment you did more for the theatre, or rather for yourself in the theatre, than you did in playing all your parts. You suffered just now; you felt deeply. Those are two things without which you cannot do in any art and especially in the art of the theatre. Only by paying this price can you attain the happiness of creation, the happiness of the birth of a new artistic value. To prove that, let us work together right now. Let us try to create a small, but real, artistic value according to your strength. It will be the first step in your development as an actress. *(The enormous, beautiful tear is forgotten. It disappeared somewhere into space. A charming, happy smile appears instead. I never thought my creaking voice could produce such a change.)*

Listen and answer sincerely. Have you ever seen a man, a specialist, busy on some creative problem in the course of his work? A pilot on an ocean liner, for instance, responsible for thousands of lives, or a biologist working at his microscope, or an architect working out the plan of a complicated bridge, or a great actor seen from the wings during his interpretation of a fine part?

THE CREATURE: I saw John Barrymore from the wings when he was playing *Hamlet.*

I: What impressed you chiefly as you watched him?

THE CREATURE: He was *marvelous!!!*

I: I know that, but what else?

THE CREATURE: He paid no attention to me.

I: That is more important; not only not to you but to nothing around him. He was acting in his work as the pilot would, the scientist, or the architect—he was concentrating. Remember this word *Concentrate*. It is important in every art and especially in the art of the theatre. Concentration is the quality which permits us to direct all our spiritual and intellectual forces toward one definite object and to continue as long as it pleases us to do so—sometimes for a time much longer than our physical strength can endure. I knew a fisherman once who, during a storm, did not leave his rudder for forty-eight hours, concentrating to the last minute on his work of steering his schooner. Only when he had brought the schooner back safely into the harbor did he allow his body to faint. This strength, this certainty of power over yourself, is the fundamental quality of every creative artist. You must find it within yourself, and develop it to the last degree.

THE CREATURE: But how?

I: I will tell you. Don't hurry. The most important thing is that in the art of the theatre a special kind of concentration is needed. The pilot has a compass, the scientist has his microscope, the architect his drawings—all external, visible objects of concentration and creation. They have, so to speak, a *material* aim, to which all their force is directed. So has a sculptor, a painter, a musician, an author. But it is quite different with the actor. Tell me, what do you think is the object of his concentration?

THE CREATURE: His part.

I: Yes, until he learns it. But it is only after studying and rehearsing that the actor *starts* to create. Or rather let us say that at first he creates "searchingly" and on the opening night he begins to create "constructively" in his acting. And what is acting?

THE CREATURE: Acting? Acting is when he ... acts acts ... I don't know.

I: You want to consecrate all your life to a task without knowing what it is? Acting is *the life of the human soul receiving its birth through art*. In a creative theatre the object for an actor's concentration is the *human soul*. In the first period of his work—the searching—the object for concentration is his own soul and those of the men and women who surround him. In the second period—the constructive one—only his own soul. Which means that, to act, you must know how to concentrate on something materially imperceptible,—on something which you can perceive only by penetrating deeply into your own entity, recognizing what would be evidenced in life only in a moment of the greatest emotion and most violent struggle. In other words, you need a spiritual concentration on emotions which do not exist, but are invented or imagined.

THE CREATURE: But how can one develop in oneself something which does not exist. How can one start?

I: From the very beginning. Not from a Chopin Nocturne but from the simplest scales. Such scales are your five senses: sight, hearing, smell, touch, and taste. They will be the key of your creation like a scale for a Chopin Nocturne. Learn how to govern this scale, how with your entire being to concentrate on your senses, to make them work artificially, to give them different problems and create the solutions.

THE CREATURE: I hope you don't mean to say that I don't even know how to listen or how to feel.

I: In life you may know. Nature has taught you a little. *(She becomes very daring and speaks as though challenging the whole world.)*

THE CREATURE: No, on the stage, too.

I: Is that so? Let us see. Please, just as you are sitting now, listen to the scratching of an imaginary mouse in that corner.

THE CREATURE: Where is the audience?

I: That doesn't concern you in the least. Your audience is in no hurry as yet to buy tickets for your performance. Forget about it. Do the problem I give you. Listen to the scratching of a mouse in that corner.

THE CREATURE: All right. *(There follows a helpless gesture with the right and then the left ear which has nothing in common with listening to the delicate scratching of a mouse's paw in the silence.)*

I: All right. Now please listen to a symphony orchestra playing the march from *Aida*. You know the march?

THE CREATURE: Of course.

I: Please. *(The same business follows—nothing to do with listening to a triumphal march. I smile.* THE CREATURE *begins to understand that something is wrong, and becomes confused. She awaits my verdict.)* I see you recognize how helpless you are, how little you see the difference between the lower *do* and the higher *do*.

THE CREATURE: You give me a very difficult problem.

I: Is it easier to curse the heavens in *King Lear*? No, my dear, I must tell you frankly: You do not know how to create the smallest, simplest bit of the life of the human soul. You do not know how to *concentrate spiritually*. Not only do you not know how to create complicated feelings and emotions but you do not even possess your own senses. All of that you must learn by hard daily exercises of which I can give you thousands. If you think, you will be able to invent another thousand.

THE CREATURE: All right. I will learn. I will do everything you tell me. Will I be an actress then?

I: I am glad you ask. Of course you will not be an actress, yet. To listen and to look and to feel truly is not all. You must do all that in a hundred ways. Suppose that you are playing. The curtain goes up and your first problem is to listen to the sound of a departing car. You must do it in such a way that the thousand people in the theatre who at that moment are each concentrating on some particular object—one on the stock exchange, one on home worries, one on politics, one on a dinner or the pretty girl in the next chair—in such a way that they know and feel immediately that their concentration is less important than yours, though you are concentrating only on the sound of a departing imaginary car. They must feel they have not the right to think of the stock exchange in the presence of your imaginary car! That you are more powerful than they, that, for the moment, you are the most important person in the world, and nobody dares disturb you. Nobody dares to disturb a painter at his work, and it is the actor's own fault if he allows the public to interfere with his creation. If all actors would possess the concentration and the knowledge of which I speak, this would never happen.

THE CREATURE: But what does he need for that?

I: Talent and technique. The education of an actor consists of three parts. The first is the education of his body, the whole physical apparatus, of every muscle and sinew. As a director I can manage very well with an actor with a completely developed body.

THE CREATURE: What time must a young actor spend on this?

I: An hour and a half daily on the following exercises: gymnastics, rhythmic gymnastics, classical and interpretive dancing, fencing, all kinds of breathing exercises, voice-placing exercises, diction, singing, pantomime, make-up. An hour and a half a day for two years with steady practice afterwards in what you have acquired will make an actor *pleasing to look at.*

The second part of the education is intellectual, cultural. One can discuss Shakespeare, Molière, Goethe, and Calderon only with a cultured actor who knows what these men stand for and what has been done in the theatres of the world to produce their plays. I need an actor who knows the world's literature and who can see the difference between German and French Romanticism. I need an actor who knows the history of painting, of sculpture and of music, who can always carry in his mind, at least approximately, the style of every period, and the individuality of every great painter. I need an actor who has a fairly clear idea of the psychology of motion, of psychoanalysis, of the expression of emotion, and the logic of feeling. I need an actor who knows something of the anatomy of the human body, as well as of the great works of sculpture. All this knowledge is necessary because the actor comes in contact with these things, and has to work with them on the stage. This intellectual training would make an actor who could play a great variety of parts.

The third kind of education, the beginning of which I showed you today, is the education and training of the soul—the most important factor of dramatic action. An actor cannot exist without a soul developed enough to be able to accomplish, at the first command of the will, every action and change stipulated. In other words, the actor must have a soul capable of living through any situation demanded by the author. There is no great actor without such a soul. Unfortunately it is acquired by long, hard work, at great expense of time and experience, and through a series of experimental parts. The work for this consists in the development of the following faculties: complete possession of all the five senses in various imaginable situations; development of a memory of feeling, memory of inspiration or penetration, memory of imagination, and, last, a visual memory.

THE CREATURE: But I have never heard of all those.

I: Yet they are almost as simple as "cursing the heavens". The development of faith in imagination; the development of the imagination itself; the development of naiveté; the development of observation; the development of will power; the development of the capacity to give variety in the expression of emotion; the development of the sense of humor and the tragic sense. Nor is this all.

THE CREATURE: Is it possible?

I: One thing alone remains which cannot be developed but must be present. It is *TALENT*. *(THE CREATURE sighs and falls into deep meditation. I also sit in silence.)*

THE CREATURE: You make the theatre seem like something very big, very important, very ...

I: Yes, for me the theatre is a great mystery, a mystery in which are wonderfully wedded the two eternal phenomena, the dream of *Perfection* and the dream of the *Eternal*. Only to such a theatre is it worth while to give one's life. *(I get up, the Creature looks at me with sorrowful eyes. I understand what these eyes express.)*

2 The Second Lesson
Memory of Emotion

You remember the lovely creature who came to me a year ago, and "simply loved the theatre"? She came back this winter. She entered the room quietly and with grace, smiling, her face aglow.

THE CREATURE: Hello!

(Her handclasp was firm and strong; her eyes looked straight into mine; her figure was well balanced and controlled; what a difference!)

I: How do you do? I am certainly glad to see you. I have followed your work although you did not come back to me. I never thought that you would come back. I thought I had frightened you the last time.

THE CREATURE: Oh, no, you didn't! But you certainly gave me a lot to work on, an awful lot. What a horrible time I have had with that idea of concentration. Everybody laughed at me—Once I was nearly run down by a street car because I had tried too effectively to concentrate on "the happiness of my existence". You see, I give myself problems like that for exercise, exactly as you told me to do. In this particular case, I was fired from my job and I wanted to pretend to myself that it didn't concern me at all. And I succeeded. Oh, I was stronger than ever. I was on my way home and made myself happy in spite of everything. I felt as if I had just received a wonderful part. I was so strong. But I didn't notice the street car. Fortunately I jumped back in time. I was scared, my heart was palpitating, but I still remembered "the happiness of my existence". So I smiled at the motorman and ordered him to proceed. He said something to me, but I couldn't understand him—he was talking behind the glass.

I: I suspect it was just as well that you didn't distinguish his words.

THE CREATURE: Oh, I see. And do you think he was right—being rude to me?

I: I could justify him. You destroyed his concentration as thoroughly as he destroyed yours. That is where the drama began. The result was—action expressed in his words behind the glass and in your command to proceed.

THE CREATURE: Oh, you make fun of everything.

I: No, I don't. I think yours is a case of drama in a nutshell. Active drama.

THE CREATURE: Do you mean to say that it helped my ability to act? My sense of drama?

I: Yes, I do.

THE CREATURE: How?

I: It will take some time to explain. Won't you sit down and first tell me why you came to me today? Is it another *King Lear*?

THE CREATURE: Oh, please! *(Blush—powder on the nose—hat off—hair adjusted. She sits down; another dab of powder on the nose.)*

I: *(As kind as my cigar permits me to be)* You needn't be ashamed of anything, especially of that *King Lear* performance. You were sincere then. That was a year ago; you wanted a little bit too much but you went after it in the right way. You just did it. You made the attack yourself. You didn't wait for somebody to push you. You know the story of the fair-haired school boy who had to walk a long way to school. Every day for years he said to himself, "Oh, if I could only fly, I could get to school so much quicker." Well, you know what happened to him.

THE CREATURE: No.

I: He flew from New York to Paris, alone—his name was Lindbergh. He is a colonel now.

THE CREATURE: Yes. *(A pause)* Can I talk to you seriously? *(She is dreaming now; she has learned to make good use of everything that comes to her. Inward or outward, she doesn't miss the slightest hint of emotion. She is like a violin whose strings respond to all vibrations, and she remembers those vibrations. I am sure she takes all there is in life as only a strong, normal being can take it. She selects what she wants to keep; she throws away what seems worthless to her. She will make a good actress.)*

I: Yes, but not solemnly.

THE CREATURE: I am going to talk to you about myself. *(She smiles.)* And ... *(Lugubriously)* My Art.

I: I hate the way you say, "My art." Why do you become so serious when you say it? You smile at yourself. Only a few minutes ago you told me that your only reason for living must be "the *happiness* of your existence". Why do people get solemn as soon as they speak of things which have no purpose but to bring joy to others!

THE CREATURE: I don't know about other people, but I am serious because art means everything to me. That is why I came here again, because I simply must make good. I have been given a part and have rehearsed for four days. I feel that I'm not very secure in it. Three days more and they may take it away from me. They say pleasant things to me, but I know I am not right—and nobody seems to know how to help me. They say, "speak louder", "feel something", "pick up your cues", "laugh", "sob", and what not, but I know that isn't all. There must be something missing. What is it? Where? Where am I to get it? I have done everything you told me to do. I think I control myself—that is, my body, very well. I've practised for a whole year. The body positions that the part demands are not difficult for me. I feel comfortable in all of them. I use my five senses simply and logically. I am happy when I act and still I don't know how! I don't know how! What shall I do? If they fire me, it will be the end of me. And the worst of it all is that I know only too well what they will all say. They will say, "You are very good, but you lack experience"—and that's all. What is that cursed experience? There isn't a thing anybody can tell me about that part—I know everything about it. I look like it, I feel every single minute of it and each change. I know I can act it. And then—"experience"! Oh, I wish I could use some of the words that that motorman used who nearly ran over me. I didn't hear them, but judging from his face, I know they would be right. As a matter of fact, I think I can guess what they were—and oh, how I could use them now!

I: Go ahead and use them. Don't mind me. (*She uses them.*) Any happier?

THE CREATURE: Yes. (*Smile. Laugh.*)

I: All right, now you are ready. Now I'll talk to you. Let's talk about your part. You will work it out for yourself, and what's more, you'll do it right. If you have done all the work you say you have and if the part is within your range, you cannot fail. Don't worry about it. Work and patience never fail.

THE CREATURE: Oh, teacher ... (*She starts.*)

I: Sit down. I mean it. For a year you have been perfecting yourself as a human instrument and gathering material. You have observed and absorbed life. You have collected what you saw, read, heard, and felt in the storage places of your brain. You did it both consciously and unconsciously. Concentration became your second nature.

THE CREATURE: I don't think I did anything unconsciously. I am a very matter-of-fact person.

I: I know you are. The actor must be—how otherwise could he dream? The only person who can dream is the person who can stand with both feet firmly on the earth. That is why the Irish policeman is the best policeman in the world. He never sleeps on duty. He dreams wide awake. And the gangster has little chance.

THE CREATURE: Please! I have a part. I want to act it and you talk about Irish policemen.

I: No, I am talking about the practicality of dreams. I'm talking about order, about system. I'm talking about harnessing dreams—conscious and unconscious dreams—all useful—all necessary—all obedient—all coming at your call. All parts in that beautiful state of your nature that you call "experience".

THE CREATURE: All right. But what about my part?

I: You will have to organize and synchronize the self that is within you, with your part. Then everything will be splendid.

THE CREATURE: All right, let's start.

I: First of all, I insist—and you will have to believe me—that you did a great deal of your work unconsciously. Now we'll start. What is the most important scene in your part?

THE CREATURE: The scene where I tell my mother that I'm going to leave her house, her poor and obscure house, for an extraordinary reason. A rich lady has become interested in me and is going to take me into her home to give me all the beautiful things of life—education, travel, friends, beautiful surroundings, clothes, jewels, position—everything. It's too marvelous. I cannot withstand temptation. I must go, but I love my mother and am sorry for her. I struggle between the lure of happiness and love for my mother. My decision is not yet made, but the desire for happiness is very strong.

I: Good. Now, how will you do it, and what does your director say?

THE CREATURE: He says that I am either happy to go away or love my mother so much that I am not at all happy to go. I cannot blend these two things.

I: You must be happy and sorry at the same time. Gleaming and tender.

THE CREATURE: That's it. I can't feel those two things simultaneously.

I: Nobody can, but you can be that.

THE CREATURE: To *be* that without feeling it? How is that possible?

I: With the help of your unconscious memory—of your memory of feelings.

THE CREATURE: Unconscious memory of feelings? You mean to say that I must unconsciously memorize my feelings?

I: God forbid. We have a special memory for feelings, which works unconsciously by itself and for itself. It's right there. It is in every artist. It is that which makes experience an essential part of our life and craft. All we have to do is to know how to use it.

THE CREATURE: But where is it? How do you get it? Does anybody know about it?

I: Oh, quite a number of people. The French psychologist, Théodule Ribot [Théodule Ribot: *Problèmes de Psychologic Affective*: Felix Actan. Paris], was the first to speak of it over twenty years ago. He calls it "affective memory" or "memory of affects."

THE CREATURE: How does it work?

I: Through all the manifestations of life and our sensitivity toward them.

THE CREATURE: For example?

I: For example, in a certain city there lived a couple who had been married for twenty-five years. They had married when they were very young. He had proposed to her one fine summer evening when they were walking in a cucumber patch. Being nervous, as nice young people are apt to be under the circumstances, they would stop occasionally, pick a cucumber, and eat it, enjoying very much its aroma, taste and the freshness and richness of the sun's warmth upon it. They made the happiest decision of their lives, between two mouthfuls of cucumbers, so to speak.

   A month later they were married. At the wedding supper a dish of fresh cucumbers was served—and nobody knew why they laughed so heartily when they saw it. Long years of life and struggle came; children and, naturally, difficulties. Sometimes they quarreled, and were angry. Sometimes they did not even speak to each other. But their youngest daughter observed that the surest way to make peace between them was to put a dish of cucumbers on the table. Like magic they would forget their quarrels, and would become tender and understanding. For a long time the daughter thought the change was due to their love for cucumbers, but once the mother told her the story of their courtship, and when she thought about it, she came to another conclusion. I wonder if you can?

THE CREATURE: (*Very brightly*) Yes, the outward circumstances brought back the inward feelings.

I: I wouldn't say feelings. I would say rather, made these two people what they were long years before, in spite of time, reason, and maybe—desire, unconsciously.

THE CREATURE: No, not unconsciously, because they knew what the cucumbers had meant to them.

I: After twenty-five years? I doubt it. They were simple souls, they wouldn't go so far as to analyze the origin of their feelings. They just naturally yielded themselves to the feelings as they came. They were stronger than any present feeling. It is just as when you start to count, "One, two, three, four," it takes an effort not to continue, "five, six, etc." The whole thing is to make a beginning—to start.

THE CREATURE: Do you think I have ... ?

I: Undoubtedly.

THE CREATURE: I wanted to ask if you thought I had memories like that in me.

I: Plenty of them—just waiting to be awakened, just waiting for a call. And what is more, when you do awaken them, you can control them, you can make use of them, you can apply them in your craft. I prefer that word to the word "Art" which you like so much. You can learn the whole secret of experience.

THE CREATURE: But not stage experience.

I: Indirectly, yes. Because when you have something to say, the experience comes so much more quickly, a hundred times faster than when you have nothing to say. It comes much more surely than when all you do is to *try* to be experienced, to "speak louder", to "feel something", to "pick up the cues", to "hold the tempo." Those are problems for children, not for craftsmen.

THE CREATURE: But how do you go about those things? How do you command them?

I: That's the spirit. You *command* them. In your particular case did you or did you not ever experience that double feeling when you are sad and happy at the same time?

THE CREATURE: Yes, yes, many times, but I don't know how to bring it back. I don't *remember* where I was and what I was doing when I felt that way.

I: Never mind where and what. The point is to bring yourself back as you were then, to command your own ego, go where you want to go, and when you are there, to stay where you went. Give me an example of your personal experience with a double feeling.

THE CREATURE: Well, I went abroad last summer for the first time in my life. My brother couldn't go. He saw me off. I was happy and at the same time I was sorry for him. But how I acted I don't remember.

I: All right. Tell me how the whole thing happened. Start at the moment you left your house. Don't omit any details. Give me a description of the taxi driver and of all your worries and excitements. Try to recall the weather, the color of the sky, the smells at the docks, the voices of longshoremen and sailors, the faces of fellow-passengers. Give me a good journalistic account of the whole thing and forget about yourself. Work outwardly. Start with your clothing and that of your brother. Go on.

(She starts. Well trained in concentration, she throws herself into the subject. She could give a lesson to any detective. She is cold, firm, exact, analytical—not missing details, not using meaningless words—giving only necessary bare facts. At first she is almost mechanical, almost a perfect machine. Then when she speaks of a traffic officer who stops the taxi and reads a sermon to the driver, and she exclaims, "Oh, please, Officer, we will be late," the first sign of real emotion comes into her eyes. She starts to be—she starts to act. It does not come easily. Seven times she goes back to facts and only facts, but gradually they are of less and less importance. When she finally tells how she ran up the gangway and jumped on to the deck of the steamer, her face and eyes are shining, involuntarily she repeats the jump. Then suddenly she turns her face, and there, not far away, is her brother down on the pier. Tears come to her eyes. She conceals them. "Cheer up, cheer up," she cries. "I'll tell you all about it. Give my love to everybody. Oh, how I hate to leave New York. I'd rather stay with you, but it's too late now. Besides you wouldn't want me to. Oh, it's going to be too wonderful ... ")

I: Stop. Now go on with the speech from your part in the play. Don't lose what you've got. Just exactly as you are now—speaking to your brother. You are what you ought to be in the part.

THE CREATURE: But I am speaking to my mother in the part.

I: Is she really your mother?

THE CREATURE: No.

I: Then what difference does it make? The theatre exists to show things which do not exist actually. When you love on the stage, do you really love? Be logical. You substitute creation for the real thing. The creation must be real, but that is the only reality that should be there. Your experience of double feeling was a fortunate accident. Through your will power and the knowledge of your craft you have organized it and re-created it. It is now in your hands. Use it if your artistic sense tells you that it is relative to your problem and creates a would-be life. To imitate is wrong. To create is right.

THE CREATURE: But while you were speaking, I lost what seemed to be that very important process of re-creation. Do I have to begin my story again? Must I go back again to that state of double feeling?

I: How do you learn a tune you want to remember? How do you learn the outline of muscles you want to draw? How do you learn the mixture of colors you want to use in painting? Through constant repetition and perfection. It may be hard for you, easier for someone else.

One person remembers a tune, hearing it just once—another will have to hear it many times. Toscanini remembers it, reading a manuscript once. Practice! I have given you an example. You can find around and within you hundreds of opportunities. Work on them and learn to bring back what seems lost. Learn to bring it back actually and make good use of it. At first it will require much time, skill, and effort. The subject is delicate. You will find the trend and lose it again many times. Don't get discouraged. Remember, this is an actor's fundamental work—to be able "to be" what he desires consciously and exactly.

THE CREATURE: In my particular case, how would you suggest that I bring back what I seem to have found and lost?

I: First of all, work on it alone. It was all right for me to demonstrate as I did to show you the way, but your actual work is done in solitude—entirely inside of yourself. You know how, now, through concentration. Think over the process of approach toward the actual moment of that real double feeling. You will know when you get it. You will feel the warmth of it and the satisfaction.

Practically every good actor does it unconsciously when he acts well and is happy about it. However, gradually, it will take you less and less time. It will be just like recalling a tune. Finally the flash of thought will be sufficient. You will eliminate details. You will define the whole thing inside of your being with certain aim, and with practice, a mere hint will make you "be" what you want. Then use the author's words and if your choice was right, they will always sound fresh, always alive! You won't need to play them. You'll hardly need to form them, they will come so naturally. All you will need is to have perfect bodily technique in order to project whatever emotion you are prompted to express.

THE CREATURE: And if the choice of my own feelings is not right, what then?

I: Have you seen a manuscript of Wagner's music? If you are in Bayreuth, go to see one. See how many times Wagner erased and crossed out notes and melodies and harmonies until he found the one he wanted. If he did it so many times, surely you can try no less often.

THE CREATURE: Suppose I don't find a similar feeling in my life's experience, what then?

I: Impossible! If you are a sensitive and normal human being, all life is open and familiar to you. After all, poets and playwrights are human too. If they find experience in their lives to use, why shouldn't you? But you will have to use your imagination; you can never tell where you will find the thing you are after.

THE CREATURE: All right, suppose I have to play murder. I have never murdered anybody. How shall I find it?

I: Oh, why do actors always ask me about murder? The younger they are the more murders they want to act. All right, you have never murdered anybody. Have you ever camped?

THE CREATURE: Yes.

I: Ever sat in the woods at the edge of a lake after sundown?

THE CREATURE: Yes.

I: Were there any mosquitoes around?

THE CREATURE: It was in New Jersey.

I: Did they annoy you? Did you follow one among them with your eyes and ears and hate until the beast landed on your forearm? And did you slap your forearm cruelly without even thinking of the hurt to yourself—with only the wish to … end?

THE CREATURE: *(Quite ashamed)* To kill the beast.

I: There you are. A good sensitive artist doesn't need any more than that to play Othello and Desdemona's final scene. The rest is the work of magnification, imagination, and belief.

Gordon Craig has a charming book-plate, fantastic, with an unusual, beautiful pattern—unknown and strange. You cannot tell what it is, but it gives you a sense of brooding, a sense of boring through, a sense of slow drive and struggle. It is nothing but a book-worm, a common book-worm, enlarged many times. An artist will find his source anywhere. Nature has not given one-hundredth part of what it still holds for you. Go and look for it. One of the most charming grotesque actors on the stage is Ed Wynn. Can you see where he began his trick of putting a windshield with a wiper before his eyes when he started to eat a grapefruit? Can't you see how he watched the mud and the water as he drove along in his car, protected by the real windshield, watched it with perfect satisfaction, feeling safe?

Then, once at luncheon, perhaps, he got an eyeful of grapefruit juice. He associated the two ideas, and the result—a charming foolery.

THE CREATURE: I doubt that he thought it out that way.

I: Certainly not. But unconsciously he went through the whole process. How do you expect to learn your craft if you don't analyze what has been already achieved? Then forget about it all and go after your own achievements.

THE CREATURE: What do you do when you find places in the part where you cannot apply that "to be" of yours?

I: You must find it for every place, but be careful not to overdo it. Don't look for "to be" when you should seek "to do." Don't forget that when you want to be an actor with all your heart and soul, want it to such an extent that you forget your self entirely, and when your technique is developed sufficiently, you can already act most of the stuff that is written. It is just like humming a tune. The difficult spots are what you should watch for and work for. Every play is written for one or at most a few "high tension" moments. The audience pays the price of the tickets—not for two whole hours— but for the best ten seconds, the ten seconds when it gets the biggest laugh or thrill. Your whole strength and perfection must be directed toward those seconds.

THE CREATURE: Thanks, I have them in my part. I know now what was wrong—there are three places which I haven't lifted above the rest of the play—that is why I was monotonous. I will look forward now "to be" in those places. Are you sure they will come out all right?

I: Sure as I am that you will soon come back to me with another problem.

THE CREATURE: Oh, I was so foolish not to come back to you right away.

I: Not at all. It takes at least a year to get the foundation for your technique. You've got enough to be an actress now. So nothing is lost. If I had told you a year ago what I am telling you now, you wouldn't have understood it, and you would never have come back. Now you have come and something tells me your next visit will be quite soon. I think I even know when—when you get a part which won't be yourself—where you will have to change yourself a little bit—where you will no longer be a mere convenient type, but must become a daring artist.

THE CREATURE: May I come tomorrow?

I: No, not until you act your part. I hope you will act it very well. And I hope you won't get very good notices. Nothing is so bad for a young artist as glorifying notices. When that happens, before you realize it, you become lazy and are late for rehearsals.

THE CREATURE: That reminds me.

I: I know. That's why I said it. Go and rehearse now. As happy and as strong as ever. You have something beautiful to work on. Meantime, remember that little story about cucumbers.

Notice everything around you—watch yourself cheerfully. Collect and save in your soul all the riches of life and the fulness of it. Keep those memories in order. You can never tell when you will need them, but they are your only friends and teachers in your craft. They are your only paints and brushes. And they will bring you reward. They are yours—your own property. They are not imitations, and they will give you experience, precision, economy, and power.

THE CREATURE: Yes. Thanks.

I: And the next time you come to me, bring me at least a hundred records of your registered moments when you made yourself "to be" what you wanted when you wanted.

THE CREATURE: Oh, don't you worry. The next time I come to you I will know my … cucumbers.

(She goes away, strong, alive, and beautiful; I am left alone with my cigar.)

I wonder who said, "The object of Education is not to know but to live."

3 The Third Lesson

Dramatic Action

THE CREATURE *and I are walking in the park. She is in a rage. She has been rehearsing a part in the talkies.*

THE CREATURE: … and then they stopped. I waited for an hour and a half. We started. This time three lines from the big scene; three lines—that was all. After that again a wait of an hour. It is impossible—simply impossible. Machinery, electricity, lenses, microphone, furniture, that is all that counts. An actor? Who cares? Acting? A miserable accessory.

I: And yet a few actors achieve quite a high degree of dramatic art.

THE CREATURE: Now and then—for five seconds—rare as black pearls.

I: If you look for them, not so rare.

THE CREATURE: Oh, how can you say so? You, who all your life advocated the magnificent, flowing, live theatre. How can you look for rare moments of beauty in talkies? Even when you find them they are separated, disjointed, cut, uneven. How can you defend those moments and justify them?

I: Tell me, have I helped you before with my talks?

THE CREATURE: You have.

I: Are you willing to listen now, with as little interruption as possible?

THE CREATURE: I am.

I: All right. Look at that marble fountain. It was made in 1902 by Arthur Collins.

THE CREATURE: How do you know!

I: It is chiselled on the rim of the base. You promised not to interrupt me.

THE CREATURE: Sorry.

I: How do you like Mr. Collins' work?

THE CREATURE: Not bad. Quite simple and clear in form. It harmonizes with the landscape; it is noble. Made in 1902, it has definite traces of modern conception. What else has Arthur Collins done?

I: This is the last work he ever did. He died—thirty-five years of age. He was a promising sculptor. Though young, he influenced many of the modern masters.

THE CREATURE: I can see it. Isn't it wonderful that he left his work behind him so that we can look at it, trace the line of creative descent, and understand the vision of our contemporaries.

I: It is wonderful, indeed. Wouldn't you like to see and hear Mrs. Siddons right now, acting the lines:

"Here's the smell of the blood still; all the perfumes of Arabia will not sweeten this little hand. Oh! Oh! Oh!"

What would you give to learn what Mrs. Siddons did with those "Oh! Oh! Oh!'s"? They say that people used to faint when she did it; we don't know. And wouldn't you like to hear David Garrick, in *Richard III*, scorn William Catesby:

"Slave! I have set my life upon a cast.
And I will stand the hazard of the die."
Or Jefferson, or Booth, or Ellen Terry? I still remember Salvini's reaction when Iago would say:

"But he that filches from me my good name
Robs me of that which not enriches him,
And makes me poor indeed."

I tried once to describe it. In vain. It is gone. This fountain speaks for itself. There is nothing to speak for Salvini.

THE CREATURE: Really, it is a pity ... *(She pauses, grows pensive, and then says, with a wistful smile—)* Well, it seems that I gave you a cue.

I: You always give me the cues. I don't invent things. I observe them and present them to you; you draw the conclusions and profit by them. The only real rules in art are the rules that we discover for ourselves.

THE CREATURE: I have discovered that it is too bad not to have the images and voices of great actors preserved for posterity. Now, I'm drawing a conclusion; because of that I must suffer in my work the mechanism and cheapness of the talkies?

I: No. The only thing you have to do is to march abreast of your times, and do your best—as an artist.

THE CREATURE: Impossible.

I: Inevitable.

THE CREATURE: It is a false vogue—a fad.

I: Narrow way of thinking.

THE CREATURE: My whole nature as an actress rebels against that mechanical monster.

I: Then you are not an actress.

THE CREATURE: Because I want a free, uninterrupted outlet for my inspiration and creative work?

I: No. Because you do not rejoice in the discovery of a great and final instrument of drama; the instrument which all the other arts have had since time immemorial, and which the oldest art, the theatre, lacked until today; the instrument that gives to the theatre the precision and scientific serenity which all the other arts have had; the instrument that demands of the actor to be as exact as the color scheme in painting, form in sculpture, string, wood, brass in music, mathematics in architecture, words in poetry.

THE CREATURE: But look at the hundreds of incredibly stupid talkies appearing each week—poor acting, insignificant action, wrong rhythm.

I: Look at the hundreds of millions of stupid paintings, songs, performances, houses, and books that have appeared since the beginning of time, that have gone into oblivion without hurting anybody while the good ones survived.

THE CREATURE: Is one good talkie worth hundreds of bad ones?

I: Be generous. The idea is worth them. It is the preservation of the art of the actor—the art of the theatre. Spoken drama equally with written drama. Do you realize that with the invention of spontaneous recording of the image, movement, and voice, and consequently the personality and soul of an actor, the last missing link in the chain of the arts disappears, and the theatre is no more a passing affair, but an eternal record? Do you realize that the intimate creative work of an actor need no longer be performed before the public eye; that there need be no more dragging the audience into a sweat and labor over your work? The actor is free from onlookers in the moment of creation and only the results of it are judged.

THE CREATURE: The actor in front of machinery is not free. He is chopped to pieces—almost every sentence of his part is separated from the previous and the following ones.

I: Every word of a poet is separated from the other words. The assembled whole is what counts.

THE CREATURE: But how can one get the flow of the part? How can one build up an emotion and rise to the unconscious climaxes of real inspired interpretation of a part?

I: In the way one should do it in the theatre. Because you have had one or two successful parts on the stage you think there is nothing more to learn, nothing more to improve or to build up in your technique.

THE CREATURE: You know that isn't so. I always want to learn. Otherwise I wouldn't be walking with you for the second time around this silly lake.

I: Well, our walk is smooth, continuous, easy flowing, building up toward a climax.

THE CREATURE: Which will be when I drop breathless on the grass?

I: Exactly, and that's the way you play your parts—rushing through them, building up emotion, and chasing the climax until you drop in a critic's lap trying to catch a breath. And you don't get much breath from them either.

THE CREATURE: Well, I can see that something is coming. What is it?

I: What was your main difficulty acting in the talkies?

THE CREATURE: Lack of springboard. Being compelled to start a scene in the middle and finish it after four or five lines, then in another hour start another scene (which in the script comes before the previous one), then again act four lines and wait an hour. I tell you it's abnormal, it's horrible—

I: Lack of technique, that's all.

THE CREATURE: What technique?

I: Of action's structure.

THE CREATURE: Stage action?

I: Dramatic action which the writer expresses in words, having that action as the purpose and goal of his words, and which the actor performs, or acts, as the word actor itself implies.

THE CREATURE: That is exactly what it is impossible to do in the talkies. I had a love scene, two and a half pages in the script, and when I was acting it I was interrupted eleven times. It took the whole day. My action was to convince the man who loved me that I loved him too, but was terrified by his father's hatred of me.

I: This on two and a half pages?—you said it in one line, quite convincingly. What did you do for the remainder of the two and a half pages?

THE CREATURE: I tried to do the same thing.

I: For two and a half pages? Thank God they did interrupt you eleven times.

THE CREATURE: That was the action. What else was there to do?

I: Look at that tree. It is the protagonist of all arts; it is an ideal structure of action. Upward movement and sideways resistance, balance and growth.

THE CREATURE: Granted.

I: Look at the trunk—straight, proportioned, harmonious with the rest of the tree, supporting every part of it. It is the leading strain; "Leitmotif" in music; a director's idea of action in a play; the architect's foundation; the poet's thought in a sonnet.

THE CREATURE: How does a director express that action in producing a play?

I: Through interpretation of the play, and through ingenious combinations of smaller, secondary, or complementary actions that will secure that interpretation.

THE CREATURE: Give an example.

I: All right. *The Taming of the Shrew* is a play where two people long to love each other in spite of their impossible characters, and succeed in their longing. It might also be a play about a man who triumphs over a woman by "treating her rough". It might be a play about a woman who makes everybody's life miserable. Do you grasp the difference?

THE CREATURE: I do.

I: In the first case the action is to love; in the second swash-buckling; in the third the anger of a vixen.

THE CREATURE: Do you mean to say that in the first case, for instance, when the action is love, you would make the actors assume the attitude of love all the way through?

I: I would make them remember it. I would ask them to have it behind every curse, every quarrel, every disagreement.

THE CREATURE: What would you expect from an actor?

I: To comply with nature's law of action, the threefold law you can see expressed in that tree. First, the main trunk, the idea, the reason. On the stage it comes from the director. Second, the branches, elements of the idea, particles of reason. That comes from the actor. Third, the foliage, the result of the previous two, the brilliant presentation of idea, the bright conclusion of reasoning.

THE CREATURE: Where does the author appear on the scene?

I: He is the sap that flows and feeds the whole.

THE CREATURE: *(With a twinkle in her eyes)* That was a narrow escape for the actor.

I: *(With a twinkle in my eyes also)* Well, if he doesn't know how to project his actions in front of ...

THE CREATURE: That's enough. I take it on the chin.

I: ... the camera and microphone, and is afraid of eleven interruptions. ...

THE CREATURE: *(She stops and stamps her foot.)* All right. All right. *(She is very much annoyed.)* Tell me how *not* to be afraid of them.

I: I need a written part or a play to show you exactly what I mean by the structure of action. I haven't one with me.

THE CREATURE: We have acted a nice little play right through, during our walk in the last half hour. Whenever we talk, we always do, as a matter of fact. Why don't you use what we have talked over as a play?

I: All right. I'm the director. You are a young actress performing a one-act play with a grumpy old man. I am that man, also.

THE CREATURE: Let's talk about characterizations later, another time.

I: At your service. Now the director is speaking: The trunk, or the "spine" of your little play, my friends (meaning you and me), is the discovery of truth about dramatic action, not on a dark stage, or in a classroom, or from learned books, or in front of an angry director ready to fire you, but in the midst of nature, enjoying air, sun, a brisk walk and good humor.

THE CREATURE: Which means quick thinking, energetic penetration, bright spirit, conviction in ideas, eagerness to understand, clear voices, fast tempo, and readiness to argue, to give, and to take.

I: Bravo! Bravo! As the director I'm through. With your help we have established the trunk or "spine". Now, let's turn to the sap.

THE CREATURE: Meaning the author … ?

I: Exactly. Is that nice?

THE CREATURE: *(Runs away from me, claps her hands, and laughs with the most childish satisfaction. I run after her, and catch her by the hand.)*

I: We are even. Let's continue, and analyze the words in terms of action. Let's take your part. What did you do at the beginning of the play?

THE CREATURE: I complained …

I: … Bitterly and exaggeratedly …

THE CREATURE: … I scorned and despised …

I: … With the charming resolution of youth.

THE CREATURE: … I piled up the evidence.

I: Not convincingly, but forcefully.

THE CREATURE: I didn't believe you … and reproached you.

I: Like a stubborn youngster. And you have forgotten that at the same time you walked, sometimes you agreed with me, you observed and studied Mr. Collins' fountain, you felt physically tired, you looked for words to oppose my arguments, you enjoyed a few Shakespearean lines, and with all that you covered about nine speeches.

THE CREATURE: *(Horrified)* Have I done all those things at once?

I: Never. No human being could. But having the main trunk, or thread of action in mind, what you did was to string on that thread the secondary, or complementary actions like beads on a string, one after another, sometimes overlapping each other but always clear and distinct.

THE CREATURE: Weren't they just intonations and inflections?

I: Where would they come from, if not as the result of action?

THE CREATURE: That's true.

I: Describing your actions, you used only verbs—that is significant. A verb is action in itself. First you want something, it is your artist's will; then you define it in a verb, it is your artist's technique; and then you actually do it, it is your artist's expression. You do it through the medium of speech—words of a ...

THE CREATURE: My own words in this case.

I: It doesn't matter, although some clever author's words would have been much better.

THE CREATURE: *(Nods silently—it is so hard to agree while one is young.)*

I: The author would have written them for you. Then you could take a pencil and write "music of action" under every word or speech, as you write music to lyrics for a song; then on the stage you would play that "music of action". You would have to memorize your actions as you memorize the music. You would have to know distinctly the difference between "I complained" and "I scorned" and, although the two actions follow each other, you would be just as different in their delivery as the singer is when he takes "C" or "C flat".

Moreover, when you know action by heart no interruption or change of order can disturb you. If you have your action confined within one single word, and you know exactly what that action is, you have it inside of you on the call of a split second, how can you be disturbed when the time comes for its delivery? Your scene, or part, is a long string of beads—beads of action. You play with them as you play with a rosary. You can start anywhere, any time, and go as far as you wish, if you have a good hold on the beads themselves.

THE CREATURE: But doesn't it happen that the same action may last for pages, or at least a very long scene?

I: Certainly, only it is more difficult for the actor to keep it going without monotony—"To be or not to be" has nine sentences with one single action ...

THE CREATURE: What is it?

I: To be or not to be. Shakespeare did not take any chances with actors. He told them right in the beginning what he wanted them to do. On account of the significance of that action and the length of the scene itself it is the hardest thing to act. To recite it is very easy.

THE CREATURE: I understand. The recitation is like the foliage of a tree without the trunk and branches.

I: Precisely—just juggling with the modulation of voice and artificial pauses. Even in the best case with a very well trained voice it is only poor music. As drama, it is nil.

THE CREATURE: What was your action when you started to enumerate the names of actors and speeches in their parts? You really looked sorrowful and wistful. Have you forgotten the agreed "spine"? We decided it must be "energy, bright spirit, quick thinking" and so on …

I: No. But what I wanted was to make you say, "It is a pity." I could do it in one way only, namely by arousing your sympathy toward my feelings. That in turn made you think about my words, and you yourself drew the conclusion that I was looking for.

THE CREATURE: In other words, you acted sorrowful to make me pensive?

I: Yes, and I acted it "energetically, with bright spirit and quick thinking."

THE CREATURE: Could you perform some other action with the same words, and get the same results?

I: Yes. But my action was prompted by you.

THE CREATURE: By me?

I: Yes. By your character rather. To convince you in anything one must approach you through emotion. Cold reasoning is inaccessible to your type of mind—the mind of an artist who deals mostly with his or other people's imaginations. If, instead of you, I had had a bearded Professor of History as a companion, I wouldn't have acted sorrowful at all. I would have tempted him enthusiastically with a picture of the past—a weak spot of all historians—and he would have yielded to my statement.

THE CREATURE: I see. So one must choose his actions in accordance with the character of the part that opposes him.

I: Always. Not only the character of the part, but also the individuality of the actor who plays the part.

THE CREATURE: How do I memorize the action?

I: After you have found the feeling through your "memory of affects". You remember our last talk?

THE CREATURE: I do.

I: You are ready for action. Rehearsals serve the purpose. You repeat the action a few times and you remember it. Actions are very easy to remember—much easier than words. Tell me right now, what did you act in the first nine speeches of our play—the one we went through?

THE CREATURE: *(Bursts into rapid energetic enumeration. All her heart is in it.)* I complained, scorned, despised. I reproached you. I didn't believe you ...

I: And what is your action now, while you are enthusiastically throwing all those hateful verbs into my face?

THE CREATURE: I ... I ...

I: Come on—what is your action?

THE CREATURE: I am proving to you that I believe your words.

I: And I believe you, because you have proved it with action.

4   The Fourth Lesson
Characterization

I am waiting for the Creature at the stage entrance. She is with a company in an important play. She has asked me to come after rehearsal and take her home. She wants to talk to me about her part.

I do not have long to wait. The door opens. She comes out hurriedly. Tired, her eyes gleaming, her lovely hair dishevelled, a tender flush of excitement on her cheeks.

THE CREATURE: I'm sorry to disappoint you. I cannot go with you. I'm not going home. I have to stay here and rehearse.

I: I saw all the actors leaving—Are you going to rehearse alone?

THE CREATURE: *(Nodding sadly)* Uh-mmmm—

I: Any trouble?

THE CREATURE: Plenty.

I: May I come in and watch you rehearse?

THE CREATURE: Thank you. I was afraid to ask you.

I: Why?

THE CREATURE: *(Lifts herself on her toes and whispers into my ear, her eyes round with horror—)* I'm very, Oh, very, bad.

I: I would rather hear you say that than "Come and see me—I'm very, Oh, very good."

THE CREATURE: Well, I'm saying that I'm bad because it's all your fault. In this new part I have done everything you told me, and still I'm bad.

I: All right, let's see.

(We pass a very old doorman in his shirt sleeves, smoking a pipe. He looks at me with deep-set, dark eyes from under bushy eyebrows. His clean-shaven face is set firmly. He is not letting anybody in. His very presence bars the entrance. He acts the part. He is not just a watchman—he is a splendid impersonation of Francisco, Bernardo, or Marcellus at his post. He raises his hand in a noble gesture.)

THE CREATURE: That's all right, Pa, the gentleman is with me.

(The old man nods silently, and in his old eyes I can read permission to enter. I think to myself "It takes an actor to be so economically gracious. I wonder if he is one?" I take my hat off as I enter the stage. It is dark. One electric bulb etches a halo in the centre of the darkness. The Creature takes me by the hand and leads me down the stairway and among the stalls into the pit.)

THE CREATURE: Sit here, please; don't say anything; don't interrupt me. Let me act a few scenes in succession for you, then tell me what is wrong.

(She goes back to the stage. I am left alone, in a space bordered by glittering dark holes of boxes, by silent rows of chairs covered with canvas, by faint outside noises. All the shadows are strange and solid. The quiet is trembling and alive. I respond to that quiet. My nerves begin to vibrate and to throw threads of sympathy and expectation toward the great promising black riddle, the empty stage. A peculiar peace descends on my mind, as if I partially cease to exist and somebody else's soul is living in me instead of my own. I will be dead to myself, alive to the outward world. I will observe and participate in an imaginary world. I will wake up with my heart full of dreams. Sweet poison of an empty theatre, empty stage and a single actor rehearsing on it.

The Creature appears. She has a book in her hand. She tries to read, but her mind is distracted. Obviously she is waiting for somebody. It must be somebody of importance indeed. She seems to tremble. She looks around as if asking approval and advice from an invisible friend. She is encouraged; I can hear her faint sigh.

Then suddenly she sees somebody in the far distance. She stiffens, draws her breath quickly. She must be afraid. She makes as if to read from the book. But it is clear to me that she does not see a single letter. Not a word is spoken. I am watching tensely and whisper to myself "Well done, well done, Creature, I'm ready now for every word you utter."

The Creature listens. Her body is relaxed, the hand holding the book hangs limply. Her head is turned slightly to one side, an unconscious help to the ear through which imaginary words enter her soul. She nods her head.)

THE CREATURE : "Good my lord,
How does your honour for this many a day?"

(There is a warm, sincere affection and respect in her voice. She speaks as if to an elder brother. Then she looks, with fear and trembling, for an imaginary answer. The answer comes.)

***

(She closes her eyes for a moment.)
"My lord, I have remembrances of yours,
That I have longed long to re-deliver;
I pray you, now receive them."

(What is it? She sounds as if she were not telling quite the truth. Expectant fear in her voice. She stands as if petrified. She looks around again as if for the support of an invisible friend. Suddenly she shrinks back as if hit by the imaginary answer.)

***

(It must have been a blow, right at the heart. Her book falls, her trembling fingers clutch one another. She defends herself.)
"My honour'd lord, you know right well you did;
And, with them, words of so sweet breath compos'd
As made the things more rich: their perfume lost,
Take these again; for to the noble mind
Rich gifts wax poor when givers prove unkind."

(Her voice breaks, then suddenly soars freely and strongly in defense of injured pride and love.)

"There, my lord."

(She seems to grow taller. It is the result of co-ordination between her muscles and her emotion, the first sign of a trained actress: the stronger the emotion, the more freedom in the voice, the more relaxation in muscles.)

***

"My lord?"

(There is an almost masculine strength in that fragile body.)

***

"What means your lordship?"

(Her fear forgotten, she speaks now as an equal. She does not look around for help or confirmation of her actions. She throws the words into the black space without seeming to wait for an answer.)

***

"Could beauty, my lord, have better commerce than with honesty?"

***

(Then a change comes over her face. Pain, tenderness, sorrow, adoration, all are in her eyes and on her trembling lips. I understand; the enemy is the beloved one. A whispered line—like moaning wind—)

"Indeed, my lord, you made me believe so."

***

(And still more quietly and sorrowfully)

"I was the more deceived."

***

(Then comes a long silence. She absorbs inaudible words of anger, shame, accusation, words which throw her to earth and remind her of somebody whom she has forgotten in her sincerity but who has power over her and who has told her exactly what to do. She is conscious of him now. She is not herself, she is an obedient daughter. She is a tool in her father's hands. Suddenly she shudders. She hears the inevitable question, the compromising question. And again a lie is the answer, a torturing lie.)

"At home, my lord."

***

(Horror lashes her; despair makes her sob from the depths of her soul, as if all her being wailed, Oh, what have I done? Then a prayer to the Only One who can help now.)

"O, help him, you sweet heavens!"

***

"O heavenly powers, restore him!"

***

(But heaven and earth are silent. The only thunder is the voice of one whom she trusted and loved. The words behind that voice are like stinging scorpions. Not a sign of understanding in them, not a sign of tenderness—not a tone of mercy. Hate, accusation, denouncement. The end of the world. Because the world for all of us is the one whom we love. When he is gone the world is gone. When the world is gone we are gone. And therefore we can be calm and empty and oblivious to everything and everyone who a minute ago was so important

and powerful. The Creature is alone in her whole being. I can see it in her contracted body and wide open eyes. If there were an army of fathers behind her now, she would be alone. And only to herself would she say those heartbreaking words, the last words of a sound mind, that tries desperately to verify all that happened a second ago. It is unbelievably painful. It is like the soul parting from the body. The separated words crowd each other, hurry one over the other in a fast-growing rhythm. The voice is hollow. The tears behind it are inadequate to accompany that last farewell; the speech is like a stone falling down, down, into a bottomless abyss.)

> "O, what a noble mind is here o'erthrown!
> The courtier's, soldier's, scholar's eye, tongue, sword:
> The expectancy and rose of the fair state,
> The glass of fashion and the mould of form,
> The observ'd of all observers,—quite, quite down!
> And I, of ladies most deject and wretched,
> That suck'd the honey of his music vows,
> Now see that noble and most sovereign reason,
> Like sweet bells jangled, out of tune and harsh;
> That unmatch'd form and feature of blown youth
> Blasted with ecstasy: O, woe is me,
> To have seen what I have seen, see what I see!"

(She sinks down on her knees, exhausted, staring into the blackness of the empty house right at me, without seeing, without registering anything. Madness next would be the inevitable and logical madness of the mind which has lost its world.)

***

(She snaps out of it all, jumps up from the ground, rubs her head and shakes out her golden hair with her hands, swerves around, and says in her youthful voice)

THE CREATURE: Well, that's my best, and as Gordon Craig says "It's just too bad that someone's best is so bad."

(She giggles. Another sign of a trained actor. It doesn't matter how deep emotion is in acting, with the return to life it snaps off and is laid aside with no perturbance.)

I: Come down here.

(She vaults over the footlights, runs to the chair next to mine, and sits down, tucking her legs under her.)

I: What do they say to you?

THE CREATURE: ... That it is overdone. That I "tear a passion to tatters". That nobody would believe me. That it is pathological hypnotism, not acting, and that I will ruin myself and my health. That with this kind of acting nothing is left for the audience's imagination, that for the audience such complete sincerity is embarrassing. As if somebody suddenly appeared naked in the midst of a dressed-up crowd. Is that enough, or is it?

I: Not only enough, but true, my dear.

THE CREATURE: *Et tu, Brute?* You are impossible. I have done everything as you taught me ...

I: And done it well, I must say.

THE CREATURE: Then I don't understand; you contradict—

I: Not at all. You have done faithfully everything that I taught you. So far I'm proud of you. So far. Now you must take the next step. It's not an exaggeration when they tell you that you resemble a naked person in a dressed-up crowd. You do. I don't mind it, because I know what it is all about—but the audience will. They are entitled to a finished product.

THE CREATURE: Does that mean more schooling and more exercises?

I: It does.

THE CREATURE: I give up. But go ahead.

I: You don't give up. If I did not tell you right now what I'm going to tell you, you would work until you found it out for yourself. It might take you a few years, maybe more. But you would work until you had mastered the next step. And even then you would not stop. A new difficulty would arise, and you would go after that.

THE CREATURE: Endlessly?

I: Endlessly and persistently. That is the only difference between an artist and a shoemaker. When the shoemaker has done his pair of boots, it is over, he forgets about them. When an artist finishes a piece of work, it is not done. It is just another step. All the steps dovetail one into the other.

THE CREATURE: If you were not so exasperatingly logical; just like an old mathematician, one, two, three, four. Disgusting. No art, just a handicraft. An old cabinet maker, that's what you are.

I: You mean emotion maker? Thank you for the compliment. Would you like me now to turn into a dressmaker and dress your emotions?

Because, as we both agree, myself and your superiors, your emotions are quite naked, my child. Quite distressingly so.

THE CREATURE: *(Laughs heartily and provocatively.)* I don't mind.

I: But I do. I don't want anybody to say that my pseudo-moralities are immoral. Amoral, maybe, but not immoral.

THE CREATURE: *(Still laughing)* I wouldn't think of such a thing. Please dress me. I'm naked—ears, nose, eyes, emotions and all.

I: I'll take care only of the emotions, if you please. And I'll start by covering them with praise. I noted carefully everything you did in building your part—your physical control, your concentration, your choice and clear outline of emotions, your power of projecting those emotions. All that was splendid. I'm proud of you. But it lacked one thing.

THE CREATURE: What?

I: Characterization.

THE CREATURE: Oh, that's simple. When I put my costume on, and my make-up.

I: Nothing will happen, my dear.

THE CREATURE: You can't say that. When I am all made up and dressed, I feel like the person I am supposed to represent. I'm not myself then. I never worry about characterization, it comes by itself.

(I must use a strong medium to bring her down from her high horse and heresy. I reach into my pocket for a small ancient book, and open to the first page.)

I: Read it.

THE CREATURE: One of your tricks?

I: *(Striking a light)* Read it.

THE CREATURE: *(Reads)* "The Actor: A Treatise on the Art of Playing. London. Printed for R. Griffiths, at the Dunciad in St. Paul's Church-yard MDCCL."

I: *(I turn a few pages.)* Remember that MDCCL. Almost 200 years, that ought to impress you. Now read here.

THE CREATURE: *(Reads with difficulty the ancient letters and spelling.)* "The actor who is to express to us a peculiar passion and its effects, if he wou'd play his character with *truth*, is not only to assume the emotions which that passion wou'd produce in the generality of mankind; but he is to give it that peculiar form—"

I: *(Interrupting)* Now read louder and remember—

THE CREATURE: *(Does so)* "under which it wou'd appear, when exerting itself in the breast of such a person as he is giving us the portrait of."

(A pause. The dear Creature slowly raises her beautiful eyes, takes out a cigarette, lights it from my lighter, and blows it out furiously. I know that she will listen now.)

THE CREATURE: Well, what does he mean, that 200-year-old anonym?

I: *(Not without a slight triumph)* That before you put on your dress and your make-up you must master your characterization.

THE CREATURE: *(Puts her arm under mine, and says tenderly)* Tell me, how? *(One cannot be angry with her.)* And if you want a cigarette, I'll give you one.

I: *(As if telling a long forgotten fairy tale)* It is like this, my child. The actor creates the whole length of a human soul's life on the stage every time he creates a part. This human soul must be visible in all its aspects, physical, mental, and emotional. Besides, it must be unique. It must be *the soul*. The same soul the author thought of, the one the director explained to you, the one you brought to the surface from the depths of your being. No other but that one.

   And the character who owns this created soul on the stage is unique and different from all the rest. It is Hamlet and nobody else. It is Ophelia and nobody else. They are human, that is true, but here the similarity ends. We are all human, we have the same number of arms and legs and our noses are placed respectively in the same positions. Yet, as there are no two oak leaves alike, there are no two human beings alike. And when an actor creates a human soul in the form of a character, he must follow the same wise rule of Nature and make that soul unique and individual.

THE CREATURE: *(In self-defence)* Haven't I done that?

I: You have done it in a general way. From your own body, mind, and emotions, you created an image which could have been any young girl's image. Sincere, convincing, powerful, but abstract. It could have been Lisa, Mary, Ann. But it was not Ophelia. The body was that of a young girl, but not Ophelia's. The mind was that of a young girl, but not Ophelia's. It was …

THE CREATURE: All wrong. What shall I do now?

I: Don't despair. You have conquered more difficult things, this is comparatively easy.

THE CREATURE: *(Satisfied)* All right. What kind of a body had Ophelia?

I: How do I know? You tell me. Who was she?

THE CREATURE: The daughter of a courtier.

I: Which means?

THE CREATURE: Well bred, well controlled, well … fed?

I: You don't have to worry about the last, but don't forget the historical elements. A body with the bearing of a chosen creature, with the power and dignity of one born to represent the best of her kind. Analyze now in detail the posture of your head, go to the galleries or look into books. Look at Van Dyck, look at Reynolds. Your arms and hands were natural and sincere, but I could have told you right away that those hands play tennis, drive a car, and, when necessary, can broil a marvelous steak. Study the hands of Botticelli, of Leonardo, of Raphael. Then your walk—almost masculine.

THE CREATURE: Well, pictures don't walk.

I: Go and see the procession of nuns in the chapel on Easter night. If you must see everything.

THE CREATURE: I know. But how do I perceive all that and incorporate it into the part?

I: Very simply. By studying and making it your own. By entering into its spirit. Study the different hands. Understand their weakness, their flower-like tenderness, their narrowness, their flexibility. You can control your muscles. Just curl your palm longwise. Do you see how much narrower it is? Two days practice and you won't even think about it, but whenever you want it, it will stay like that as long as you wish. And when, with that kind of hand, you grasp your heart, it will be a different gesture than the one you made. It will be Ophelia's hand clutching Ophelia's heart, not Miss So-and-So's hand grasping Miss So-and-So's heart.

THE CREATURE: Can I study and interpret just one picture or can I use different ones?

I: Not only different ones, but living, contemporary personalities as well, in the whole or in part. You can borrow a head from Botticelli, a posture from Van Dyck, use the arms of your sister and the wrists of Angna Enters (the last not as a dancer but as a person). The clouds driven by the wind can inspire your walk. And all of this will make a composite creature, just as a tabloid makes a composite photograph of a person or event from a dozen different photographs.

THE CREATURE: When is one supposed to do this?

I: As a rule, the last two or three days of rehearsal, right at the stage where you are now. Not before you are well settled in the part, and know its structure well. But there are exceptions. Some actors prefer to start with characterization. It is more difficult, that is all. And the result is not so subtle, the choice of elements not so wise as it might be if you followed the inward thread of the part first. It is like buying a dress without being measured.

THE CREATURE: How do you make those things acceptable to your own nature? How do you blend them all together? What do you do to make them represent one real, believable person?

I: Let me answer you with questions. How did you acquire your good manners? How did you learn to eat with a knife and fork, to sit straight, to keep your hands quiet? How did you adjust yourself last winter to short skirts and this winter to long ones? How do you know how to walk on the golf course in one way and on the ballroom floor in another? How do you learn to use your voice in your own room in one way and in a taxicab in another? All those and hundreds of small changes make you what you are, so far as your physical personality is concerned. And for all those things you drew living examples from the life which surrounds you. What I propose is the same thing, done professionally. That means organized study and the appropriation, through intensive practice, of all the elements which will make you, in your part, a distinct and unique physical personality.

THE CREATURE: That is why you told me at the very beginning of our talks that I must have absolute control of every muscle in my body so that I would be able to learn quickly and remember all those things?

I: Exactly! "Learn quickly and remember," because to acquire good manners you have a lifetime; to create your part physically but a few days.

THE CREATURE: How about mind?

I: Characterization of the mind in the part on the stage is largely a question of the rhythm. The rhythm of thought, I should say. It does not so much concern your character as it concerns the author of that character, the author of the play.

THE CREATURE: Do you mean to say that Ophelia should not think?

I: I wouldn't be so rude as that, but I would say that Shakespeare did all the thinking for her. It is his mind at work which you should characterize while acting Ophelia, or for that matter, any Shakespearean character. The same goes for any author who has a mind of his own.

THE CREATURE: I never thought of that. I always tried to think the way I imagined the character would think.

I: That is a mistake which almost every actor commits. Except geniuses—who know better. The most powerful weapon of an author is his mind. The quality of it, the speed, alertness, depth, brilliancy. All of that counts, without regard to whether he is writing words of Caliban or those of Jeanne d'Arc, or those of Osvald. A good writer's fool is no more foolish than his creator's mind, and a prophet no more wise than the man who conceived him. Do you remember *Romeo and Juliet*? Lady Capulet says about Juliet "She's not fourteen". And then a few pages later Juliet speaks.

"My bounty is as boundless as the sea,
My love as deep; the more I give to thee,
The more I have, for both are infinite."

Confucius could have said that, or Buddha, or St. Francis. If you will try acting Juliet's part in a way which characterizes her mind as a fourteen-year-old mind, you'll be lost. If you try to make her older you'll ruin Shakespeare's theatrical conception which is that of a genius. If you try to explain it by the early maturity of Italian women, by the wisdom of the Italian Renaissance, and so forth, you will be all tangled up in archaeology and history, and your inspiration will be gone. All you have to do is to grasp the characterization of Shakespeare's mind and follow it.

THE CREATURE: How would you describe the quality of it?

I: A mind of lightning-like speed. Highly concentrated, authoritative, even in moments of doubt. Spontaneous, the first thought is always the last one. Direct and outspoken. Don't misunderstand me, I'm not trying to describe or explain Shakespeare's mind. No words can describe it. All I am trying to do is to tell you that whatever character of Shakespeare you perform, its mind (not yours but the character's) must have those qualities in its manifestation. You don't have to think like Shakespeare, but the outward quality of thinking must be his. It is like portraying an acrobat. You don't have to know how to stand on your head, but all the movements of your body must convey the idea that you are able to turn somersaults whenever you wish to do it.

THE CREATURE: Would you say the same if I had to act in a Bernard Shaw play?

I: Precisely. More so in Shaw's case. His peasants, clerks, and girls think like scholars, his saints and kings and bishops like lunatics and monsters. Your portrayal of Shavian character would be incomplete unless the mind of that character, embodied in its ways, continued attack and defence, continued provocation for argument, right or wrong.

THE CREATURE: Sort of an Irish mind.

I: There you are. You have explained it much better than I.

THE CREATURE: How do you apply that practically to a part?

I: As I have told you before, it is mostly the rhythm or organized energy of your delivery of the author's words. After studying him and rehearsing him for a length of time, you ought to know the movement of the author's thoughts. They must affect you. You must like them. Their rhythm must infect yours. Try to understand the author. Your training and nature will take care of the rest.

THE CREATURE: Can you apply the same rule of characterization to the emotions of a character?

I: Oh, no. The emotion of a character is the only sphere where the author should pay attention to the actor's demands and adjust his writings to the actor's interpretation. Or, an actor is justified in adjusting the author's writing to achieve the best results for his own emotional outline of the part.

THE CREATURE: Don't say that aloud. All the authors will murder you.

I: The wise ones won't. Emotion is God's breath in a part. Through emotion, the author's characters stand alive and vital. The wise author does everything to make this part of creation in the theatre as harmonious as possible, without ruining the idea and purpose of the play. Gilbert Emery told me that he threw out two and a half pages from his play *Tarnish*, in a big scene between Ann Harding and Tom Powers. He did it because Ann Harding could bring herself and the audience to tears much better by simply listening silently, than by answering every speech of Powers with another speech of the same importance. Gilbert Emery chose wisely between the emotion of an actress and his writing. Clemence Dane gave me permission to cut out every superfluous word in *Granite* for stage presentation. No, the authors won't murder me. They know that you, and I, and all like us work for them in the theatre.

THE CREATURE: But emotions must be characterized just as clearly as body and mind. What is the proper way to do that?

I: When you have mastered the general human emotions in the part, as you have in your Ophelia, when you know when and why anger comes, or pleading, sorrow, joy, or despair, whatever the case demands, when it is all clear to you, start to look for one fundamental quality: freedom in expressing your emotions. Absolute, unlimited freedom and ease. That freedom will be your characterization of the emotions at hand. When the inward structure of your part is well prepared and built, when you have mastered its outward appearance, when the manifestation of the thoughts of your character is in perfect accord with the author's way of thinking, watch during rehearsals to see when and where your emotions rise and flame with difficulty. Look for reasons. There may be many.

Your fundamentals may not be strong, you may not understand the action. You may be physically uncomfortable, the words may disturb you—their quality or quantity—the movement may distract you, you may be lacking in the means of expression. Find the reason for yourself and eliminate it. Let me give you an example. What scene in Ophelia do you feel least comfortable in?

THE CREATURE: The third act, the performance scene.

I: All right. What is the action?

THE CREATURE: To be insulted.

I: Wrong. To preserve your dignity. Ophelia is a courtier's daughter. The Prince of the reigning house is making unsuitable remarks to her publicly. He is master of her life, the more because she loves him. He can do whatever he pleases. But even if it pleases him to kill her, she will die with the dignity appropriate to her state. Your main action is not to break down, not to show weakness, or to *display publicly your intimate emotion.* Don't forget, the whole court watches Ophelia. Take all that now as your action. Can you find it in yourself easily?

THE CREATURE: Yes.

I: Is the rest all right? Are you comfortable in your seat? Do words come easily into your mind? Are you vital enough to think with Shakespearean boldness?

THE CREATURE: Yes, yes. I have it. Let me do it for you.

(Suddenly behind our backs a voice arises. An old, shaky, but trained and rich voice, trembling with the expectation of something big, decisive, half absent from its own sound.)

"Lady, shall I lie in your lap" ...

(I turn around. The old doorman is standing behind us.)

THE CREATURE: *(Like a frozen sea. Calm and terrific in its rigidity.)* "No, my lord."

THE DOORMAN: *(Still tense with expectation, but I can sense a trace of sorrow and pity toward the beloved one.)* "I mean, my head upon your lap."

THE CREATURE: *(You are my master. You are within your rights.)* "Aye, my lord."

THE DOORMAN: *(The pain is behind that voice now. He must go on with assumed madness. He must hurt one he doesn't want to hurt, to convince the others.)* "Do you think I meant country matters?"

THE CREATURE: *(The apotheosis of dignity. If I have to die, I will think nothing, my lord.)* "I think nothing, my lord."

(A few speeches more, and the scene is finished. Fast, terrific, tense. Just right. The Creature jumps from the seat and whirls along the aisle.)

THE CREATURE: I have it, I have it now! It's so simple. I felt easier than ever before. It's just nothing.

THE DOORMAN: *(His sad old eyes blinking at her)* It's nothing, Miss—when you know it.

THE CREATURE: Oh, Pa, you were very good. How do you happen to know all the cues?

THE DOORMAN: I have played with all the big players for the last forty years. I have played almost every part in all the big plays. I studied them all, I worked hard. But I did not have time to perfect myself or to think about all the things this gentleman has told you. Now, when I have time to think, and I plunge back into years gone by, I know all my mistakes, and the reasons, and the ways of doing. But there is nothing to apply them to; I try to keep my door shut the best I can. And when I see and hear the young actors struggling, I think always ... Oh, if youth knew, and if age could do, what a wonderful world it would be. I have enjoyed your talk, sir. Everything was true, very true.

I: I am honored, sir.

THE DOORMAN: Now begging your pardon, would you please take your leave, sir. It's time for rehearsal. *(He finishes with a sly, dreamy smile which covers his old face with wrinkles.)*

"The actors are come hither, my lord—
The best actors in the world ... "

5   The Fifth Lesson
Observation

We are having tea, the Creature's Aunt, "who knew Mr. Belasco personally", and myself. We are expecting the Creature at any moment. The tea is excellent.

THE AUNT: I think it charming of you to take such an interest in my niece. The child is so absorbed in the theatre. Especially now that she is successful. Can you imagine, she is getting a regular salary. I never thought it possible in the theatre.

I: Just the law of supply and demand.

THE AUNT: I must confess, I don't understand what she wants from you now. She is a "professional". She has received good notices. She has a good part. What else can she ask? Not that I don't enjoy the pleasure of your company, now and then. And I'm sure my niece does. We both adore the theatre and its people. The late Mr. Belasco—what a charming man he was—said to me once when I considered taking a part in one of his productions "Madame, you belong to opening nights. Your presence in an orchestra seat is just as vital to the play's success as the best performance of all my actors." It was so cute of him. The man was a genius. Would you believe that I never miss an opening night of a successful play?

I: It's very kind of you, Madame.

THE AUNT: Not at all. I'm doing everything to promote—*(she almost sings it. ... The tea is unbearably hot.)* a b-e-a-u-t-i-f-u-l art of the theatre. Shakespeare. ... Noel Coward. ... And what an actor Alexander Woollcott has turned out to be.

I: He has studied hard, Madame.

THE AUNT: Unquestionably. And in the right way. He watched actors for years. He remembered their tricks. Then he took a part and started to act it. Now, if he would just act and act every day as much as he could, he would be remarkable.

*(I gulp the tea which, for some reason, gets hotter and hotter. I am
preparing to ask for another cup when the Creature enters. She stops
in the middle of the room to look us over. There is doubt in her
expression.)*

THE CREATURE: And may I ask what you two were talking about?

THE AUNT: About the theatre, my dear, about *(she sings again, and rolls
her eyes)* a b-e-a-u-t-i-f-u-l theatre.

THE CREATURE: *(With a slightly grim humor)* Then I hope you agreed.

I: We were getting ready to disagree when you entered. Your Aunt, my
dear, just made the statement that all that is necessary to become an
actor is to act, act, and act. Am I correct?

THE AUNT: I know that I am right. I don't believe in all the theories and
lectures, psychological analyses, and brain-befuddling, exercises
my niece has told me about. You'll have to forgive me; I'm a
straightforward person. And I adore the theatre. But my theory is:
To be an actor one must act. So act all you can,—as long as it pays.
When it doesn't pay,—stop acting. And that's that. If one has talent,
like this child here ...

THE CREATURE: Auntie ...

THE AUNT: That's all right, my dear. Talent needs advertising like
everything else. If one has talent the pay will last for a long time.

I: I'm glad, Madame, you give talent such a boost. But, if I may ask,
don't you consider that talent needs cultivation, that only through
cultivation can one discover the presence of talent?

THE CREATURE: *(Picking up my thought heartily)* Auntie, dear, it's just
like a wild apple and a cultivated apple. They are both apples,
but one is green, hard and sour, and the other red, soft, sweet, and
fragrant.

THE AUNT: To argue with poetical comparisons is unfair, my dear. An
apple is one thing ...

I: *(Continuing quickly)* And talent another. You are quite right. Let's
not compare. Let's have a pleasant teatime. May I ask for another
cup? Thank you. *(I receive a full cup of delightful tea, with cream
and sugar, then I continue.)* May I ask you, Madame, if you ever
heard of a new delightful game which is played much in German
Kindergartens, called *Achtungspiele?*

THE AUNT: No, what is it?

I: A very simple game. The teacher makes the children repeat snatches
of their activities, things they have done today, yesterday, a few
days ago. It serves the purpose of developing the pupil's memory,
analyzing his actions, and sharpening his sense of observation.

Sometimes the child is allowed to make its own choice, and then the teacher makes her conclusion as to what direction the child's interest takes, and either develops it or warns the parents and other teachers about it. For instance, the child who chooses to remember how it destroyed a bird's nest is not punished, but an effort is made to shift its interest into a different sphere.

THE AUNT: *(Like a glacier)* Very interesting.

I: Oh, not half as interesting as when you try it on the grown-ups. Interesting because it shows how little we grown-ups use a wonderful natural gift, the ability for observation. Would you believe that very few persons can remember how they have acted for the last twenty-four hours?

THE AUNT: Incredible. I can tell you exactly what I have done for the last twenty-four years.

I: Oh, yes, you could *tell* me, I'm sure. But the game is not to tell but silently to perform, to re-enact. Silence helps concentration and brings out hidden emotions.

THE AUNT: I could do it silently if I wanted to. Though I'm not so sure that I would want to. I'm a straightforward, outspoken person.

I: Why not try? It's just a childish game. Would you be willing?

THE AUNT: Oh, I'll try anything.

I: Splendid. We all will try. Let us start on something easy. For instance ... for instance, may I ask you to re-enact the process of serving me with that delightful cup of tea which I received from your hands a minute ago—

THE AUNT: How ridiculous. *(She laughs heartily.)* A very cute idea. You want me really to go back to Kindergarten.

I: Not at all, Madame. It's just a game. The next test will be mine or your talented niece's.

THE CREATURE: Oh, please, Auntie, I'm curious.

THE AUNT: All right. It's a gloomy afternoon anyhow. Now observe me. *(She begins like a high priestess or Macbeth's witch, almost rolling back her sleeves.)* Here is the cup ... *(I interrupt.)*

I: Silently, please. No words, just actions.

THE AUNT: Oh, yes, I forgot. The mystery of silence. *(She is a sarcastic old lady. But she has made up her mind, and she is going to show us up—she begins. Her forehead is wrinkled. The thoughts are working. She takes a cup in her right hand, reaches for a teapot with her left, realizes her blunder, exclaims candidly "Oh, my God", puts the cup back, takes the teapot in her right hand, holds it in the air. I whisper between two sips of tea—)*

I: Don't touch anything, please. Just go through the actions. ...

THE AUNT: I'm doing that exactly.

I: Then kindly put down the teapot.

THE AUNT: Oh, yes. *(She puts it down and lays both hands on the table, jerks them off immediately, and with maddening speed indicates the motions of taking the cup and pouring a drop of tea into it. Then without placing the pot on the table adds imaginary cream and lemon from respective containers, and hands me the cup by its handle, obviously having forgotten the saucer and the sugar. The Creature shrieks in unrestrained laughter, and throwing her arms around her Aunt's neck, kisses her many times. I finish my cup of tea.)*

THE AUNT: It's just silly, that's all.

I: No, Madame. It's just an uncultivated gift of observation. Will you allow your niece to re-enact your actions of the same event? And as you know, she couldn't foresee that I would choose this particular one. So she will have to do her best unprepared, please.

THE CREATURE: Can I tell it? I'm so excited,—at you and Auntie getting along so nicely, that I couldn't possibly keep silent.

I: Yes, you can tell it, because it's somebody else's action. If it were your own I would insist on your re-enacting it in silence. The gift of observation must be cultivated in every part of your body, not only in your sight, and memory.

THE CREATURE: Auntie, when B. asked you for a cup of tea, you smiled at him. Then you looked at the teapot as if trying to make sure that there was any more tea, then you looked at me and smiled again as if saying "Isn't he cute?"

THE AUNT: *(Booms loudly)* I did not.

I: You did, Madame. I remember it well. It was my only encouragement from you.

THE CREATURE: Then you looked again at B. as if waiting for him to hand you his cup. But he did not.

I: I'm sorry.

THE CREATURE: Then you held your wide right sleeve with your left hand and reached over to the tray for a fresh cup. Took it, holding it on the saucer, and placed it in front of you. Then, still holding your sleeve, you took the teapot. It was quite heavy, so you put it down and got a better grip on the handle. Brought it over the cup, let your sleeve go, took the strainer,—placing it over the cup. Then, holding the cover of the teapot with the fingers of your left hand, you started to pour the tea. The cover was hot and you changed your fingers one after another. When the teacup was three-quarters full, you placed the teapot nearer to you and smiled again, this time at nobody in particular. Then you poured cream with your right hand and drop-ped in two lumps of sugar, holding the tongs in your left. You handed the cup to B. and placed the tongs on a dish with lemon, right where you can see them now.

THE AUNT: *(Seriously offended)* One would think you were in the thea-tre, you must have studied me.

I: No. Please don't be cross. I assure you there was no premeditation. *(I turn to the Creature.)* You forgot to mention that your Aunt could not find the cream right away, and for a fraction of a second looked all over the table for it.

THE CREATURE: Yes, and you were playing with your napkin all the time.

THE AUNT: *(Laughs heartily. She is a good sport, after all.)* Aha! So you didn't escape scrutiny either.

I: I didn't try to, Madame. I was intently watching your niece exercising her gift of observation.

THE AUNT: And you taught her that childish game just to watch her pranks.

I: Madame, I did not teach her anything. We both work in the theatre. And the theatre is one place where teaching and preaching are absolutely excluded. Practice is what counts, and only practice.

THE AUNT: Just what I say. Act! act! and you'll be an actor.

I: No. To act is the final result of a long procedure, Madame. Practice everything which precedes and leads toward this result. When you act, it is too late.

THE AUNT: *(Caustically)* And what, if I may ask, has that gift of observation to do with acting, if you please?

I: A great deal. It helps a student of the theatre to notice everything unusual and out of the ordinary in every-day life. It builds his memory, his storage memory, with all visible manifestations of the human spirit. It makes him sensitive to sincerity and to make-believe. It develops his sensory and muscular memory, and facilitates his adjustment to any business he may be required to do in a part. It opens his eyes to the full extent in appreciation of different person-alities and values in people and works of art. And lastly, Madame, it enriches his inner life by full and extensive consumption of every-thing in outward life.

It has the same effect that one banana and a handful of rice, as a day's food, have on a Hindu follower of Yoga. Consumed rightly, getting the maximum energy out of that miserable amount of vitamins, that food gives to a Hindu immeasurable energy, spiritual power, and vitality. We consume a steak at lunch, and imagine at dinnertime that we are hungry. We go through life in the same manner. We think that we see everything, and we don't assimilate anything. But in the theatre, where we have to re-create life, we can't afford that. We are obliged to notice the material with which we work.

THE AUNT: So you tell my niece to notice how her Aunt pours a cup of tea, and then you both make fun of her. *(I see a twinkle in her eye; she is a good sport.)*

THE CREATURE: Oh, Auntie, dear, not at all. He was just joking.

THE AUNT: I know a joke when I see it. He is darn serious, and so am I.

I: No, you are not. Otherwise I wouldn't read in your eyes the invitation to continue. You are amused. I appreciate that. I cannot teach, but I will endeavor to amuse you. Your gift of observation will do the rest.

THE AUNT: *(Graciously)* If you want another cup of tea, pour it yourself.

I: Thank you. *(I do it, and Auntie watches me like a hawk. After I am through—)* Madame, I realize that for the first time you have given me your full attention. I'll make use of it. You adore the theatre. We, your niece and I, work for the theatre and in the theatre. When you go to an opening night, you go out shopping and choose the most suitable dress. We shop in life every day and choose the most suitable things for every night that we spend in the theatre. To us, they are all opening nights. They all command us to be at our best. The actor who has his gift of observation dulled and inactive will appear in wornout dress on a gala occasion. As a rule, I believe that inspiration is the result of hard work, but the only thing which can stimulate inspiration in an actor is constant and keen observation every day of his life.

THE AUNT: Do you mean to say that great actors walk through life spying on all their acquaintances, relatives, and passers-by?

I: I'm afraid they do, Madame. Besides, they spy on themselves, too.

THE CREATURE: How otherwise could we know what we can do and what we can't?

THE AUNT: We are speaking about *great* actors, my child.

THE CREATURE: Oh, poor me, poor me. What a blow. *(She pouts humorously.)* Auntie, are you through with advertising me?

THE AUNT: You are a spoiled creature.

I: She is a marvelous creature. Allow me to advertise her a little. I won't overdo it. I'll tell you only how we both developed, and made important observations in our craft. Your niece had the part of the blind girl in *The Cricket on the Hearth*. She rehearsed it well, but nobody ever believed that she was blind! She came to me and we went out to find a blind man. We found one on the Bowery. He sat at the corner. He did not move for four hours. We waited for him to go because we wanted to see him walking,—finding his way. To ask him to move wouldn't be good. He would be self-conscious. For the sake of art we risked hunger, pneumonia (it was chilly), loss of time.

Finally the beggar got up and went home. We followed him there, it took another hour, gave him a dollar for his involuntary service to us, and left highly enriched in experience. But the price of it, not counting even the dollar, was too big. In the theatre, one cannot spend four hours waiting for beggars. One must pick up and store experiences for all emergencies at all times. One must start from the beginning so ...

THE CREATURE: I decided, Auntie, on a plan, and B. approved of it.

I: Exactly. Go ahead and tell it, it's your contribution.

THE CREATURE: I decided that for three months, from twelve to one every day, wherever I happened to be and whatever I might be doing, I would observe everything and everybody around me. And from one to two, during my lunch time, I would recall the observations of the previous day. If I happened to be alone I would re-enact, like the German children, my own past actions.

I do not do it any more except occasionally, but in three months' time I became as rich in experiences as Croesus in gold. At first I tried to jot them down, now I don't even need to do that. Everything registers automatically somewhere in my brain, and through the practice of recalling and re-enacting I'm ten times as alert as I was. And life is so much more wonderful. You don't know how rich and wonderful it is.

THE AUNT: You ought to change your career, my child. You ought to become a detective.

I: Madame, isn't every produced play and every acted part a discovery of hidden values and treasures? The unveiling of virtues and vices, the control of passions? A fourth wall removed from a room? A battlefield exposed? The grave of "Poor Yorick" dug out?

THE AUNT: Well, well, well. (*Not entirely convinced*) Still, somehow, it doesn't sound real to me. Very theoretical. Bookish. In my estimation the ways of the theatre, and all other arts for that matter, ought to be natural. We don't do those things in life.

I: Forgive me, let's drop the subject. Your niece tells me your sister has just come back from abroad. Did you find her rested, looking well, when you met her at the pier?

THE AUNT: Oh, yes, thank you. She was rested all right, but as for looks!—That woman will be the death of me! She is the champion worst dresser in New York. Can you imagine; she had on a beige Eugenie hat with a dull mauve plume. And a narrow purple satin ribbon flecked with silver. Even tiny silver marcasite clasps on the side. She wore a travelling outfit of checked velveteen—small checks, first a brown line, then a grey, then a purple, on a background of a dull mocha color ...

I: *(Interrupting rudely)* Madame, what you have said just now shows a gift of observation, cultivated and used quite naturally in real life. In the theatre we do the same thing, making our circle of observation as wide as possible. We use everything, and everybody, as an object, the only difference being that we never talk about it, we act it.

THE AUNT: *(Sighs softly, and changes the subject of the conversation to the Horse Show at Madison Square Garden. We finish tea in peace and mutual agreement. The Creature is silent and thoughtful.)*

6   The Sixth Lesson
Rhythm

The Creature put it to me bluntly.

THE CREATURE: If you have any longing for beauty you'll go with me and see it.

I: The only time I indulge in a longing for beauty is between seven and eight in the morning. ...

THE CREATURE: *(Even more bluntly)* I'll be at your door tomorrow morning at seven-fifteen.

***

At twenty minutes to eight today the Creature and I find ourselves standing at the top of the Empire State Building. Far below, innumerable arms of stone are desperately reaching for the sky. In the distance, the same sky is gently descending toward green fields and a pearly sea but they seem to make no effort to reach it. The Creature and I are most entertainingly silent. After a while we sit down.

I: I'm certainly grateful to you.

THE CREATURE: I knew you would like it. ... *(Suddenly, very shrewdly)* ... And I knew you would explain it to me. You will have to explain it to yourself anyhow; that is, if you register "all this" emotionally the way I do.

I: Suppose I am not able to explain? And suppose I register "all this" emotionally quite differently from you?

THE CREATURE: Exactly what I hope will happen.

I: May I ask why?

THE CREATURE: You may. First, because if you are not able to explain a thing you always lean on me for support, proof, or clarification. I am your "Exhibit A." This makes me feel important and wise.

A marvelous feeling, almost like receiving a fan letter. I think I'll be able to help you—this time as usual. *(In her gaze I feel a deal of pride and gratitude. Well hidden though, behind a youthful challenge.)* Second, if you feel anything differently we will plunge into an argument—and I rather think you profit by my arguments. As a matter of fact, without my arguments, I cannot imagine what you would do. *(She must be happy. She is positively defiant today.)*

I: Probably I would invent arguments.

THE CREATURE: An extremely difficult and dangerous procedure. You might not be able to invent them and even if you did, they might not be real and convincing. It is only human to be prejudiced toward one's own arguments.

I: It is only human to be prejudiced toward arguments used against us, as well.

THE CREATURE: Yes, but that kind of prejudice is an incentive for one's own strength and convictions. Isn't it?

I: In life, yes. And in the arts, the straightest and most practical answer is also yes—especially in the theatre.

THE CREATURE: Is that because on the stage, resistance and conflict of actions are the essential elements of its life?

I: Precisely. Suppose in the first act of *The Merchant of Venice*, Antonio should pay the money on the dot, change his religion, and ask for the hand of Jessica. ... Don't laugh. I am serious. That is an exaggerated example. Here is a legitimate one:

"How all occasions do inform against me,
And spur my dull revenge!
... Rightly to be great
Is not to stir without great argument,
But greatly to find quarrel in a straw
When honour's at the stake."

Which is *Hamlet*—Act IV, Scene IV. All through Shakespeare you can find those marvelous sign posts for the actor. They are wisely concealed in the text of the plays—not displayed in a multitude of boastful directions. In those two lines—the first which come to mind—you see the straightest advice: No action without conflict!

THE CREATURE: And is that stimulant of action the sole secret of a successful play or acting?

I: Oh, no. This is only a theoretical beginning. An A. B. C. so to speak. In the theatre I call it "Mr. What"—rather a deadly personality without his mate, "How". It is only when "How" appears on the stage that things begin to happen. The conflict of actions may be *presented* on the stage and remain there petrified awaiting an answer to the question: "What is the theme of the play?" In which case it is not theatre. But the same conflict may be *created* with unexpected spontaneity, with uncalculated impulse and it will plunge the audience into a feverish state of partisanship toward one side or another. It will force them to find their own living and excited answer. This will be theatre. And the secret is not in the question: "What is the theme of the play?" but in the statement: "This is how the theme perseveres or does not persevere through all obstacles."

THE CREATURE: You are, of course, speaking about what happens in performance itself when you mention the "unexpected spontaneity and uncalculated impulse". You don't mean during the preparation of the play and the working rehearsals. You have always told me that inspiration and spontaneity are results of calculation and practice.

I: I am still inclined to believe so. I am speaking about the performance itself.

THE CREATURE: All right. Now I want an explanation from you. Why do we stand, for I don't know how long, here on the top of the Empire State Building; silent, awed, bewildered, exhilarated? The view from here is remarkable but not unexpected. I knew it before I actually saw it—from hundreds of photographs and newsreels. I have flown over Manhattan in an airplane; moreover, I live in a twenty-third story penthouse. I have seen it before. Why is the impression so great?

I: Because that remarkable "How" has had a finger in the affair.

THE CREATURE: You seem to be enthusiastic about this "How". I'll be jealous.

I: You may well be. Let me show you "How's" ways and means as opposed to those of "What". "What" would take you from the street level of that boiling, screeching, clanging, arguing city of New York to the window of the first floor of the Empire State Building. He would open the window and say to you, "This, my child, is the first of the hundred and two floors of this building. As you see, the difference between the level commonly known as the street level, and the first floor is slight. Exactly twenty feet. You hear the same noises. You see almost the same view. You do not feel much separation from the squirming mass of humanity below. Let's go to the second floor."

THE CREATURE: *(In horror)* What?

I: "To the second floor, my child," is the answer of "What", and no sooner said than done. You *are* on the second floor. A slight change in the analysis of the height and difference in view follows. Then "What", with appropriate explanations, takes you to the third floor, fourth floor, and so on until you reach the hundred and second ...

THE CREATURE: Oh, no. I beg your pardon. He does not take me to the fourth floor, and so on.

I: "What" is very persistent, I assure you.

THE CREATURE: That doesn't matter. On the third floor, exactly, I take him gently by the neck and push him over the window-sill toward the level "commonly known as the street level". Curtain.

I: But suppose you did go with him through all the hundred and two floors? Can you imagine your emotions then, in the face of this splendor?

THE CREATURE: I presume there would be none.

I: Why? Where would be the difference? Let us try and find out. You would climb each step logically. You would understand where you were and how high you were. You would realize the gradual change. You would be, as a matter of fact, thoroughly advised on every detail of this remarkable structure. Why do you think there would be no emotion?

THE CREATURE: I really don't know, but I hate the very idea of it.

I: May I ask "How" to bring us here?

THE CREATURE: Please.

I: We are taken along the street. The City rushes to work. No, more than that. It stampedes toward the havens of existence, to the places of its "jobs". "Jobs" which will give to every man in the city—bread, a roof, hope in the daytime, quiet sleep at night. Those things seem as precious to them as black pearls to a diver. Everybody is afraid to miss the time-clock, to lose his work. Terrific tension in steps, gestures, faces, and words. There are exactly so many minutes to make so many miles. One cannot stop for a second and compare his own frenzied speed with the serene speed of the sun or wind or sea. To give oneself courage one must shriek and yell and laugh loudly and falsely.

As if not satisfied with that manifestation, all the conceivable means of sound production lash one's eardrums. Rivets, horns, bells, grind of gears and highpitched groans of brakes, whistles, gongs and sirens—all seem to yell in a steady rhythm, "Go to work—right away. Go to work—right away." It is like two-fourths time in music repeated endlessly—with ever increasing volume. We are part of that rhythm. We walk faster. We breathe faster. Whatever words you say to me, you flash like radio signals. I answer you with speed. Finally we arrive at the door of the Empire State Building and we find ourselves struggling. It is so difficult to tear ourselves away from the surging currents of arms, legs, and faces, and turn inside. It takes an effort, but we do it.

In a flash we find ourselves in a box of an elevator—cut off as if with a knife from the world behind. I could compare that feeling with the *forte fortissimo* of an orchestra, cut off by the master hand of a conductor, to be resumed by the tender *sostenuto* of violins. How long it lasts, we do not know. We are alone. We shoot up through space. We change elevators. We shoot up again. The upward flash of those hundred and two floors seems like two winks of an eye. Almost two seconds in silence—in repose. The door opens. We find ourselves here, suspended from the sky by man's genius—separated from the earth by the result of his labor.

Wherever we look, space flows, inviting to the eye and thought. We are not forced to accept any direction, any command, any limits. We are yanked out from the measures of Scriabine's *Prelude*, in fifteen-eighths time, with its torturing temptations, and thrown suddenly on a broad, streaming magic carpet, to float in the air to the rhythm of a steady wind which seems to sing out, in measured intervals, one word, "Space". Our spirit is raised in an upward flash from torment to bliss.

THE CREATURE: And "How" is responsible for that upward two-winks-of-eye "flash"—which seems to produce such a remarkable result.

I: Aren't you grateful? And don't you realize "How's" importance?

THE CREATURE: Yes. *(Slowly thinking)* Importance to what?

I: To our profession.

THE CREATURE: Are you serious?

I: As serious as if I were telling you a joke.

THE CREATURE: How do I know—maybe you are. After all, "How"—it's ridiculous.

I: Do you want a learned, much abused, common name for "How"?

THE CREATURE: I'll be delighted.

I: *Rhythm!*

THE CREATURE: *(Her usual, charmingly humorous self)* I've heard the name somewhere—but I've never had the pleasure.

I: Neither had I. Jaques Dalcroze told me a great deal about Rhythm in Music and in Dancing, two arts in which it is the essential and vital element. I found a book on Rhythm in Architecture; it is not translated into English. Those were the only two reliable and practical guides to that great element of every art. Critics occasionally mention rhythm in painting and sculpture, but I have never heard it explained. In the theatre the mechanical word "Tempo" is substituted, but it has nothing to do with Rhythm. If Shakespeare had cast those two, he would have written:

> Rhythm—the Prince of Arts.
> Tempo—his bastard Brother.

THE CREATURE: Splendid. Now I want to know all about both of them.

I: You would never believe the countless hours I spend trying to define Rhythm so that it can be applied to all the arts.

THE CREATURE: Have you succeeded?

I: Not yet. The nearest I have come to it is *the orderly, measurable changes of all the different elements comprised in a work of art—provided that all those changes progressively stimulate the attention of the spectator and lead invariably to the final aim of the artist.*

THE CREATURE: Sounds methodical.

I: Because it is the beginning of a thought. I do not claim that it is a final definition. I beg you to think about it and find a better one. Put it to your friends. I'll be grateful for it. We will all be. Meantime, I would like you to attack mine. It will give me a chance to defend it.

THE CREATURE: All right. You say first: "Orderly and measurable"—but suppose I am creating "Chaos"? How can it be orderly and measurable?

I: You forget the word "changes". Your work of art, "Chaos", if it is such, must consist of a number of conflicting actions. They may be as disorderly as your genius will let them be. But the "changes" from one to another must be orderly. And that is exactly what only a genius can make them. If you remember Michelangelo's frescoes on the ceiling of the Sistine Chapel, you remember that from the floor looking upward they give a perfect impression of "Chaos", prototype of creation. Take a reproduction of those frescoes and spread it before you on the table. One look will be sufficient to convince you that it is "Chaos" composed of the most "orderly and measurable" changes of all the elements involved.

THE CREATURE: I do remember. You are right. But I'll be scrupulous. What do you mean by "changes"? Fluctuations?

I: No, not fluctuations. Precisely changes. Perhaps I can explain myself more clearly by another example. You recall Leonardo's "Last Supper"?

THE CREATURE: I do. Very well, indeed. I studied the movement of all the hands in it. I knew them by heart and could use all of them freely and naturally.

I: Very well then. The element here is *the hand*. It changes its position twenty-six times. Twenty-three visible and three invisible. If you knew all the positions by heart and could freely change from one to another, building up their significance with each change, you would achieve a Rhythm of that particular masterpiece.

THE CREATURE: Isn't that exactly what Isadora Duncan did, and what Angna Enters does now?

I: It is.

THE CREATURE: I see. One more question. On the canvas of the "Last Supper" the hands change, but at the same time they are stationary. How can you apply the word Rhythm to them? Isn't Rhythm applied to movement?

I: There is no limitation. A glacier moves two inches in a century; a swallow flies two miles in a minute—they both have Rhythm. Expand the idea from the glacier to a theoretical standstill and from the swallow to a theoretical light-speed. Rhythm will include and carry them all within its scope. To exist is to have Rhythm.

THE CREATURE: How about its "elements"?

I: That is simple. Tone, movement, form, word, action, color— anything a work of art can be made from.

THE CREATURE: How would you apply "orderly and measurable changes" to colors on canvas?

I: Take Gainsborough's "Blue Boy". The dominating color is blue. It varies an infinite number of times. Each time the change is clean cut and almost imperceptible. It is orderly. Countless copyists have tried to measure the amount of indigo in each change. They generally fail, but that does not mean that it is immeasurable, because it was done once.

THE CREATURE: Continue with the same example. How does the change in blues "stimulate progressively the attention of the spectator"?

I: Simply by arousing his curiosity to look at that which is *not* blue.

THE CREATURE: You mean …

I: … the pale and refined yellowish-pink face of the "Blue Boy".

THE CREATURE: True. And at the same time it "points to the final aim of the artist", that same boy's face.

I: Must you run ahead of me to the conclusion?

THE CREATURE: I wouldn't be a woman if I didn't love to have the last word.

I: The least I can do is to make you believe you have it.

THE CREATURE: What do you mean by "make me believe"?

I: I have not told you all about Rhythm yet.

THE CREATURE: Oh, that is all right. That only means I'll have many more last words.

I: Let us hope so.

THE CREATURE: I am sure of it. And to prove it to you I will even have a few *first* words. Here is one. While I was working in the theatre— legitimate theatre, mind you—in stock companies and on Broadway, I found that old reliable "Tempo" very helpful. You abused it a few minutes ago. As a matter of fact, it saved me many times when I did not know what to do. ...

I: *(Oh, how pleased I am!)* Yes—exactly—when you did not know what to do! You just sped over the embarrassing moments until you knew what to do. Marvelous! I have seen performances when actors apparently never had an idea what to do because all the elements I could discover in three acts were "Tempo" and that other savior of embarrassing moments, "Intonation". *(I pat her on the shoulder humorously.)* My dear friend, stick to last words.

THE CREATURE: You are horrid. In stock, the poor actor often has no time or opportunity to find out what to do.

I: Let him not lie. Let him sketch the situation lightly. Let him glide over it truthfully—then he may, on the spur of the moment, discover what to do. Such things happen in life. You meet somebody you did not know was in town and whom you do not want to meet, and spontaneously you start to act. You get your cue and you answer. After all, that is what the author wants from you. Spontaneous answers to his cues.

THE CREATURE: But where does one get that spontaneity?

I: In a developed sense of Rhythm. Not from Tempo, surely, which means slow, medium, fast. That is far too limited. On the other hand, Rhythm has an endless, eternal swing. All created things live by Rhythm, by a transition from one definite thing to another greater one. Take this speech, for instance:

"You lie, in faith; for you are call'd plain Kate,
And bonny Kate, and sometimes Kate the curst;
But, Kate, the prettiest Kate in Christendom,
Kate of Kate-Hall, my super-dainty Kate,
For dainties are all cates; and therefore, Kate,
Take this of me, Kate of my consolation;—
Hearing thy mildness prais'd in every town,
Thy virtues spoke of, and thy beauty sounded,—

Yet not so deeply as to thee belong,—
Myself am mov'd to woo thee for my wife."

And this, as you well know, is *The Taming of the Shrew*—Act II,
Scene I. This speech can be the most deadly, monotonous affair,
delivered by an actor without a sense of Rhythm. And speed or
Tempo won't save him. The faster he goes—the duller he will
sound. But I have heard this speech spoken by an actor who knew
the value of "changes" from "plain" to "bonny"; from "curst" to
"prettiest"; from "Kate-Hall" to "super-dainty"; and so forth.
I assure you I never heard a shorter speech in my life. It was an
avalanche of changes; a dose of admiration—which is the shortest
measurable time in the theatre. The most brilliant test of the difference between "Tempo" and "Rhythm" is the first soliloquy of
Claudius in *Hamlet*, which begins:

"O, my offence is rank, it smells to heaven;
It hath the primal eldest curse upon't,—
A brother's murder!—Pray can I not,
Though inclination be as sharp as will:
My stronger guilt defeats my strong intent;
And, like a man to double business bound,
I stand in pause where I shall first begin,
And both neglect. ... "

Study it sometime. Do you see now?

THE CREATURE: I see one thing. More exercises are entering my busy day.

I: Well, the last word is yours—what shall it be?

THE CREATURE: Anything that will enable me to "Stimulate progressively
the attention of my spectators".

I: Bravo! You are a willing victim. In that case, the workout will be
simple. For an actor, the business of acquiring a sense of Rhythm is
a matter of giving himself up freely and entirely to any Rhythm he
happens to encounter in life. In other words, not to be immune to
the Rhythms which surround him.

THE CREATURE: But to do that, one must know and realize what Rhythm
is. Suppose I am Rhythm-deaf or, will you say, unconscious? What
should I do?

I: "To a nunnery, go; and quickly too. Farewell."

THE CREATURE: Oh, please—I really do think I have no sense of Rhythm.

I: You are mistaken. There is not a stone in the universe without a
sense of Rhythm. A few actors, maybe, but very few. Every normal

being has it. Sometimes undeveloped, in a dormant state, true. But a little work will bring it forth.

THE CREATURE: Don't torture me now. Tell me how.

I: Do not hurry me. It is one of the hardest subjects to explain because it is so simple and universal. A child is born with the manifestation of Rhythm present. It breathes. A fair start which nature provides for all. After that, development follows. First in walking, second in speech, third in emotions. One step, one word, one emotion changes into another and then another, each with the same allegiance, a final aim in view. This is the first level of Rhythm—consciousness. The second level arrives when outside forces impose their Rhythm on you. When you walk or move or gesture with or for others. When you walk in line; run to meet a friend; shake hands with an enemy. When your words answer other words; sweeping you with them or holding you still. When your emotions are the direct answer and result of somebody else's feelings.

THE CREATURE: What is the third level?

I: When you command and create your own Rhythm and that of others. It is perfection. It is a result. Do not hurry to achieve it. The student must start with the second level. He must not do much at the start. All that is required of him is to notice these manifestations in real life and store them away in his brain. Special attention should be given to the results of different Rhythms. The best thing to start with is music, where Rhythm is most pronounced. Go to a concert; a street organ, if you prefer, will do just as well. But listen to it with all your being, entirely relaxed and ready to be swept by the definite measures of the music. Give yourself up to the emotions it brings to you. Let them change with the changes in the music. Above all, be attentive and flexible. Follow music with the other arts, these with every-day occurrences.

THE CREATURE: *(In ecstasy, as always when she discovers that two and two are four.)* I know now. That is what has happened to me here, on this height. I gave myself up entirely to the terrific change of Rhythm performed so quickly, so masterfully.

I: So impressively. An elephant would stagger under the effect of that change. No great virtue for you.

THE CREATURE: Very kind of you, dear Sir, but that is not going to be your last word. Suppose after a while I am sensitive to music? Where do I go? To what should I be sensitive next?

I: You are already sensitive to a trifling jump of some thousand feet in the air.

THE CREATURE: Please!

I: You are sensitive to the Rhythm of the New York streets. You nearly ran me out of breath.

THE CREATURE: But I won't be sensitive to your humor! It's rather annoying.

I: I am sorry to disappoint you again. (*I suspect that she is serious.*) You *are* sensitive to my humor because you changed the strength of your voice; the speed of your words; the amount of demand in your request. You changed your Rhythm.

THE CREATURE: One day I'll learn to argue with you. Please tell me: what shall I pay attention to after I respond to music freely and easily?

I: (*She pleads so tenderly that I follow my own recipe and change my Rhythm. I take her by the hand and lead her to the balustrade.*) Don't look at me now, my dearest friend, look into space and listen with your inner ear. Music, and the other arts which follow naturally, will be only an open road to the whole of the universe. Don't miss anything in it. Listen to the waves of the sea. Absorb their sweeping change of time, with your body, brain, and soul. Talk to them as Demosthenes did, and don't weaken after the first attempt. Let the meaning and Rhythm of your words be a continuation of their eternal sound. Inhale their spirit and feel at one with them, even for an instant. It will make you, in the future, able to portray the eternal parts of universal literature. Go through the same experience with woods, fields, rivers, sky above—then turn to the city and swing your spirit to its sound as you did to its creative rattle. Don't forget the quiet, dreamy, small towns—and above all, don't forget your fellow men. Be sensitive to every change in the manifestation of their existence. Answer that change always with a new and higher level of your own Rhythm. This is the secret of existence, perseverance and activity. This is what the world really is—from the stone up to the human soul. The theatre and the actor enter this picture only as a part. But the actor cannot portray the whole if he does not become a part.

THE CREATURE: (*Very thoughtfully and sadly*) I am mortified.

I: Why?

THE CREATURE: Thinking how busy I shall be for the next few months.

I: Yes. But you will always know "what to do next". Isn't that a consolation?

THE CREATURE: Rather! My regards to "How"! Shall we go?

(*We do. The elevator whisks us down. The street swallows us—and we change our Rhythm.*)

The "Creative Theatre" Lectures

Editor's note: As far as can be discerned, these are the lectures given by Boleslavsky at the Princess Theatre in 1923 during the New York visit of the Moscow Art Theatre; as such, they are the first public presentation in the US of Stanislavsky's approach to acting and the theater. The original document—the actor Michael Barroy's initial transcription and edition—is held by the New York Public Library Theater Collection at Lincoln Center. Intended for a general audience of theatergoers, these lectures are an earlier version of some of what appears a decade later in *Acting: The First Six Lessons*; they provide a general context and clarification for the book. This present edition corrects some misspellings and typographical errors in the original to facilitate ease in reading; in some instances, as with the Lincoln Center manuscript, marginal notes in hand have been incorporated, while material in the original that has been penciled out has been omitted.

Introduction

Man can not live without art! At first it sounds like an aphorism, – but you'll soon see my point. Wherever we turn we always find traces of art. It was so in ancient times, as well as today.

A knife of the stone age of a prehistoric man, the statue of Venus de Milo, the Cathedral of Notre Dame of Paris, even the Rolls Royce car, – everything created by man bears upon it the mark of art.

"Man cannot live by bread alone," said Jesus Christ ...

"The designs on the wings of a butterfly are dearer to me than all earthly treasures," said Confucius.

People usually divide art in two classes:

(1) *applied* art and
(2) *pure – real* art.

Applied art is supposed to refer to the practical things of life such as furniture, clothing, household articles and the like.

Pure art – is supposed to serve for one purpose only – *delight*, as sculpture, painting, music, dancing, poetry, the theatre.

As if one could divide art.

As if art were not the only, the real, the eternal ...

Try to divide the ocean. To say – this part is for navigation, this for scenery. You couldn't do it.

The ocean will be always both beautiful and useful.

So is art. It is both – beautiful and useful. And what is more, art is absolutely indispensable to us. The only trouble is that we have not enough of it in life. We miss it, we long for it constantly. That's why we decorate with a design even a match box, we have carvings on our woodwork, flowers painted on our tea cups and saucers and so forth.

And what about candies? Don't we prefer them packed in pretty boxes, to those in plain paper?

This is the reason why the manufacturers all over the world are spending fortunes in decorating their products.

This peculiarity of man to embellish his life, his eternal striving toward beauty, is the seed of the divine in a human nature. It is the thing that distinguishes man from other mammals.

The striving of man to beautify his life is the only trace that he leaves behind him through the ages. We know only about those departed peoples, which left after them some works of art – as monuments, drawings, sculpture, literature, etcetera.

Nations who had no art are really and thoroughly dead, to us.

We know much more about the primitive life of the caveman by the simple drawings of animals on the walls of his cave and by the broken fragments of pottery, than about the life of ... let us say the Chaldeans, who left no works of art behind them but who, according to their neighbours, the Egyptians and the Phoenicians, were a powerful nation with a complicated system of government.

People enter history only through the record of their genius in art. What would the world know about Russians were it not for Tolstoy, Tchaikowsky, Pavlova?

The Poles – were it not for Kopernikus, Chopin, Paderewsky and Kosciushko (or at least his statues in public squares)? Of Americans if *we* would not have a Poe, a Sargent, a Mary Garden, a Walt Whitman. (I almost said Paul Whiteman) – But why bring up names. – Let us take the modern Greeks.

Now tell me honestly what do you know about them, beside the fact that they had some kind of a revolution, that one of their princes sought refuge in America and that they are running most of the lunch rooms in Chicago? I see you are laughing, but I am certain that you do not know much more about them. – I, at least, must confess I do not.

But now I will put to you another question. What do you think of the Greeks who lived 3000 years ago, who built the Acropolis, who made the statue of Venus of Milo, who created the Doric, the Ionic, the Corinthian Capitals (orders) or composed the *Iliad* and the *Odyssey*?

I am certain that your mind gets a thrill of the mere thought of those creations. – Those were men! Only because of that great past you care at all for their modern princes. But I feel that I am deviating from my main theme – the theatre.

You see – each art, in order to exist demands two things:

(1)   an artist-creator and
(2)   the material

As long as man reproduces his kind we'll always have creators. But man is a cautious being! We became afraid that some day he would not have sufficient material to create his works of art, that it might give out.

Yes he got scared – In spite of the fact that all he needed for drawing on the walls of his cave was a tusk of a boar, – that Appeles used for his pictures only two or three or primary colours, – even that for building pyramids there was no use for steel or concrete – in spite of all that man became worried that he might lack some day in material and he decided to insure himself against such occurrence. So he said to himself: "I do not need a thing, neither the paints, nor the tusk, nor the stone or the strings – nothing. I will be the material of which I myself will create a work of art. I – with my voice, my body, my soul, with my eternal striving toward better life, – I am the material which I'll use to make a masterpiece I am afraid of nothing," said he and with joy at his own smartness he started to dance and to sing.

Thus was born the theatre.

The Theatre! What a magic word!

From the very moment of its birth, man got infected and is still afflicted by it. It's like a chronic illness of mankind. It is the only art of all and for all. Art of kings and paupers … Geniuses and buffoons.

There was not a king, especially among those who felt how short their reign would be, such as Nero, the Medicis, the mad King of Bavaria, who would not maintain magnificent theatres.

During my life in Europe I've never seen a beggar who wouldn't stop in the street before an acrobat turning somersaults.

In Paris I observed some of the midinettes, little working girls earning around $5 a week, freed at noon for their lunch hour, to spend that hour in front of a street singer, buying with their last pennies a copy of the song in order to sing in chorus "J'en marre!"

I take my hat off to them! They created art, out of themselves – for themselves.

They were creating their own theatre! The theatre is *vital* like a salamander and does not burn in the fire scorching pages of history.

On the contrary, the more horrible the day, the more alluring are the lights at night by the portals of the theatre.

Louis XIV, the Sun King, who said: "Apres nous le deluge" – was doing all he could to support the blazing sun of Moliere's genius.

Nero, to whom the crowd, losing patience, boldly cried the immortal slogan "Bread and Circuses," did not always supply the bread, but never failed to provide circuses, especially as the actors, who were the Christian martyrs devoured by lions, were not demanding big salaries.

The reign of the virgin Queen Elizabeth, rich in brilliant events and characters, could not overshadow the reign of Shakespeare.

Napoleon brought along with him to Moscow the French Theatre headed by Mme George. Napoleon is known as being defeated of Moscow, but Mme George returned to Paris in full splendor of her glory.

At the time of the great French Revolution the so-called "saviours of the people," while saving their citizens during the day by the "guillotine," were resting at nights in theatres, enjoying classical tragedies with the great Talma.

During the Great War with Germany there were over twenty new Shakespearean productions, which were holding the repertoire.

The conflagration of the revolution entirely scorched Russia, but could not consume the theatre which is flame in itself ... A flame eternal and holy. A flame of the human soul. (Mute agreement between the red and the whites not to touch the Moscow Art Theatre. Theatres were heated.)

The theatre can be suppressed by no one, not even by those who have a chance to do it. I am speaking about ignorant producers – or as my late friend Hartley Manners, author of "Peg o my Heart," used to say, "Glorified Janitors".

I must tell you a little story which happened to me when I came to see one of the foremost Broadway producers just a few weeks before the first arrival of the Moscow Art Theatre: example – My interview with a Broadway producer concerning the "Would be Gentleman."

1   What is the Theatre?

The theatrical literature has many definitions of that word, but here is one used by my master Stanislavsky which served as a corner stone for the entire theory of the Moscow Art Theatre School: "The theatre is the result of that natural striving of mankind to correct and improve the reality."

The theatre creates an imaginary but beautiful illusion instead of an unsatisfactory reality. The theatre in all its aspects and manifestations (that is: games, dancing, parades, pageants and whether it be a circus-tent show or a religious mystery play) has for its motto: there is something which is better than the ordinary, every day life – come and watch it!

This call is so powerful and answers so strongly to the natural needs of mankind, that all the first performances in the whole world are overflowing with an eager and, generally, well disposed crowd that is ready to absorb everything offered just like a child waiting to be presented with a new toy.

But often, mostly because of the producers' ignorance, the theatre goer is witnessing a performance which is not better but sometimes even worse than reality. In such cases the spectator gets bored, dissatisfied and leaves the show quite disappointed … and waits for another chance to see a performance that would improve the reality.

People often say: "I want to relax – let us go to the theatre", or "I feel so lonesome – let us see a show" – or else "let us see John Barrymore – he is a wonderful Hamlet." In other words, most of the people go to the theatre in order to rest, for diversion, to see an impersonation of some fictitious character – to get away from reality and our every day life.

The theatre is the real enemy of the humdrum actualities of life. It shows our life in the past, present or future, but *always* better and more beautiful than it is in reality.

Shakespeare's words about the theatre as being the "mirror" of life should not be taken literally. The word "mirror" implies by itself the idea of " reflection" of "improvement." An artist holds his picture in front of a mirror in order to discover its defects and to correct them. We look in the mirror to improve our appearance – to look better.

You've noticed, of course, that people going to the theatre are getting all dressed up – they try to look better than usual.

Nowadays it has become simply a custom, a kind of vanity – but this custom comes to us from ancient times from those theatrical festivals when the actors and the audiences were not separated when they represented, but one enthusiastic crowd which gathered bound by only one desire – to create a bit of *improved* better life.

You have heard of the theatre being the "school of life" which educates and uplifts people. We may acknowledge this statement but we must not pursue it as our aim.

As a matter of fact the theatre is a marvelous teacher but only because it does not want and does not try to teach us. I mean the real creative theatre – not the "propagandizing" one! It fascinates the crowd by merely showing the beautiful illusion of life. – In discussing this question my pupils were often asking me to show this illusion in a play like for instance Gorky's "Lower Depths." I succeeded in proving to them during our class exercises that every tramp presented there was an "idealized" – an "ideal" and that a truly *realistic* performance could not be accepted on any stage in the whole world.

As I said before, the theatre is one of the most ancient and complicated arts in the world. You probably will be surprised if I tell you that the theatre and architectures are the only arts *practiced by animals*. Oh yes – I mean it.

Take for instance a cat, – not a kitten, but a wise old Tom cat – Have you ever tried to play "mouse" with such a cat – If you'll attach a piece of paper to a string and will drag it on the floor in front of the cat – you'll find very few that would not respond. It would give you an actual performance of chasing a mouse. It will deliberately *act* in front of you, knowing perfectly well that it is not a real mouse. Then, suddenly the old cat gets bored, – in the middle of a somersault it stops playing and sits down quietly without another glance at the fake-mouse. – The curtain fell down. It's intermission.

And what about a dog that feels in fault and falls on his back seeing the approaching master. The dog wags its tail, *pretends* to be extremely unhappy and miserable. Isn't that the purest form of theatre. I should say it is.

And a bird trying to escape from the hunter, pretending, to have a broken wing. Theatre! A peacock spreading its tail and showing off in front of its mate – theatre! ... If you are observing, I'm sure you will find hundreds of such examples around you.

As for the monkey, being biologically nearer to men than the rest of the animals – its longing for the theatre is quite pathetic. – It never loses a chance to act and to impersonate something that's lacking in its own life.

It seems clear to me that the theatre is an integral part of all the higher forms of life. That's why the word "theatre" does not mean a building, with an audience, orchestra seats, a stage and a group of people putting make up on their faces every night and reciting by heart lines composed by someone else. – Not at all! It is a tendency – an innate longing of every living being toward improved life, toward an ideal.

That's why there is a close kinship between the actor and the priest – two professions that used to be years ago but one. Both are having for their subject – striving toward a better life.

Before finishing this first little chat about the theatre I must say that the most important part of the theatrical *science* – (I emphasize – science) is: The ability to give a *most accurate, faithful* yet *enthusiastic* representation of the life around us.

Because, in order to create something that is *better*, one has to know to perfection what is like the actual thing. For instance, before making a cover which is better than this one, I have to know to perfection the way this one was made.

Now I wish to thank you for the attention you gave to my little chat and to thank you for the brilliant performance you gave as an audience.

2 What is a Play?

One of the most important parts of the theatre is the theme, the plot, in other words the "*play*".

If you whistle to your dog and say: "come on for a walk!" and your dog starts jumping and cavorting around you – at that very moment your dog gives a performance having for its theme: delight with nature, joy or gratitude.

Each pantomime, each dance must have a certain theme. Without a theme your dance will become a series of contortions.

The theme, the plot or the play is the author's idea about better life or about a certain phase of it put into a concrete form.

The centre of life is the soul or the human spirit in all its simple or complicated manifestations.

A worth while play is much more concerned with the inner life of the spirit than with the external happenings of our everyday existence.

The actors call some of their roles "grateful" and others "thankless", which means that there are parts full of spiritual significance to which the actor's soul responds easily and enthusiastically and gives him the opportunity to create an image – a living character and other parts constructed only externally, without any inner spiritual logic. Such parts are hollow and an actor finds it extremely difficult to make anything out of them.

Life teaches us, that each feeling, each desire to attain something – has to be "performed" or "enacted."

If I beg you to do something for me I have to "perform" my request. If I call you for "help" – I have to "perform" the danger which threatens me.

If I try to persuade you in some idea, I have to "perform" all the advantages of my thought in other words show you why I am right.

This is really the basis of each play.

The Moscow Art Theatre in its teachings uses the expression "The man-role", – It's like Pirandello's six characters. – Let us call it the "living character." So – each "living character" in a play must possess a spiritual urge striving toward a definite aim, and expressed in a form that gives the actor the opportunity to demonstrate this urge most convincingly. How could you, for instance, impersonate convincingly a dying man if the author supplies you with a lengthy monologue, relating the reasons of this death.

The author can create a real play only if he takes as a basis for his "living character" a real human feeling. He might invent the form, the way of expressing this feeling, but he can not invent the feeling itself.

The laws of nature are immutable and eternal.

But nature in its divine opulence expresses them in many different ways.

The laws of nature teach us; that our entire life is nothing else but a series of struggles for an ideal for the better things of life.

The dog struggles for a bone. So does sometimes a man, especially if the bone has a piece of steak attached to it.

Yet mostly man struggles for his spiritual ideals.

Every living being, starting from a microbe, is in a constant struggle. As soon as the struggle stops life dies.

The author offering his creation must follow this law. There can't be a play without a struggle of ideas, passions, feelings, and desires. In life such struggle is expressed by a series of will problems, dictated by our intellect and our spirit and carried out by our physiological apparatus.

I am ambitious – I struggle to satisfy my ambition. I am in love – I struggle to have my love returned. And so forth down to the smallest problems.

I wish to wash my face – I am struggling, with wash cloth and soap, to attain my end.

In other words our whole life consists of a series of problems expressed by two factors (thesis) which follow each other: (1) I want it and (2) I do it.

A play can not exist (either) without these two factors. Unless we can apply them to any part of the actor's role we have not a play but just a gathering of words.

If you'll take a real classical play you'll see that you can apply these two factors to any of its parts. Sometimes, true, with certain difficulty as for instance: "I want to relate, I want to explain", – but penetrating carefully into the spirit for the play you'll be always able to discover its problems and its action.

In life we are generally confronted with two kinds of problems:

(1)   *Main problems*; filling the entire existence of a man during a certain period of his life. As for instance love, ambition, etc.
(2)   *Secondary* or *auxiliary* problems, problems of our daily existence – as: request, lie, caress, persuasion ...

The same is true regarding a play. We have there one, or at most two, main problems, filling the entire play and being the main theme of nearly all the parts and a number of secondary problems helping to bring forth the main problem.

In Shakespeare's "Twelfth Night" for instance, the main problem is: The faculty of enjoying life, the appreciation of the joy of living. This problem runs throughout the entire play and through almost every part. The secondary problems help to develop the main one.

The discovery of the main problem in a play is extremely important. – In a real creative work, one half of the rehearsal time is devoted to it, but as soon as the main problem is definitely found, the whole play becomes clear and harmonious with one single aim, which is a most necessary condition for every work of art. Unfortunately, many authors, being extremely careful regarding the literary side of the play, are forgetting to be true to its "life problems".

As examples of such plays I could take some of the French "romantic" and so called "pseudo-classical" plays by Corneille, Racine and even Victor Hugo, plays with long tirades and pompous monologues, – plays abundant in words and showing not the "better life," but ostentatious, bombastic people brought by the author into artificial, pseudo-tragical or comical situations.

And only because on the stage, as in a fairy tale, everything is permitted, – some authors following their "library-imagination," which often has nothing to do with the "truth of life," supply the actors and the audience with an artificially invented *main problem*. They have for their object merely the demonstration of a novel and "trick" situation, – instead of an improved bit of life. This, of course, makes the actor seem unnatural and the very word "theatrical" becomes the synonym of "artificial." In Shakespeare's "Tempest" all the imaginary characters are as plain and natural as the tempest itself, or the wind, the flower, the tree, because the human feelings in it reflect the characteristics of nature itself.

3   What is the Audience?

What could be more beautiful than our childhood? That period of the human life when the entire world seems to be nothing but a huge riddle, when everything appears so full of mystery and when the little childish heart beats so anxiously before a mechanical toy, burning with desire to find out what is hidden inside of that toy, – when the whole life seems to concentrate in the questions: what is it? and why? – When there is no other life problems but "to know" and "to understand."

But, the older we grow the less there remains for us to discover – most of the secrets of our toys are disclosed and we have ready answers to most of those "whys." In other words, our life comes down to the simple fulfillment of our daily problems, which are no longer riddles for us but are long since definitely set and solved in our minds.

And yet, the divine spark in our nature is so powerful, that we cannot rest and find satisfaction in things that have become clear to us, that are solved – and like children we continue to look for new possibilities that will confront us with another mystery, which will arouse in us again the eternal question "why" – something that will be better than the past or the present and that will help us in our eternal search for perfection, for an ideal.

For the sake of that pursuit, man, like a child, longing for a new toy, gives up his life in scientific research, founds new sects for the complete perception of God, embellishes his life with works of art and cherishes a naïve though almost unconscious love for the theatre, where the mystery is presented in such bright colors and life seems to be so beautiful and alluring and so unlike the actual one.

The theatrical audience is nothing but a child in front of a new toy. All the emotions of such a child or the feelings of a savage watching a modern invention you'll find in hearts of people gathering rightly in theatres. Just look at the audience a few moments before the show has started. What animated faces! What an enthusiastic anticipation! And then that hush which passes through the audience calling everyone to attention at the rise of the curtain. If the performance is a truly creative one, this excitement increases by the minute and it is not the public's fault if toward the end of the show such a frame of mind dies away, giving place to dissatisfaction and boredom. It only means that this time the theatre has not disclosed the mystery and did not answer the child's question: "What is there inside of the toy?"

Have you noticed the air of importance about most of the people, telling their friends that they are going to an opening night? It sounds almost as solemn as when a man says, "Tonight I expect to become a father!" I don't know of anyone (with the exception perhaps of theatrical critics) who is reluctant to go to an opening. Even the disappointment of the theatregoer, unfortunately very frequent, can't kill his eagerness to witness something new. That's why the theatre can always find an opening night audience. The attendance of the following performances depends entirely upon the play, the actors and the whole theatrical organization.

There is a peculiar childlike quality of trust about the theatregoer. He buys his ticket for an unknown play almost blindfolded, with complete confidence that his favorite author, actor or producer will not disappoint him. I am certain that you will not buy a pair of shoes, even of the best make, without trying them on. And see what a lot of absurdities are good-naturedly overlooked by the public:

Wobbly stone walls.
Moonbeams chasing the leading characters all over the stage.
Ignorance of lines!
Houses ridiculously small compared to the size of the actors and trees growing out of the floor.
Lovers shouting tender declarations loud enough to make all the neighbors come running.
Country girls in silk ginghams and wearing large diamonds.
Growling villains knowing no other feelings but intense hatred.
Eloping couples with several pages of dialogue in front of the approaching danger.
Brandished wine cups remaining filled to the brims contrary to all natural laws.

And so forth, and so forth. There are hundreds of examples and one cannot be safe from such absurdities even in foremost commercial theatres. And all this is willingly overlooked by the public if there is only the tiniest bit of truth about the performance, the smallest particle of that "improved" life for which mankind is constantly longing.

And what about that adoration surrounding the favorite players, an excessive adoration, almost out of proportion in comparison with the merits of many benefactors of the human race.

It's not without good reason that Victor Hugo said: "The greatest people are those who make the world smile." And though the actor after his death is comparatively soon forgotten by the public, – I do not know of any profession whose members could boast of a greater popularity than the theatrical one. It seems to be that all this is enough of a proof of the essential necessity of the theatre for the human race.

What is, then, the natural deduction from all this? Let us see:

> We have a public, – a gathering (group) of friendly and, as a rule, well disposed people, who are ready in advance to overlook many of the shortcomings and mistakes committed on the stage. They are bringing you their money in advance and in advance they are prepared to believe in all you are going to tell and to show them. They feel a craving for spiritual food, for a bit of improved life, and they are hoping that during the two or three hours of the perform- ance the theatre will conscientiously fulfill their expectations.

Don't you think that the theatre has a serious moral obligation toward this trusting crowd? – That every member of the theatrical profession from a stage hand up to the star has to do all in his power to carry through the problems of a creative theatre?

Before I finish this little talk regarding the theatrical audience I wish to say a few words about that peculiar relationship between the actors and the public during the performance. It is like what the French call "un cercle civieux" (a vicious circle). The better the actor incarnates his part and "lives it," the more responsive grows the audience and vice versa, – the more intense and enthusiastic is the public, the more inspired becomes the actor in his performance. A mysterious invisible bond is created linking the audience with the stage, and as a result we get a truly inspired and creative performance. This is the reason why witnessing the same show twice in succession you may be entranced by it once and dissatisfied and bored with it next time.

I'll always remember the words of Otis Skinner, with whom I was touring the country in the play "Sancho Panza." Addressing the public in his curtain speech he used, sometimes, to thank *them* for a brilliant performance. It is not far-fetched as it might seem to you at first, because the behavior of the audience is 50% of the success of the play, and if everyone on the other side of the footlights were initiated into this little secret the number of flat and uninspired performances would be considerably lessened.

A most striking example of this mutual bond between the actors and the audience I observed in Russia during my association with the Moscow Art Theatre. The patrons of this remarkable group had a deep, almost religious attitude toward this theatre and its players. A death silence was reigning in the audience during the show. The late comers would never think of taking their seats while the act was on, and were patiently waiting in the corridors for an intermission. The actors, on the other hand, were most considerate toward their public. The kidding on the stage, so frequent even in the best commercial theatres, was a thing unheard of. Each of them realized that he couldn't possibly give an emotional, spirited performance, if a moment before in the wings he would tell funny stories or discuss ball game. Too, there existed an *unwritten backstage law*, according to which one half hour before curtain time, the actors backstage had to be made up and keep complete silence, sitting quietly in the green room or in their dressing rooms and "concentrating", or, according to Stanislavsky's expression "entering into their circles." If someone would ask him at that moment a question, he would either not understand, or kick back at the inquirer.

"Misfortune of being clever." [Editor's note: This refers to Aleksandr Griboyedov's play *Gore ot uma*, typically translated *Woe from Wit*.] Stanislavsky, playing the host, asked Bailiff (then super) playing one of the guests, what he thought of the hero's (Kachalof) mental condition. B., thinking Stanislavsky meant Kachalov's interpretation, replied naively that K. was nervous because of Grand Duke's presence. After show B. got a terrible bawling out by Stanislavsky for giving an answer which had nothing to do with the play, while he was on the stage.

To them the theatre was nothing but a temple. I never saw anyone keeping on his hat upon crossing the threshold of the stage door, – as one would never think of dropping in for a chat into a church, no one of the Moscow Players would ever think of coming to the theatre for anything else but for the sake of art. If an actor would drop into the theatre during a rehearsal, even a private one, organized by the actors themselves (another thing unheard of in a commercial theatre) he would enter on tiptoes into the audience, sit down quietly and watch the work of his comrades.

In some instances, the Moscow Players went a little bit too far in their fanaticism. When, during the bolsheviki terror, Moscow lacked absolutely any kind of fuel, and a glass of water left at night on the table was turning into ice by morning, the only building in Moscow, supplied with heat was, besides a few houses of the leaders of the Revolution, – the Moscow Art Theatre. After a meeting held in the theatre Stanislavsky offered the actors to sleep in their dressing rooms. A unanimous refusal was the answer. The theatre, like the church, was not a place to sleep in. As a result was the death of Koreneva, one of the leading women, who caught pneumonia in her apartment.

A few weeks later, during the bombardment of Moscow by both the "Reds" and the "Whites," when every building was either plundered or confiscated or destroyed by shells, there was a sort of a silent agreement between both parties to protect "their theatre." Cordons were established from both sides of the theatre, nothing in it was touched, and not one shell came flying in that direction. It was a *theatrical audience* that came to a mutual agreement in protecting their own theatre.

4 What is an Actor?

Can a theatre exist without a scenic designer? – Yes –
Without music? – Yes –
Without an author? – Yes –
Without an actor? – Never –

The theatre is the actor, and the actor is the theatre.

The actor combines in himself two entirely different entities, – the "artist creator" and the "material" of which he creates his works of art, in other words, – himself. In this combination lies the main difficulty of the actor's profession. In order to be an actor it is not enough to possess the first of those faculties, as I know a lot of people with refined, artistic taste who could explain to perfection how a certain role should be played, and yet they would never be able to enact it.

To create in an actor the first of the above mentioned entities is impossible, and it can't be taught. This personality in the actor has to have 18 qualities. The first is talent. If one has *that*, the other 17 do not matter.

The second personality of the actor, namely, the "creative material," is entirely in his power and it could and should be developed. This material consists, in its turn, of two parts, the external and the inner one, both requiring a thorough study and training. The external part, – the plastique of arms, legs, and the whole body; control of every muscle of the body; strength, flexibility and precision of voice; complete control of one's nerves.

The inner part is much more complicated and less known as material for training and study. It is: the *intellect* the *will* and the *emotions*, – three separate parts which allow the actor to attain the chief essential in his art, the ability to "*live* through his role." Only the actor who is able to "*live*" his part can expect to create a bit of "better life." Only by developing his intellect, his will and his emotions can he learn how to "live" his parts.

The difference between an actor who "lives his parts" and one who "imitates life" is the same as between a *living person* and a *mechanical puppet*. No matter how precise he may be, trying to copy life, if he doesn't live through his emotions he'll never be able to get hold of the spectator, to entrance him. He might astonish, even amaze him but he'll never be able to penetrate into his soul, and stir it and to leave there an impression. In other words, he will not show to his spectator the "better life" but merely a "reflection", an imitation of it.

5   What is a Theatrical Designer?

We call a theatrical designer a man who brings into the theatre a visual picture of "better life," created by means of colors and forms, – *in order to include it as a component part into the general production*. This is what distinguishes an ordinary designer from a theatrical one.

The theory defining art as the "creation of better life" can be applied to every art and consequently to the art of painting, – but not every painting, picture or architectural motive can be called "theatrical." They might be called so, only if they were created for the purpose of including them in the theatrical "ensemble," and are qualified to remain in it. It means, – they must not overpower nor be crushed by the other elements of the theatrical production, which are: the human voice, the plastique of movements, music, the struggle of feelings, the dialogue, etc. The ideal of "better life" is *harmony*, the substance of our actual *daily life – chaos*. That is why, in a theatre which strives to show the "better life," the artist-painter should be an integral part of the general harmony. A performance lacking in general harmony can never be successful.

But how can one expect general harmony in a commercial theatre, if the procedure in getting together a production consists usually in the following: The manager who has decided to produce a certain play, picks out his actors, a stage director, a scenic designer and a composer, not because of the spiritual response he might expect of them, but only according to his own financial resources. After the question of their respective salaries is settled, he usually calls a general meeting for all these people, with the exception of the actors. (Sometimes, though, he invites to this meeting the stars of the production.) During the meeting he simply tells them what to do, often even without asking for their suggestions. Then starts an amicable little chat, during which most of those present agree with the opinion of the producer, who pays them the money, though shortly before he might have been a successful grocer.

By the way, saying this I don't try to be funny, as I was once myself in a New York production run by a rich grocer. Then, having established a superficial plan of work they start *everyone separately* on a conscientious fulfillment of his tasks. How often had I to pity these honest efforts wasted in vain! What good is there in a beautiful set, when it is delivered to the director just before the opening night? When the actor has to act without knowing what is behind his back? How can an actor be successful and play with ease a complicated scene on a bridge, or let us say, on a stairway, if it is for the first time that he has to walk upon a shaky and badly adjusted construction, and if until then had to rehearse only between four old chairs?

I once saw from the wings the opening night of "Romeo and Juliet." The actress representing Juliet stood on the balcony, and playing the greatest of female lovers was furtively glancing toward the side wing, where stood the head-carpenter, responsible for the erection, just in time for the performance, of the wobbly balcony. Standing in a heroic posture and watching the scared Juliet, he was whispering reassuringly, "Don't fret, if you'll come down, I'll catch you anyway!" I wonder who was at this moment Juliet's real hero, – Romeo or the stage carpenter?

No one could feel at ease wearing for the first time a pair of brand new shoes! Yet they want the poor actor to feel at home and to be in a creative mood, in perfectly strange and unfamiliar surroundings. For instance, the director rehearses the actors in a forest scene during a night storm. They struggle in vain to find the necessary mood, to express the feeling of fear, chill, discomfort, of the wet swampy ground under their feet, of the rain streaming down their necks. There is such a scene in "King Lear." Who, if not the artist with all his scenic effects could help the actor in such case? Because the actor certainly needs assistance, having before him a most difficult problem, that of finding the basic feelings of his part. You cannot after all, wallow them in mud or pour water on them, in order to furnish them the necessary mood. No one but the artist by his drawings and his sets, creating the impression of an "ideal storm" can help the actor to get into the mood of feeling an "ideal" horror in front of a raging nature.

How often the actor spoils his interpretation, not knowing until the last moment what the physical appearance of the character he plays should be, or, which is still worse, when during the dress rehearsal he comes to the conclusion that the looks of his "living character" have nothing in common with the character he had in his mind. He must have the same sensation as a traffic policeman, standing at noon on a busy corner, all dressed up in ballet skirts.

The artist, no more than any other member of the production, has the right to miss any of the meetings concerning this production or any of its rehearsals. He must be initiated in all the troubles, all the attempts and attainments connected with the work. As much as the artist assists the director and the actors in their work, they should inspire him and help him in all his searches and doubts.

The artist should make his sketches for the make-up and the costumes, while watching the actors rehearsing. By all means while they rehearse, as the actor incarnating a part, brings sometimes most surprising results, creating a personality often directly opposite to his offstage individuality.

The same holds true in regard to the stage furniture and the props. It is extremely important, for instance, to an actor, playing a scene in his own home, to be surrounded by furniture and articles responding to his individuality. Do you think it is possible to furnish in the same way the rooms of Shylock and of Othello only because it's Venice and more or less same period? And do you think that the room of Othello as played by Salvini, quick and alert with a tiger-like personality, throwing around the furniture, could be set in the same way as the room of Othello – Mounet-Tully, classically calm and majestic in his tragedy of an outraged lion.

And shouldn't an actor playing Hamlet have a costume, a sword, an armchair, responding to his individual interpretation of the part? Yet one often hears at theatrical costumers and workshops such expressions as "Macbeth's armour," "King Lear's Throne," as though they were serial made articles, or else a "forest drop," or a "royal crown" – for any old king at all.

Sometimes, though, the following happens: A producer secures the services of some talented scenic artist, who stirred merely by the author's literary work, secludes himself and creates inspiring and beautiful sets, giving truly the illusion of "better life." The actors and the director were rehearsing, in the meantime, using as a foundation for their work the common everyday life. The images created by them are trivial and commonplace, while those of the artist are fanciful and unusual. Their stage mechanics do not go farther than "right" and "left," while the artist's sets are full of charm, of unexpected curved lines. The tone of voice they are using is realistic, loud and even, while the sets are full of mystery and delicate transitions from one mood to another. As a result we say that the artist has crushed the actors, that he does not take them into consideration and that the whole production is nothing but an exhibition of that artist's masterpieces. Only an artist who works hand in hand with the actors and the other members of the theatrical production, who subordinates his creative power to the requirements and needs of his theatrical colleagues, can be called a theatrical designer.

Example – Macbeth in Auditorium.

6   What is a Theatrical Composer?

It is not an easy task to find the right place for music in a dramatic production. It's because the music by itself is too much of an independent art. Music, as such, is almost the incarnation of the "better," the "ideal" life. Music helps us to move in rhythm; it helps our work; our mood changes under the strain of a certain air; even death seems to be easier with musical accompaniment; otherwise why should all the armies in the world maintain such splendid bands? Music is the most complicated and abstract art in the world as well as the most independent one. To give its full expression it does not require any kind of assistance, and yet it is brought into a dramatic production as something supplementary. Its great power must be subordinated to the general problem of the production.

That is why it is a great mistake to include in a dramatic production any previously written musical composition which is not specially composed for that particular production, but is, doubtless, written according to purely musical laws. They try to squeeze it into the production, cutting it down, shortening and rearranging, which, as a rule, arouses lots of misunderstandings between the director and the composer. The composer following the laws of musical theory, construction and harmony. The director and the actors being subject to the laws of theatrical theory, construction and harmony. Two entirely different realms.

Why are most singers such poor actors? Because they have to submit themselves entirely to the musical laws, sacrificing to them the truth of life. It is only natural that an exalted human feeling would be expressed, through an orchestra or a single musical instrument, by a sharp powerful note of a brass or a stringed instrument, while the human soul expresses the same intense feeling by deep silence, a pause full of impressive meaning. Yet the musical laws demand that the actor should take together with the orchestra the same powerful note taken by the brass instrument, a note which requires all his spiritual and physical forces and distracts him completely from "living through his part," which is the only thing that really matters in a creative performance. If, on the other hand, the actor pays too much attention to the "spiritual interpretation" of his part, they usually say that he neglects the music, is careless with the composer. This is the reproach made frequently to Chaliapin, who, while on the stage, always follows the laws of his own spirit.

One of the theatrical conventionalities is the orchestra playing during the intermissions in the pit, in front of the lowered curtain. You see the musicians drifting in, greeting each other, blowing their noses, you hear them discussing their private affairs, we hear them tuning their instruments. In other words, we see them violating one of the fundamental theatrical problems – the disclosing of mystery. Why shouldn't we see then, the actors putting on their make-ups, and costumes in front of the public? Why don't we see the stage hands setting the stage? The music in the intermissions of a dramatic production is certainly an incongruity. What could be in common between a serious dramatic play and a jolly tune, even by a good composer, played between the acts?

In opera as well as the operetta music occupies the leading position. In such production the theatre is submitted entirely to the baton of the orchestra leader, even if it is not in accordance with the baton of "life." In such case the art of the theatre is subordinated to the art of music, which possesses a clear and harmonious theory with unfailing laws, while the theatre, as exercised in such kind of entertainments, is nothing but a collection of artificially put together separate works of an author, an actor, a designer and a director, without a general linking aim, and lacking in definite laws and regulations, because – "everything is allowed in a theatre".

In a dramatic production, on the other hand, music occupies an entirely different situation. First, with all its unfailing theory it has to be entirely subordinated to the main problem of the theatrical production. Secondly, it must be thoroughly understood, that in a real, creative, dramatic theatre music occupies only a secondary place and is nothing but one of the colors of the whole production, if not merely a background. The third stipulation is that the number and the kind of instruments in such orchestration as well as the strength of tone of a certain instrument must be entirely in accordance with the general strength of tone of the production.

As an example let us take Hauptmann's "Hannele." The main problem of that play is the protection of a child's soul and the expression of enthusiasm at its faith in God. This play has, as musical accompaniment, choirs of angels, the voice of Christ, the dreams of a delirious child ... Could we use here a large brass orchestra? Certainly not.

"Hamlet" ends by the funerals of the Prince of Denmark. It would be appropriate in order to produce a stronger impression, to use here a military funeral march. Should such a march be composed according to all the rules of musical theory, with a developing of the main theme and a climax? In other words, – should it constitute an independent, finished musical piece? No, we should hear now and then a few chords, just enough to give us the full impression of funerals and to increase the mournful feeling from the hero's death.

The best way to depict the storm in "King Lear" is through the medium of music, but I doubt if any of the numerous "storms" known in our musical literature would fit the occasion. Indeed, no matter how great might be the actor playing the "Jester" or the "King," – his voice will always be drowned by the sound of four trombones, and the most important part of this scene – the grief of a man that has lost everything and has no shelter during a stormy night – would be killed.

There is another musical possibility that could be used to great advantage in a dramatic production and that gives sometimes splendid results. It is music produced not by musical instruments but by means of different sound-devices, depicting various manifestations of life. This realm is practically unknown in the contemporary theatre. In one of the plays, produced by the Moscow Players, they were searching for music to represent the awakening of spring. It was a fairy tale – and according to the construction of the play, this scene was of the most vital importance. It was the main problem of the act, and from its successful representation and impression produced on the public was depending the whole play. For days they were struggling in vain, rummaging through the world's musical literature in order to find something suitable. Nothing! The theatrical composers were exhausted trying to compose a piece to fit the production. The results were deplorable, – it was either too weak or too powerful – to the point of crushing this whimsical scene. And yet the actors succeeded in giving a splendid performance of that particular act, – they were full of genuine spring, you could almost smell the resinous odor of the pine trees, the aroma of the grass on the meadow, they were light and alert as a beautiful spring morning, – but the music was killing all their efforts. It was lyrically sentimental, with high violin "pizzicatos" according to the sugary, conventional routine of a theatrical spring, but there was nothing to suggest the real spring. A great disappointment reigned in the theatre. Suddenly Stanislavsky got an idea. He suggested to turn toward the primary source – nature. So they started to analyze; what is the music supplied by nature at springtime? What are the sound combinations that one hears in the fields or in the forest at dawn, and what are the instruments that could reproduce those sounds? It proved to be that there is a tremendous amount of those sounds, but that in order to reproduce them a special instrument for each one of them should be devised.

Here are some of the sounds that have been discovered as produced by nature in spring: The rustle of leaves, the bursting of tree buds, the knocking of branches against each other, the creaking of trees, the hissing of the wind, raindrops falling on the large burdock leaves, the buzzing of insects, the singing of different birds, ducks splashing in the water, the murmur of brooklets. Added to all this was a whole series of confused sounds as though coming from a distant village. When, after a painstaking research, a number of instruments reproducing all these sounds were fashioned, when the composer has arranged them, according to the musical laws, into a regular musical scale and has used as a background a simple shepherd's air played by an ordinary flute, – then and only then, was created a music that responded entirely to the spiritual moods of the actors and expressed at last the feeling they were after.

After the opening night the musical critics and the composers did not recognize the result of these efforts – but the public said, that there was a distinct aroma of spring in the air during the performance and were asking curiously by what trick had this been achieved? The members of the company were merely smiling as they knew that the odor in their theatre was exactly the same as in hundreds of other theatres, – but they also knew that they had been faithful disciples of nature and that following its footsteps they refused to deceive the public by a "mock" spring but gave them the best that was prompted to them by nature itself.

If we'll try to listen carefully to the life that surrounds us, and will lend our spiritual ear to all the sounds produced by life, – we shall discover an unexpected amount of them, and will come to the realization that there are no set instruments to reproduce them. Think of the city noise, the noise coming from a factory, the clamor of an excited crowd. All these sounds in nature are waiting for their Stradivarius and Paganini, but they will be discovered only by the theatre and for the theatre. The theatre of the future, no matter how funny this may seem to a professional musician, will be filled with new instruments and new sound-combinations. It may even create a gamut and a new rhythm – not that of a metronome, but the rhythm of human feelings, heart and soul.

7 What is a Collective Work in a Theatre?

In order to illustrate the results of collective work, I will use three separate examples from life. Let's go over the laws of creative work and let's try to apply them to the theatre which is the most outstanding example of such work.

The first example: *Rowing on a ten oar boat with a coxswain*

All the participants of such work are submitted to the only will of the coxswain, who leads them, gives them a certain direction, changes the rhythm and prevents them from using their energy and ability on anything else but their direct duty – in this particular case – the rowing. The maximum efforts of the 10 oarsmen are collected into one unit and applied and used by the only will of the leader. The whole success of this work depends on the harmony of action between the oarsmen.

Second example: *The construction of a building*

This work is submitted as well to one will, in this case the will of the architect. But here, this single will goes into action much earlier. The work starts by purely individual creation. The architect begins to create the plan of a future house or a bridge while staying at this own home, having nothing but a pencil and a piece of paper. After this, he starts to act in the direction of the following contributors to his work: engineers, geodesists, masons, etc. Little by little he involves all of them into his work, and subordinating them to his single will, he makes them take part in the creation of the building. The difference between this and the first example is that *here* the creative period of the leader's single will is terminated while the work is still in progress.

The coxswain creates during the very process of rowing, while the architect, during the erection of the house, has already terminated his creation and merely supervises its execution. To succeed in his work he does not use all of his co-workers simultaneously but in succession, turn by turn, – the work of each of them depending on the careful and thorough work of the preceding. The right walling depends on the well measured land, as well as the carpenter's work depends on the right walling, etc. Here is a collective work with one single will, but with a successive fulfilment of the problems of this will.

Third example: *A symphony orchestra concert*

Again a case of submission of individual creators to the one single will of the composer, who having created personally and individually his work of art, has stepped aside and has entirely transmitted his will to the orchestra leader. The orchestra leader has become from that moment on, the only person qualified to express his single will. This particular collective creation is submitted to his will, while he is submitted in his turn to another single will. He acts on his co-workers both simultaneously and in succession. It is a combined action, a successive one at first, turning later into a general one.

The orchestra leader has to work out at first individually his creative program; he must understand the single will of the composer, he must work it out in his own spirit, he must find forms for its interpretation. Then, bringing all this spiritual material to his co-workers, he must entice at first by his will, each of his co-workers separately, which he does during the rehearsals, and then during the concert at the moment of the creation, he must, like the coxswain, lead them, giving them the proper rhythm and direction and getting out of them the maximum of their creative power and ability, from each variety of instruments, separately. The leader's single will does not permit anyone to act on his own responsibility. He must keep everyone in the limits of the general problem and lead them all by the power of his will to one clear and definite aim. What are the general features that we may find in these examples and what are the qualifications of a collective creator?

In the first place we see a definite and absolute submission to the leader's will. I've never heard of a rower who would try to row faster or differently than required by the coxswain. I never knew of a bricklayer making his portion of the wall higher than indicated by the architect. And I never heard a musician taking a different tempo from the one given by the orchestra leader.

Too, the *submission to one single will is the first stipulation* for a collective creation. *The second stipulation is: Lending the maximum of personal participation even in the smallest component part of the collective work.*

The weakening of any component part weakens the entire body. If one of the ten rowers will not lend to his oar, even for one second, all his strength – the speed of the boat will diminish. The same holds true regarding the construction of a house or a symphony concert. This condition may be very hard for the artist's ambition. Who thinks of a bricklayer admiring a beautiful building, or of a bass-violin that gives during the entire symphony a few extremely low notes resembling nothing else but the droning of a bumble bee. And yet they are indispensable, as a necessary part of the whole.

In nature each tree-leaf fulfills its function and if it does it badly, nature rejects it and it falls dead on the ground. Everyone in a collective creation, besides lending the maximum of his strength, must have a complete control of his forces and be a real master in his specialty. Taken individually a poor artist-painter is not dangerous; he does not spoil the work of others and will be simply unsuccessful because of his bad work. But in a collective creation the same artist represents a most dangerous element, as he spoils not merely his own work, but the work of a whole corporation of a branch of artistic life.

An unskilled artist, lacking in talent, or one who does not lend all his forces for the common cause, has no right to be a member of a collective creation.

The third stipulation is: The special ability of a collective creator to penetrate into the significance and nature of that particular collective work, – I would say – the self-sacrifice of his personal creation for the sake of the general success. The adaptation of one's own talent to the talents of all the rest of the creators as a whole; the understanding of which one of his special qualifications is required for that particular moment.

The continuous struggle with his own feeling that carries him on his individual path, the oarsman must feel the amount of strength he should apply to produce a certain speed with a particular crew of people – and though he personally could row twice as strong and as fast, he must submit himself to the force produced by the crew. A mason building a house might see a much simpler solution for constructing a window-arch than that given by the architect – yet he cannot adopt it. He must understand why the architect insists on this particular arch instead of the one which seems to be better. He must be able to penetrate into the very soul and idea of the construction and submit himself to it.

An orchestra musician, possessor of an unusually strong temperament, while playing a soft, lyrical piece, has to understand that his individual manner does not fit for that particular piece, and penetrating into its spirit, he has to develop in himself a different way of playing.

Let us pass now to the theatre, where the "collectivism" plays the most important and indispensable part, – "The theatre of collective creation." It consists of the following workers: playwrights, actors, directors, musicians, dancers, artists, sculptors, architects, costumers, decorators, carpenters, etc.

Being the perfect form of collective work the theatre must be completely submitted to all its laws:

The first law: The one single will. One might think that in the theatre, as well as in music, the director should be submitted to the single will of the playwright. Yet it is not quite so. The one single will in a creative theatre belongs to the stage director. The playwright is merely a component part of the production. If he is alive, the director has the right to submit him to his will as far as it concerns the general problem of the production. He may demand of him to make the necessary changes, cuts and alterations. In case the author is not alive, the director has the right, no matter how famous that author's name may be, and how great his classical reputation, to submit to his own will the playwright's literary masterpiece. If, in such a case, the director misinterprets the spirit and the problems of the author and fails to create a harmonious production, – it is bound to be a flop, and he is the only one to suffer from it, – but if he succeeds in getting a new interpretation of the author's visions in addition to getting the main problems of the work, the more power to him. The theatre has accomplished its task.

In book form the author may create his individual work, based on his personal understanding of the given theme, without taking into consideration anyone else, but in the theatre during the staging of this play he must submit himself completely to the one and only will of the theatrical autocrat – the stage director. It's rather useless to emphasize how completely this submission extends to the other members of the production. Even in the poorest theatres the director's will is a law for the rest of the co-workers. Only those productions which bear the expression of only one will – that of the stage director – will be complete and successful.

The second law: The maximum of personal efforts for the sake of the common cause, – has to be observed in the theatre more than anywhere else.

The theatre has a great amount of obscure and unnoticeable participants whose efforts give but little self-satisfaction to their creation; the stage director, as well, pays sometimes but little attention to their work. I am talking about the extras, the back stage musicians, the stage hands and others, unseen by the public, but whose efforts are very important for the success of the production. Pertaining, so to say, to the second rank of the production, some of them have a certain nonchalant attitude toward the importance of their work, based on the feeling that no one can see them anyway. This indifference is encouraged, sometimes, by the attitude of the directors themselves.

For instance, – the leading characters are dressed, in some of the productions, much more elaborately than their closest friends and relatives, if these are played by extras. I have seen a production where the heroine, the star of the show, playing the part of a beggar's daughter, appeared on the stage with her deaf-mute father, – a part performed by a super. She was dressed in silk-rags with silk stockings, while her father wore ordinary theatrical tatters. Yet, according to the play, they belonged socially to the same class.

I once heard a director yelling at the extras: "Eh – you back there, don't act. You're distracting the attention from the leading characters!" I felt like saying: "Eh – you there in front, stage your play so that no one could be in anybody else's way. Then everything will be O.K.!"

Example – John Barrymore's Hamlet with Bernardo and Marcello [sic]. His reaction would be much stronger if he would lead this scene with real actors instead of wooden puppets.

The secret to obtain a creative performance is not as complicated as it seems. Everybody in the theatre must have and know his place and give to the production the maximum of his efforts. Then we will have the harmony that is so necessary for a good performance. The poet Altenberg said: "Even a button, if it is sewed on by a loving hand, stays on better!" This holds true especially in reference to the stage. Even the most unnoticeable of its coworkers has to give the maximum of his devotion, energy and ability to the task where his contribution, no matter how small it is, will be of any benefit to the common cause; but in case his assistance is not indispensable it would be much better to do without him altogether, than have him hang around the stage where he would be only in everyone's way.

An "ensemble" performance is a performance where the director succeeds in squeezing out of each participant the maximum of his talent and ability and knows how to show to advantage even the smallest of these talents.

The third law: The ability of each participant to penetrate into the spirit of the general work is especially important in the theatre. One of the most important problems of the actor is the so-called ability to catch the tone of his partner and the mood of the play, which is nothing else but the ability to adapt one's self to the common cause, to find in one's self the necessary color for this particular collective work.

8 What is a Theatrical Performance?

The theatrical performance is a *collective creation* that expresses in *visible, audible* and *rhythmic* images some *real* manifestations of *imaginary life, places* and *people*, by means of *clear, precise* and *natural feelings* and *emotions* of the human soul.

Let's take the stage production of "Hamlet" and let's analyze it according to the above definition. It is a *collective* creation because it is the combined work of actors, artists, musicians and other theatrical workers, all of them submitted to the single will of the director.

It's a *visible* image because it is through the medium of our eye that we receive the impression of sets, costumes, make-ups of the actors, etc. It's an *audible* image because our ear receives the impression of all the lines delivered by the actors, as well as the musical tunes played on the stage. It is a *rhythmic* image because the above proceedings are confined to a certain lapse of time, during which the tempo of the action changes from slow to rapid according to the pulsation of the artists-creators, or the musical requirements of the piece.

Through *real* manifestations, because people on the stage use their eyes in order to see, their throat and tongue to talk and their legs and arms to move; the scenery is painted on canvas or cardboard with brushes and paints mixed according to the artist's actual will. In other words, everything that occurs on the stage is *real*.

An *imaginary life* because every artist in his desire to create a bit of "better life" uses his *imagination* to improve reality. Shakespeare's Venice is much better than the real one, and all the drunkards in the world could not beat the "ideal" drunkard Falstaff.

An *imaginary place* because the artist painting the set of a battlefield does not travel to Waterloo to get the actual scene of this place but uses an *imaginary* and more impressive landscape.

Imaginary people because none of the historical characters created by the *imagination* of poets, playwrights and actors has anything to do with their original prototypes. Caesar, Anthony, Cleopatra, as imagined by Shakespeare are certainly different from those who actually existed.

Clear feelings;, because only a clear and plain human feeling can be accepted and understood by the audience. As a chord of an instrument would respond only to a pure tone of an identical tuning, so would a human soul respond only to a clear and kindred feeling.

Precise feelings,; because every art is knowledge, and knowledge does not accept any haziness or inexactness. A fanciful idea can be accepted only if it has a precise foundation. The King, while hating Hamlet, asks him not to leave for Wittenberg. He expresses his request in a mild and tender way. It may be a request of a snake, but still a request, which should be expressed with precision. Otherwise it would be merely craft and pretense. An artist may design a fantastically long arm, but it must be still an arm with a hand, on which one could lean.

Natural feelings, because the human mind can never invent such variety and abundance of feelings as supplied by nature. The musicians of the whole world will never be able to use all the combinations that they could bring out from the eight fundamental tones known in music. The same holds true regarding the few fundamental human feelings; the greatest genius in the world would not be able to *invent* a new one, – all he can do is to make combinations of those suggested to him by nature.

Emotions of the human soul; because the theatre is the art of investing the spiritual emotions of man in a visible form. If a man does not know how to enjoy himself he cannot impersonate joy on the stage, just as an artist cannot design an arm if he has not seen a real one. If, on the other hand, an actor tries to represent joy without actually having experienced it, but just imitating its outer expressions, he would not be an actor but merely a parrot or a photographer.

9 What is a Mechanical Performance?

It is a performance which instead of being based on new, specially discovered for that particular play, creative principles, is produced according to an old commonplace routine. The only standard rule in such kind of a theatre is the motto: "The public likes it!" Yet the public likes the theatre anyway, and attends it not because it likes to see something that it has seen hundreds of times, but simply because man cannot exist without the theatre.

The best example of a mechanical production is a musical revue as staged in nearly all the theatres in the world. With a few exceptions the recipe for such a show is almost the same. All its members know in advance what it is going to be like. The author of the book and the lyrics knows that there must be two acts with a dozen disconnected scenes in each; that the sketches, no matter how insipid they are, will go over big, providing the producer has secured the services of a popular comedian. The director knows that the show girls should be tall and goodlooking, even though they could not sing a note nor make a step on the stage, but that the dancing girls, on the other hand, must be fast steppers. The scenic designer knows that the sets should be flashy and bright to the point of hurting one's eyesight. The costumer knows that the less will the girls be dressed, the better will the producer be dressed.

And so forth and so forth. The recipe for such a production, as I said before, is not very complicated. Serious theatres, especially the very serious ones, are sometimes also purely mechanical. The theatre has a less definite scientific theory than the rest of the arts collaborating with it. That is why it gets easily influenced by the authority of some of them – especially by the art of literature. Very serious theatres, building their repertoire on important classical plays are often timid in their searches and attainments. As an example let us take the famous theatre of the "Comedie Francaise" – the first governmental theatre of France. The plays of Moliere and other classics, as staged there, have turned into pompous and tedious orations of a "museum-like" nature. Being full of reverence towards the classical author, they are killing, at the same time, his masterpieces by traditional and purely mechanical repetitions of acting, that could have been appealing a hundred years ago but not now. Then, too, everyone knows to perfection how Moliere should be staged, in what sets, and "*how*" a certain line should be delivered. They have a ready explanation for everything: "This is the way it was played by so and so," "that was done by Moliere himself," "this set is an exact copy of the set of the period." They forget that the theatre is an inalienable part of our life and as such must first of all struggle, seek and strive toward new achievements instead of trampling on, on old grounds.

The mechanical theatre is a theatre of set types and seniority. I don't mean to say that the respect for rank and discipline should not exist in an ideal theatre. On the contrary it is quite essential, but it has to be based only on talent and on the necessity of that particular actor for a certain part. What could be sillier than the set type of a "hero-lover" of a stock company, who plays every leading part, whether he fits it or not. The mechanical theatre is a theatre that gives an accurate imitation of human feelings as though they were custom made articles: jealousy, grief, happiness, hatred are presented, each time precisely in the same way, as though bearing a certain stamp and label. It is the precision of primitive, illiterate and unimaginative means. The mechanical theatre is a theatre of trade, but not of art.

10 What is a Creative Theatrical Performance?

The creative theatrical performance is a performance created by spiritual and physical means especially discovered for that particular play. It is achieved through a tenacious collaboration between the author, the actors and the director, and is presented nightly, using live, fresh feelings that should be each time created anew, but never repeated as something external, learned by heart. It is a performance of the human spirit, of its spiritual life, spiritual imagination, spiritual knowledge and spiritual memory. A performance where all the outer qualities are subordinated to the inner ones – and are merely their direct result. The main difficulty of a creative performance consists in a special education of the actor as well as in a particular atmosphere of the theatre. My following lectures will be dedicated to the education of the creative actor.

The atmosphere of a creative theatre depends entirely on the serious attitude of all the members of such an organization towards their problems. Requiring from an actor a clear, flexible and free spirit – the creative art demands of him as well to maintain this spirit pure, both morally and physically.

Called to incarnate the "better life" the artist's spirit must possess a clear conception of it. Having to incarnate beautiful and pure images created by great people in moments of ecstasy and perfection of their hearts – the spirit of the actor could not accomplish it were this spirit soiled and uninspired. All the lofty feelings, all that is beautiful in nature and art, should be cultivated in the actor's soul. All the petty human feelings and weaknesses must be in a state easy to conquer. God forbid that I should preach bigotry and puritanism or complete renouncement and annihilation of human faults. A man is a man and would not be complete without his shortcomings, – but as a prize fighter who, training his body, protects it from different harmful excesses, knowing that an extra glass of brandy might unfit him, – so the man who struggles in his spirit for the attainment of "better" life must protect his soul from unhealthy excesses. Small, spiritual failings are inherent to us all and I am not talking about exterminating them altogether. God preserve me from a prudish and saintly actor – he is acquainted merely with half of our life, but the point is, that a real creative actor should know how to struggle with his faults.

Here I may be using a paradox when I say that the more faults he has, the better it is, because the stronger the struggle for victory and the more intense the spiritual penetration into life and closer the acquaintance with the life of the human spirit. Just as the "Converted Sinner" of the Scripture is more precious than the "Saint," so an actor who has conquered his own sins and passions is of greater value than one who being perfectly dependable is commonplace and uninspiring. The contemporary life does not help the actor in his spiritual improvement. The continuous struggle for his existence does not make him very particular in finding ways to attain success, and leaves him but little time for meditation. Yet the actor of a creative theatre where the human spirit plays a most important part, must devote as much time as possible to meditation and strive as hard as possible to improve his inner qualities.

It is especially important owing to the fact that the conditions of our modern life make the actor go from the sublime to the ridiculous, jump from triviality and petty worries of his daily existence into the finest, loftiest and most ideal feelings, evidently to their detriment.

A Hindu – a man of great talent and knowledge, asked me once to describe to him step by step the program of my day. After I finished, he looked at me and said: "But when do you meditate on God?" I had to answer, that almost never.

Most of the actors never give a thought to it and would, probably, consider my words as a strange whim of a "nutty" dreamer. True! What is there in common between the acting of Charlie Chaplin and the meditation on God? I would say there is a lot.

I am sure if you'll ask any really talented and successful actor what were the subjects he was thinking mostly of in his life, he'd answer you: "About my roles," – in other words, about *his art*, which is *his God* no matter where the temple of this God might be, should it be in the theatre, on the screen or in a circus.

11 The Qualifications of a Creative Actor

An ideal actor has to combine in himself the following qualities:

1. Talent
2. An apt mind
3. Education
4. Knowledge of life
5. Observation
6. Sensitiveness
7. Artistic taste
8. Temperament
9. Voice
10. Good enunciation
11. Expressive face and gestures
12. Well built body
13. Dexterity
14. Plastique of movements
15. Tenacity in work
16. Imagination
17. Self-control
18. Good health

All these qualities with the exception of the talent could be and should be developed by the actor. But this development must be done gradually in a definite and logical sequence. To start with the actor has to realize the three different planes of this development: the *spirit*, the *intellect*, and the *body*.

What must he do for the development of his spirit?

First: He has to train his own will power to the point of becoming complete master of his soul. This can be achieved by developing a quality known as "Spiritual Concentration".

Second: He has to make his spirit sensitive and flexible. This, again, can be achieved by developing another quality called the "Spiritual" or "Affective Memory."

Third: He has to educate his spirit in order to have it strong and healthy in feelings. This could be accomplished by daily exercises on the *"fulfillment of spiritual problems."*

What must he do to develop his intellect?

He has to educate his artistic taste and sensitiveness by frequent *contact and study of all possible works of art*. He must increase his knowledge of life by constantly training his *observation*. Develop in himself to the greatest extent the faculty of *imagination*.

What must the actor do for the development of his body?

He must train his *voice* by vocal exercises; his *body* by dancing, fencing, different kinds of sports and by control of his muscles; his *face* – by make-up; his *speech* – by diction and enunciation. Besides the above mentioned exercises he must develop in himself the *art of inner and outer mimicry and incarnation*.

To get a knowledge, even though an elementary one, of the first principles of the Psycho-Analysis of Human Feelings, using any popular manual of Psychology (Ribot).

12 What is the Meaning of "Living the Part?"

All the qualities of the actor mentioned in my last lecture are essential for him in order to "live his part." An actor who "lives his part" is a creative actor, the one who simply imitates different human emotions without feeling them each time is a "mechanical" one. The difference between them is the same as between a human being and a mechanical puppet, or as between an artist's painting and a photograph. No matter how fine a photograph may be it could never be a work of art. It is nothing but a copy, a mechanical repetition of life, a stamp, – while a painting is unique, being an individually created bit of "better" life.

An actor who "lives his part" uses each time, playing his role, a brand new, fresh feeling. Sometimes he expresses it in an entirely different manner, merely following the fundamental lines of his main problem, but without adhering to the once set stage mechanics.

The creative actor, being sensitive and responsive to his surroundings, should be able to find the life's truth in all circumstances and situations. Example: – the scene in Heyerman's "Good Hope," when the mother, trying to persuade her son not to be afraid of the sea and sail on the next boat, shows him a couple of beautifully carved coral earrings; promising to give them to him in case he sails, she describes their beauty, pointing to the carved ships. On the opening night the property man forgot to put the earrings in the drawer. The actress playing the mother did not lose her presence of mind and holding the imaginary earrings started to describe them so eloquently that the public actually believed seeing them. After the show a couple of people asked Stanislavsky where in the world had he acquired such a remarkable set.

A creative actor lends his ear exclusively to his soul, and does not try to *invent* new feelings, but merely invests his own in different forms prompted by his imagination. He is never concerned in the external effect of his part but merely in the inner, spiritual side of it. According to Stanislavsky's expression, – "He does not love himself in art, but loves art in himself." He controls his art always and everywhere. He does not look for any artificial excitement furnished by the footlights, the public, the applause, the costume, the sets, a girl friend in a box and so forth, – the only thing he needs is to have in front of him a definite problem.

A creative actor is generally inclined towards beautiful literary works with great and eternal themes – because those are the only ones that would supply him with spiritual food. Such an actor belongs to the class of "artists-creators" of the living theatre, while the "actor-imitator" of human feelings will always remain among the so-called "utilities" of the theatre.

"Living one's part" means a complete spiritual and physical self-abandon for a definite period of time, in order to fulfill a real or fantastical problem of the theatre.

13 What is "Spiritual Concentration?"

The main condition for each work is the ability to surrender one's entire being or at least the maximum of one's strength and energy to this particular work or creation. Life and nature supply us with a number of examples, starting with a cat that steals up to a bird, and ending with Balzac who composing his novels was forgetting to take his meals. The most valuable quality of a good tradesman is attention. An ordinary actor is usually very attentive towards his lines or his stage-business. But this is merely an outer attention. According to our theory, the main attention should be paid to the "life of the human spirit" or the "life of our inner feelings."

I cannot play Hamlet if I have never been afflicted by the loss of anyone dear to me, if I do not know what a deep grief means and have not developed this feeling in my soul. The discovery and the development of such feelings is the main work of a creative actor. As any other work, it demands a great deal of concentration, which in that particular case is called *Spiritual Concentration.*

The "Spiritual Concentration" is the ability to say to any of your feelings: "Stop, and fill my entire being!" This faculty can be developed and trained as much as one can train a human body, – and this training is the main problem of a creative school of acting.

The spiritual concentration is the energy produced by the entire human physiological and psychological apparatus, concentrated on one definite single problem.

A hunting dog, pursuing game, spends all his energy in dashing rapidly back and forth in order to discover his prey. The very moment the hound comes upon the scent he stops as if petrified. He commands all his feelings and energy to stand still and concentrates on one single thought: to trap the animal and to leap upon it at the proper moment. At this moment the entire muscular and spiritual energy of the dog is concentrated on three senses: seeing, hearing and smelling. All that hinders him in the way of the complete and utmost functioning of these feelings is removed and forgotten. You can see it particularly by his muscles; the tail is dropped, the lifted paw hangs in the air as though broken, all the muscles of his body are relaxed and do not deprive him of even a single particle of his energy that is concentrated on nothing but these three senses.

This is an example of ideal concentration of one's primary feelings. As far as it concerns us – humans – there are two things that are in the way of our complete abandonment and concentration. They are our muscles and our contemporary spiritual and physical life. We may counteract the opposition of our muscles by certain daily exercises, but the task of conquering the resistance of our modern life is much more complicated.

How are we handicapped by our muscles?

Let us take a look back at our childhood. On the way we were taught to carry ourselves, the conventionality of our clothes and shoes; on the unnatural way of our modern locomotion comparing it to the one indicated by nature itself. Think of the rush hour in street cars or subways, when we travel for hours suspended like grapes, falling over each other at each jerky movement of the car, – and you'll understand how much energy we are wasting and how far we are removed from the free body of an ancient Roman, or an animal!

Compare the free stride of a savage with the walk of a modern girl. You will not find much difficulty in conquering the opposition presented by your muscles. The only thing you have to do is to think of them constantly, to relax them as soon as you feel any tension and to develop them by using some specially devised daily exercises. You must watch yourself all day long, whatever you do, and be able to relax each superfluous tension of your muscles, letting work only those of them which are indispensable to the performance of a certain physical problem.

An ideal example of co-ordination between the muscles and the soul are mostly all the images of the Meditating Buddha. You may plainly see that there is not one muscle in the whole body which prevents the rising of his thoughts toward God. A modern expression of that state you will find in Rodin's "Thinker." If it lacks the Buddha's complete calm of the beyond, it has on the other hand the logical relaxation of muscles capable of a tremendous labor, but majestically calm for the moment in order not to prevent the labor of the spirit.

Here is a list of exercises which should be done daily in order to relax your muscles from useless tension.

1. The concentration of your thoughts on each separate group of your muscles, bringing them from the state of tension into the one of relaxation.

2. The verifying of your muscles in the sense of supplying them only with the necessary amount of strength during the performance of the following exercises: walking, sitting down, the lifting up of different articles from the floor, taking down of same from a high shelf, pointing at different things, calling, greeting, lighting a cigarette, the handing of a burning match to someone while a third person tries to blow it out, kicking with your foot articles of a different weight, lacing a shoe, any physical exercise, followed by complete rest, the taking of an intricate position followed by an immediate relaxation of all the muscles with its natural result – the fall of the body, the giving of a blow, the defense from a real or imaginary blow.

In doing all these exercises you must follow exclusively the example of nature and perform all of them in a high spirit and in a joyous frame of mind. You must understand as well that the *relaxation* of your muscles does not mean by any means their *weakening*. You must train your muscles every day without making of it a meaningless series of physical exercises. Each of your muscles must understand the reason for its particular training.

Let us see now what are the manifestations of our modern life that are in the way of our *spiritual concentration*. First, it is the constant struggle for our existence that subordinates us to those on whom depend our livelihood and does not leave us any time for meditation on *our God*, absorbing our whole mind in worries about our next meal. How can we struggle against such a cruel and seemingly inconquerable condition?

Only by a boundless faith in our vocation, and the continual support of our spirit through close communion with the geniuses of humanity who suffered for the triumph of their ideals. Think of Cervantes, who died in prison; of the destitute youth of Dickens; of Savonarola burned at the stake; of Mayor McSweeney of Cork, and hundreds of others whose examples teach us the conquest of life.

No one expects you to retire from life and be sinless, – but the important part is to be conscious of your own shortcomings and to be able to combat them.

The contemporary life prevents us from concentrating also because of its crazy outer rhythm created by man. I'd like to see Hamlet saying his "to be or not to be" around 8:30 P.M. on the corner of Broadway and 42nd Street. Speaking of Hamlet – I remember poor John Barrymore, who with tears in his eyes, was trying to say from the Longacre Theatre stage: "Oh, that this too … too solid flesh would melt, thaw and resolve itself into a dew … " He almost had to yell this sentence in order to be heard through the clattering of a huge truck that stood just in front of the exit No. 6, while the driver was continually tooting his horn. At this moment I felt more pity for "poor Hamlet on Broadway" than for "poor Yorick."

Try to say, while riding on an elevated [train] during the rush hour, even in a whisper, the "Sermon on the Mount", this greatest piece of world's literature.

And, while looking up from the street at a train running over this very elevated [train], try to reconstruct in your mind the details of the Athenian Acropolis.

Try to show me a single real masterpiece born during the years of the last great war. Where can you find the harmony so necessary for your spirit in this mad whirlpool of our modern life? Where is Leonardo Da Vinci, who spent seven years in painting his Mona Lisa? Where is the Cathedral of Notre Dame of Paris, which was for over 500 years in the process of construction? Where are the roads of the Roman Legions which are still used by the peasants of Southern France to bring into town milk and vegetables? Where is the fourth order to follow the Ionic, the Doric and the Corinthian Capitols? Has not 2000 years been time enough in which to create it? Where are all these accomplishments?

Yet this is the only thing that distinguishes man from animals. Only through the creations of his spirit has he developed in himself the ideas of humanity, of truth, of beauty and of all without which he would be nothing but a blind mole digging in the ground.

How can we return to the great creative rhythm and spirit of humanity? Only approaching nature, by loving it and by constant meditation about it.

Cast your eyes at a piece of blue sky among the skyscrapers of Broadway and you'll understand where the truth lies. Lend your ear to the beat of the surf and you will understand where is the real key for the appreciation of music. Look at a rushing mountain brook or at a falling star and you'll understand the meaning of speed.

I am certain that any architect could create a much more beautiful building if instead of working in the city he secluded himself for a few months in an isolated house somewhere in the mountains surrounded by a rustling forest.

Don't miss any chance you have, to concentrate and to think of nature. Don't cast away (reject) a flower or even a tree leaf without entering into communion with it and penetrating into its mystery. Listen to the twittering of each bird, watch the thoughtfulness of each small fish in an aquarium; do not repulse any animal that approaches you to be caressed; gaze as often as you can at the stars – and all this will help (facilitate) you in your struggle for spiritual concentration.

The third opposition in this struggle, and perhaps the most serious one, we find in our own passions, emotions and desires.

How to withstand our ambitions, our craving for priority? How to resist our personal grief when we have to rush to the theatre to play a merry comedy. How to renounce the petty things of life obstructing our mind – a new hat, a drink of whisky, flirtation, etc.

All this too has its remedy. Example – Pedro de Cordoba.

You must always remember that you – actors are the material, the clay of which you yourself have to mould your works of art; well, – then consider yourself as such, – as the material which must not be spoiled or soiled. And don't forget to invest, whatever you do, with a colorful, – more than that, – with a beautiful form! Even if you are getting drunk, don't let it seem ugly let it have a touch of beauty, to be imbued with that striving towards better life. When you are getting angry try to supply that petty human feeling with something that would remind you of the perfect scorn of Jupiter or Nemesis.

Don't let any of your passions take hold of you without reason and do not make the consequence more important than the cause, in other words don't get hysterical because of a ruined gown or a broken pipe. Remember that most of the things in life are of no consequence, except the perfection of spirit and that you may "trace the noble dust of Alexander till you find it stopping a bung-hole," but that the life and deeds of Alexander the Great may still serve us as an example.

In other words, if we learn how to control our muscles and to dominate life that surrounds us, we shall develop and begin to get hold of our Spiritual Concentration.

Just as the hand of a pianist or a violinist requires daily exercises, so does our spirit with the only difference that the exercises of our spirit are much harder than those on a piano or a violin.

Do you remember how simple it is to play the flute:

HAMLET: "Govern these vantages with your fingers and thumb, give it
   breath with your mouth and it will discourse most eloquent music."
GUILDEBRANDT [SIC]:   "But I have not the skill, my lord!"
HAMLET: "There is much music in this little organ, yet cannot you make
   it speak. I'blood, do you think I am easier to be played on, than a
   pipe?" Etc.

Let this quotation prompt you how complicated are the human feelings and how difficult it is to play on them, in other words how difficult it is to be an actor.

Be prepared, that the first exercises for the development of your spiritual forces are very tedious and not easy to master just like the playing of scales which requires a long and painstaking practice before it shows us any results.

Be ready for disappointments and ridicule in this abstract and purely spiritual work, and think of Paganini who all his life exercised seven hours a day and then perhaps you will not mind spending the miserly half an hour which I ask you to devote to the following exercises:

1. *Bring yourself into a happy frame of mind and complete spiritual ease, concentrate on your primary feelings: seeing, hearing, feeling, smelling and taste.* (The first three with real objects, the last two with imaginary ones.)
2. Remember all the details of the day and mark every one of its sad or happy moments.
3. Remember last New Year's day, and decide whether during the (course) of it you experienced more sad or gay moments.
4. Remember the gown you had on, the day you experienced an event of great importance.
5. Say mentally the "Lord's Prayer", realizing the *vital significance of every one of its words.*
6. *Inhale and exhale evenly and deeply several times in succession trying to feel and to understand the work of your lungs.*
7. *Listen to the beating of your own heart trying to understand its work.*
8. Transmit mentally to any living person your blessing and the wish for complete happiness.
9. Recall you last anger or irritation, trying to justify it or to reproach yourself for it.
10. *Remembering your last strong emotion try to retain it for a certain definite period of time.* (The time should be gradually increased from a few *moments to several hours.*)
11. [skipped]
12. Compare two paintings or two pieces of sculpture trying to discover the essential difference between them.
13. Try to analyze and to understand the mood of a certain person you have just met.
14. Create in your mind a mental picture of all the sets in full colours and other details of a play you have just read.

15. Recall in your mind any time you wish and try to retain for a certain time the mood that particular strain generally brings to you.

16. As you walk or while you do some physical exercises, keep different moods, beginning with the simplest ones and increasing them gradually up to the most complicated rhythms of your inner feelings.

17. Take a certain pose and keep it for a specified period of time without moving.

18. Transmit mentally to someone an order (don't expect an immediate result)

19. Go over one of the roles you have studied or over a familiar poem without saying the lines aloud but simply using the corresponding moods and emotions.

20. Arouse in yourself according to your own choice a certain feeling, then transmit it to some imaginary being like a spirit of a deceased friend, or a phantom of a forest and get a response from it that will bring to you the state of peace or alarm.

All these exercises should not be performed one after another. Take a good rest after each of them in order to start the new one with a perfectly fresh and relaxed mind. It would be much better to produce just a few exercises or even one at a time than many without the required feelings.

It is advisable to perform all this in your usual, distracting surroundings, instead of shutting yourself up in your own room where nothing is in the way of your concentration. Only in the very beginning, while you are groping in the dark, trying to make yourself familiar with that elusive "spiritual concentration," should you perform these exercises in complete solitude.

But as soon as you succeed in finding your way and get hold of that feeling you must take it out in to the open and continue the training of your spirit exposing it to all kind of dangers and temptations. Do it wherever you can, during your walks, your meals and even while resting.

Only after a month of daily persistent work may you expect to feel the first results of that training, in other words only after a month of the most strenuous work will you begin to realize the meaning of "Spiritual Concentration."

14 What is the Spiritual or Affective Memory?

This feeling was mentioned for the first time about forty years ago by the French psychologist Ribot. According to his terminology the affective memory is the ability of the human organism to retain imperceptibly for man himself different psychological shocks and emotions and to live them all over again in case of an identical repetition of outer physical occurrences.

For instance, while returning home with a bunch of freshly gathered lilies of the valley, a girl finds out about the tragic death of her beloved fiancé. The very moment she was hearing the news she was inhaling the aroma of these flowers. Many years have passed since then. She was married and has lived in perfect happiness, – but each time she smelled the scent of lilies of the valley she would become nervously excited just as she was at the time of tragedy, without even being conscious of the fact. More than that, unconscious tears were coming to her eyes at the mere sight of these flowers. Later on this became so much of a habit that it remained with her until the end of her days.

Second example:

A young man made his love declaration, proposed and was accepted by a young girl while walking in the country throughout a large vegetable garden. They were eating fresh cucumbers, just picked from a border-bed. They returned home with the taste of cucumbers in their mouths and carrying a basket full of them.

Many years they were married and forgot about that particular incident. – Yet each time they saw fresh cucumbers or had cucumber salad, a nice, kindly feeling came upon them. They grew gay and tender toward each other, no matter how discontented they had been a moment before.

Third example: that I observed myself in New York.

An old civil war veteran putting on his uniform on decoration day felt much stronger and healthier than the rest of the time. The uniform was performing a real miracle with the old man. He was carrying himself much straighter and his gout was not bothering him. His grandchildren discovered that secret and whenever he grew especially grouchy they used to take out his uniform.

Every one of you going carefully through your memory will discover I am sure, lots of examples of "Affective Memory".

The "Affective Memory" is one of the most important factors of our art.

The actor can use it in order to reproduce in himself all kind of feelings and fill his stage creations with the "life of the human spirit."

With the help of that feeling he does not have to "imitate" the outer manifestations of actual life but can take an active part in the creation of that beautiful, "better" life entering thus into the ranks of independent and individual creators.

No art can tolerate amateurishness and dilletantism!

That is, if you bring it out before the public instead of keeping it for home consumption. – In the latter case you may do anything you wish! You may play Lady Macbeth at 16 and Juliet at 50. I don't care.

But if you bring it before the public, if you try to satisfy the utmost necessity of humanity to beautify its daily life – you have to do it honestly, taking the full responsibility of it on yourself.

The members of a theatrical organization should be especially conscientious toward the performance of their duties remembering that the theatre is a *collective* or *co-related* art, where everyone is responsible for everyone else. Unfortunately this last stipulation is forgotten because of the seeming easiness of the theatrical work and the absurd "star" system.

The absurdity of this system as applied to a whole production, is evident because of the following logical reason: The whole, consisting of several component parts can be harmonious only if all these parts have a definite mutual connection one with another.

How can you expect to have a good watch if it has only a fine steel spring and all the rest of its parts are "tin"?

A show can not be successful if it has only one fine leading actor and the rest of the cast is terrible (example – Hamlet – Bernardo – Marcello [sic])

The collective creation is submitted to three laws:

1. The single will of the leader
2. Even the smallest component part has to lend the maximum of its energy for the sake of the common cause.
3. Each of the participants has to penetrate into the spirit of the general work.

All the greatest creations in the world like the Acropolis, the three orders in Architecture, The Foremost Creative Theatres were submitted to these three laws during the process of their actual creation.

Let us see the one and only normal way that should be used in a theatre.

What are the leading elements of a creative production? A production which has for its main problem to present the life of the immortal human spirit.

The "better" life, created by the imagination of great people in the moments of elevation of their hearts.

Such performance consists of the following elements: The author, the director, the actors, the scenic artists, the musicians and the stagehands.

And finally of the most important, which is the *special atmosphere* surrounding such production, expressed in a certain *convincingness* and *resistance* to the physical outer obstacles that might be in the way of creating such a performance.

(Description of such work by each group of participants)

The Author: The logical truth of feelings. Eternal themes. Subordination to the director, Harmony with actors. Clearness of action.

Director: Clear expression of each part of the production. The style of the production. The bringing out of the actors' individuality. The using of new stage forms of expression through painting, architecture, lighting, sounds and rhythm. Control of the ethical side of the show.

Actors: Professional will. Truth of feelings – based on affective memory. The development of outer means. Characterisation. Golden Casket. Ethics.

Scenic Artist: Truth in forms and colours. Connection with actors, author.

Musician: His place in a dramatic production. Themes. Strength of sounds. Submission to the spiritual rhythm.

15   How to Use the Affective Memory in Preparing a Part

After having decided what is the feeling necessary for a certain part of his role, the actor tries to find in his affective memory a recollection similar to that particular feeling. He may use all kinds of means in order to bring that feeling to life, starting with the actual lines of the author and finishing with experiments from his own life, recollections from books and finally using his own imagination. Then by a series of gradual exercises and rehearsals he brings himself into a state, enabling him to arouse in the strongest degree the necessary feeling by a mere thought of it and to retain it for the necessary period of time.

For instance, an actor playing Othello comes to the conclusion that a certain part of his role is filled by the feeling of jealousy. He searches in his so-called "Golden Casket of feelings" for some recollections having to do with jealousy and discovers several of them having to do directly or indirectly with that feeling: for instance having read in a paper a criticism about a very successful performance of one of his colleagues, he experiences a feeling of acute envy, similar to that of jealousy. This feeling brought him into a mood expressed by excessive irritation and exaggerated amiableness toward his colleague. Then, he remembers, that once his wife has received a letter addressed in a strange handwriting. For some reason she did not tell him its contents while he, on the other hand did not want to question her about it. This has aroused in him quite a number of new feelings: watching the behavior of his wife, the inner struggle between the desire to find out the contents of the letter by reading it while she was away and a feeling of respect towards her that wouldn't allow him to do so.

Another case, – when arriving to the theatre he found his seat occupied by another person and how, being certain that it belonged to him he was claiming it and defending his right to it.

Sometimes the mere recollection of a feeling enables the actor to live it all over again and, as in the above mentioned case, his heart begins to beat faster at the mere recollection of the success of his colleague. In such case, the only thing he has to do is develop that feeling by continuous repetition of that recollection, until it will become near and familiar to the point of getting hold of him at any moment according to his order.

But sometimes the mere recollection would not be sufficient and the actor has to arouse his affective memory by purely physical means as for instance the sight of his wife reading anything at all, would bring to him the feeling he experienced while she was reading that mysterious message.

Sometimes, though, the actor has to use purely his imagination. As in this case – a persistent thought of a lost article he was fond of, might supply him with the necessary feeling.

In other words – this work consists in finding and developing of necessary feelings but not in their outer reproduction.

We may call this work, the actor's "home-work" – the preparation of the pallete and its supplying with necessary colours. –

He must not think during this work *how* he is going to reproduce a certain feeling, – his only concern should be to *find it, to sense it with his entire being, to get used to it and to let nature itself find forms for its expression.*

The next period of the actor's work is when after having discovered and developed in himself the necessary feeling he starts to apply them to the lines supplied by the author. This is one of the most beautiful moments of our work.

If until then the actor, who has collected all the familiar colours of jealousy and developed them to the point of making them near and vivid, did not dare to touch the Shakespearean text, – he can begin to do it now.

Aroused to the heights of exaltation, in full possession of all the shadings of his new feeling the actor begins to pronounce in the solitude of his workroom the immortal words of the author.

Timidly to start with, as though not daring to touch them he begins to invest them with new forms, prompted not by the rules of elocution but by the great creative mind of the author in complete union with his own creative spirit.

By this time the actor knows perfectly his part, and the words come to him easily as though prompted by feelings. He never touches the words without being aroused and moved by feelings. He never reads or repeats his role, *he actually lives it.*

If the actor succeeds to find the right feeling at once the author inflames him still more by the force of his talent and the actor begins simply to "Bathe" in them; if on the other hand, the actor took at first a wrong feeling, he will have to search all over again through his "golden casket."

But a real artist should not be afraid of that work – it has so many creative possibilities which, according to human nature, are the real source of joy, that he can not help but feel happy while doing it.

If the author has expressed his feeling in the right way, the actor can not change or add a single word to it, their feelings have to be in harmony and their hearts must beat in the same tempo. – If this does not take place, the director's business is to discover it and to correct either one or the other, according to whose feeling is more valuable.

In his search for the affective feelings the actor sometimes can not find in his "golden casket" the right one.

Actors often say: "How do I know the sensations of a murderer"? or "how do I know what Salome felt holding the head of John the Baptist – I never had a severed head in my hands –"

In such cases one has to use very extensively the *"similar"* affective memories and the *imagination*.

Similar affective memories help us a great deal if we analyze thoroughly and in details the necessary feeling and try to understand its nature.

Here is a rather simple example of such an affective memory:

Cleopatra before her death takes in her hand the deadly asp and it should be very important for the audience to feel that the Queen has in her hands a real snake instead of a piece of overstuffed canvas. But where from can the actress get such an affective memory if she never had and probably never will have in her hands a poisonous snake? Certainly only through a *similar* affective memory!

Everyone of you probably remembers how you were shaking from a little bug or a caterpillar crawling along your neck. This recollection has the same foundation as has the feeling experienced by Cleopatra holding the asp.

The actor has, probably, never killed anyone, true, – but has he never killed a mosquito with the same ire that most likely is the embryo of the feeling experienced by Hamlet killing his uncle. Has he never seen a chicken killed?

The actor has not the right to be superficial or inattentive so to say of the events of his own life or to the life surrounding him, but has to penetrate into the deep meaning of everything that happens in front of him and store every one of his new emotions in his "golden casket" of feelings.

Here is an example of a complicated feeling which you may find through a series of simple feelings. You have never seen a ghost, – consequently you do not understand how to "live your part" in feeling the reverential fear of Hamlet meeting the ghost of his father.

But have you never experienced a feeling of uneasiness from unknown reasons? Were you never startled at night by a sound from the next room? Don't you remember the feeling you had entering a room where was the corpse of a dead person? Did you never walk at night through a deserted place peering intently through the darkness, being on the look out, listening to the slightest noise in front or in back of you? Were you never startled by the sudden appearance of a person you did not expect to see? Have you never tried to conceal yourself – so as to remain unnoticed?

Boleslavsky Lectures from the American Laboratory Theatre

Undated (c. 1925–26)

Editor's note: I believe the following to be lectures that Boleslavsky gave at the American Laboratory Theatre early in its existence. Stella Adler provided original copies of these to Jerry Roberts, who edited them and who provided a copy of them to Robert Ellerman, from whom I received a copy. Pages and even lectures are sometimes missing (e.g., these materials begin with Lecture 3); to my knowledge, these have been lost. Like the Creative Theatre Lectures, these provide a significant context and clarification for principles taken up in *Acting: The First Six Lessons*. I have corrected some misspellings and formatting for ease of reading.

1 Lecture 3

In my last lecture I spoke to you about the memory of feeling. I told you that memory appears in our system according to the same laws of our common memory. The laws of the memory of feeling, though they are more difficult to trace, and less attention is paid to them than to those of common memory, just the same they are of the same order and kind. With practice, exercise and technique, you can develop your memory of feeling to such an extent that it will be just as easy for you to handle your feelings as it is for you to handle telephone numbers, street numbers, etc.

Then if you will remember, I told you how you can use that memory in working on a part. I told you you could find it and use it in an actual part. There isn't a feeling which you don't experience in your life, if not the actual feeling, then a substitute. Substitutes, when handled by an artist, can embrace a very wide scale. From the murder or killing of people to the killing of mosquitoes is just one road. One is as far from the other as it can be yet at the bottom it is of the same quality.

Suppose an actor has to play despair at the sickbed of a child, and suppose the actor never had a child. But the actor may have had a sick puppy, and the elements, the foundations, the beginnings of the theory of the feelings toward the puppy and the feelings toward your child are more or less of the same nature. You can start from them and build them up and bring them to the required strength. The use of substitutes is a thing you must understand very well because very seldom in preparing a part will you have the colors at hand. Very seldom will you find that everything in the part was experienced by you. Always you will have an "I don't know that," especially when you have a creative part, when it isn't pure realism.

When you approach writers like Shaw and Shakespeare you will find that you need something more than your actual life experience. You will find that you need things which you have never experienced in your actual life. You will have to substitute these things with the things which belong to your cultural, spiritual and moral life, and to others. The things belong to your whole life and you will have to hunt them out from the whole atmosphere which surrounds you, and not only around you personally but sometimes far back.

I saw Herman Themig in *The Servant of Two Masters*. There is an example of what I am telling you now. Of using the memory of feeling only from the substitutes, not from his realistic life, though maybe he is a cheerful and happy fellow who likes to run around. His actions of being a servant in trouble doesn't disturb him at all. The whole style of his actions, the adjustment which he takes to every action which happens in the play is of a certain quality, absolutely strange and foreign.

What I mean is that the whole production is a sort of reproduction of the *commedia del 'arte* from the modern point of view. He probably got his character from essays, articles, books, etc. The spirit of *commedia del'arte*, the spirit of foolery and spontaneous entertainment is just as far removed from the German theatre and the German actor as it can be. But thru intuition, thru analysis and thru clever and honest preparation they realize what the spirit is.

In the case of Themig, you forget everything and feel as if you were fed with nice peaches or apples. He just puts them into your mouth one after the other, and you don't think, "What is he doing?" You don't think, "How and where is the actor able to get that?" The difficult thing to understand is what it is. It's easy after you know the game but what about before? Where would you get your feeling for every kind of extreme and grotesque way of eating spaghetti or sealing a letter? Only thru substitutes, and substitutes in comedy are very different.

To create a human soul and to give it life on the opening night is, once again, this ideal.

Let us say that we are all human souls. What if we start to analyze ourselves, what will strike us as very definite, fundamental matter? That life is action. When I am lying in the undertaker's office, I am through – finished. From the minute I wake up in the undertaker's office, I start to act. The very first minute you are born, you start to do something. You start to act. In every human being, no matter if it is simply an embryo or a developed human being, action is the first symptom of life. What would you say then is the function we can build on in our creation of the human soul? Do you think it is the action of acting? Let us go thru the everyday life of a human being.

You wake up in the morning and without any knowledge on your part, you realize that it is morning, that it is very early or it is late.

But before you realize that condition there is a certain action. You see and are conscious that it is light, that the weather is clear, that your watch shows 6:30 or 10:30. The next thing that you realize is that you are late or early for some particular job and you say to yourself, "I must dress quickly," or, "I may dress slowly as I like." Do you not wish? I do. This happens all the time. What I am doing now is to wish to explain certain things. Your wish is to or not to understand the things I am explaining to you, but it certainly is a wish or action. From all this it is a very simple thing to realize and understand what a part or play is. A collection of problems in which you wish or do. When you can say, "I know how to do it. I can have a wish every moment of my life and I can fulfill exactly what I wish," nothing else can be said to you by any teacher or stage director in the world.

You will then need only talent. One may have a strong will, but if he has not talent, he can't do what he wants to do. Talent cannot be taught, it must be in the person. It must be held at certain times under glass and cared for. Sometimes it is killed by rough living which does not give it what it wants to live on. If you put a southern plant in the north it will die. I am not now taking about your latent taste, but about those things which are strongest and most necessary, the knowledge that you do those first elemental things in human life. "I wish – I do. I wish – I do." This is from whence come all the exercises which are given you to do. That is why you must learn to do that which is ordinary for you, and that which you are ordered to do. From whom and how the order comes, I will explain to you, but the order must be given to you. The days when artists tramped around the world, creating only when they were inspired are gone. Now the artist must be on the job like everyone else. Now you get an order that at the seven o'clock you must play a certain part tonight, or the order comes on Friday and you must play on Monday and you must be ready. You must have your technique as the musician must have his note and the painter his brush, and you must know how to the last possibility to create a human soul.

Now let us analyze and see who the creators are and who gives us orders. Some people say that the trouble with dramatic art is that everyone gives orders. On the other hand, some say that the artist himself gives the orders and no one else. Let us try to find the real persons who may and should give orders. Who do you suppose is the first person to give the actor the order to act? Quite obviously it is the author. Is it possible that the actor himself may give the first order? In the history of the theatre, there was a period of a couple of hundred years when the actors were the authors themselves. Now that is lost and the author is the first person to give the order.

I shall take a book and try to read an order given by the author. You will recognize the play. I want you to think about the author's order in this particular moment.

Act I, Scene 1.
Elsinore. A platform before the castle. Francisco at his post. Enter to
   him Bernardo.
B. Who is there?
F. Nay, answer me, stand and unfold yourself.
B. Long live the king.
F. Bernardo?
B. He.

And so on during the scene. What are the author's orders? You must know how to find them and carry them out. You cannot say, "All right, Mr. Shakespeare," and go ahead. The first thing is the presence of danger and the guard against it. The clever actor asks from whence comes this danger? He may be answered that it is from the ghost. If that enemy were human he would come from the north, east, south, or west, but here it is otherwise, because of the ghost. Before you open your mouth you must realize that you are on guard and nothing must escape your observation. Moreover, you must prevent anything which would disturb the normal passage of time. Do you feel that you could play two hours guarding this place, being always ready to repel danger? You have your sword or pike in your hand. This figure ready to turn down any danger represents action.

There comes a question when the guard hears a sound: "Who is there?" That means that the watcher hears all things and that he has heard something. The next action will be to penetrate the air and find out who is coming. This scene cannot be merely shouted. It must be played with feeling and action. The mistake in *Hamlet* is that the guard usually walks about the stage in open spaces. In this scene you cannot, so that the feeling of truth will give you the right thing to do immediately. You will find a corner from which you can watch. In such a situation when I hear the question, "Who is there?" my thought is, "No I will not say who I am since it may be danger. I will first find out who this man is. I will not tell him, but will ask who he is. If he is part of the guard, he will answer, 'Long live the King,' and I shall know that he is one of the guard." Attention and readiness to defend changes the guard into a thoughtful person, who speaks in the play to the man who comes in.

I don't know whether I have been clear enough in showing you step-by-step the little actions which fill out this none too significant scene.

It should be evident that even in this scene, every step is action and if you will not use too clever words, not too sophisticated speeches, and if you do not use what we call "professor's stuff," which will make you able perhaps to write books but unable to say, "Who is there?" probably you will be able to say everything.

The first thing, then, is a platform. Elsinore. What else does the book say? You will find the scene full of meaning and danger, and instead of a nice, strong-looking super, you will have an actor who will act and do. Let us go on with the discussion of the danger.

It is here a supernatural danger, which is different from that which comes from sword or bullet. One is afraid to be seen by the ghost, or to be killed by it. Here your imagination must go to work. What sort of feeling is this? I have never seen a ghost in my life. In later talks we will discuss affective memory, which will show you how to find substitutes for any feeling. Let me say, however, that you can find a real substitute to use towards the ghost which will be a special one for that particular circumstance.

Then Shakespeare gives you another order. "It is cold, and I am sick at heart." Do you not think that these things are very clear? All these little things give you orders which are cues for action, which if you are trained you will be able to do easily and play right away.

Let us take the next man to give the order. He is a strange creature called "stage director." I call them moodmakers. They are the people who create the mood. The actor is the one who should have an open heart to them, because these people open the doors of mood to you. All the rest must come from you. All you have to do is to listen to and believe what these people say to you. For when you are expecting the command from the author you may get it from them. It is not an order or command which the stage director gives you. He helps you rather than orders you. The result which you will get from him will help you to start to create and build a picture which is prepared in your heart by your study at home.

The next one to give an order is the scene designer. Probably you have not had much time to meet him, but in a few years you will know what he does for you when you have to play a light part and this clumsy creature puts you in no less than fifty pounds of satin and brocade and then says, "All right now, go ahead." The poor actor only realizes at rehearsal that he has to put these things on and play. When you play a part you should know from the beginning what costume you are going to wear, what scenery you are going to play in, and what generally the artist thinks from the visual point of view. So you can go on with your work, and not be surprised to find something at the last moment you hadn't thought about.

The last person to give you orders is yourself. You have to deal with him and rely on him because he is the only one who will tell you what to do. Who is yourself? That depends on your education, your will, your artistic development, and your talent, all of which you must realize do exist. I would like to speak more about giving orders to yourself.

The trouble we had with *Twelfth Night* was that all the people are working hard, trying to do their best and to do all that is asked of them, but they have not enough faith in their best friends – themselves. The trouble is that they have not had enough time to develop their own ego and their own personalities in order to say, "I will do what I believe is right." I hope they will wake up and create their own souls. Everything that could be explained has been. The mood-maker has told them things and given them moods. All that is left is for them to show their own judgment in situations. Someone has fixed a trick with a chair and they honestly follow it out, but they do not ask, "What can I do with it? Must they tell me to turn it so I can play with it? Shall I do it this way or that? It depends on me."

It is clear now that those little problems are as necessary to the art of acting as A, B, C, D are to music and anatomy to design. One statement can be made: that our life is the chain of certain problems in succession and that all these problems are in action. When you do nothing you are not alive. The next statement is that you must have an aim – a goal. I *want* a glass of water – must *find* a glass of water. The glass is the first object; then the water. Without an object there is no problem.

"To be, or not to be" – here is the object. You may speak to yourself, to God, to your mind. You may analyze the thing that happened in Denmark, but you must have an object. When I tell you that your object is not strong enough when you say, "Juliet, I love you," it is because you are reciting it – not saying it to Juliet. The audience will say that you are not talking to each other.

The next object is the feeling of truth in the problem. The moodmaker will say to you, "You are in a bad mood. Let us say that you lost your best friend. In this mood you will take a cup of hot coffee from the pot." Generally, the actor will talk with his eyes full of tears. He will take the hot coffee and drink it without feeling because he is in the mood. He must have this feeling of truth.

You must also have connection with your object. What connection is cannot be explained – it is nothing that can be touched. It is not made. At this moment I have connection with everyone of you and no-one in particular. But if one were to ask me a question I should have a direct connection with him and forget everyone else. The power of connection is very necessary, and you must learn to connect yourself with the one who is given to you by order. Let us say he is the ghost – I am Hamlet. From the moment he appears I should know that nothing else exists.

The last thing is adjustment. What is adjustment? If I am speaking to you, I have a certain way of approaching you. To some one else my way of approach is different. These adjustments do not concern only people, but everything around you. You are sitting here and listening in one way. In another room you would be listening in another way. The soul adjusts itself to circumstances.

You must do these problems given you by order, either by the author, stage-director, or designer, because these orders will help you to obey that which makes you do necessary things. The result will be the development of your artistic will.

There must be action in the problem; without action it is not a problem. There must be an object. When you act you must know toward what point you act and where you will receive your answer. There must be a feeling of truth. When you speak to a lion differently than you would to a hare. You adjust yourself in a different manner to a cup of hot coffee than to a cup of cold coffee. There must be a connection between the object and yourself. It is not enough to act toward the object. You must have a real connection with it. There must be adjustment. The individual person is creative and improvises an adjustment in every problem he does. You may pick up a pin in such a way as to show people your personality, because it is not a mechanical action.

2   Lecture 5

Today I will try to tell you (I don't know what will come of it) to show you how to apply memory of feeling to practical work, how to look for feeling, how to combine and develop them, how to use imagination, substitutes, etc. I am purposely taking a theme which is unprepared by me, so that you will not get the impression of a mind which is working with a thing that does not have to be found. I could take a scene from a play which we have already done, but I think that from my looking for the things really as if I were working on the play you will get much more.

The play is *The Scarlet Letter*, and probably all of you know about the scene where Hester Prynne is set up for public shame, which is to say led through the crowd to the market place and put on the scaffold to stay twelve hours – from dawn to sunset – with the scarlet letter on her bosom. While this is going on, her husband is entering the town after being absent twelve or fifteen years. The first thing he sees in the town is his wife standing on the scaffold with a child in her arms which he knows is not his child. I shall read you the scene:

CHILLINGSWORTH: I pray you, good sir, who is this public woman? Wherefore is she set up here to public shame?
TOWNSMAN: You must needs be a stranger in this region, friend, else you would surely have heard of Mistress Hester Prynne and her evil doings. She hath raised a great scandal, I promise you, in godly Mister Dimmesdales's church ...
And so on to the end of the scene.

This is the scene. Now I will try to go through the part of Chillingsworth. First of all, I am not taking the whole play, but only this scene, to try to find what will be the action, the spine, the line which will direct me in my doing, in my action, in this scene.

Ques: Is it too much to ask the actors merely to imagine themselves in that situation. Ans: I don't know a man in the world who can do it unless he builds the situation as I am trying to do it now. The imagination will not give you enough food for it. For instance, you will say to the painter who wants to paint this picture, "Imagine that." He will do it, but he will imagine it in one way only, which gives him a foundation. In the theatre, we have only imagination, and this lacks that foundation.

From the words, from the many questions that are in this little scene, you may conclude that the acting would be that one tries to explain to him, to the best of his ability, to help in finding out, but he cannot and the thing is not explained. Having under consideration only this one scene, I am taking only this spine: that the both of them are trying to find out, to expound a riddle – How did it happen? What he says here, "who is guilty," etc. This is the simple, common, elemental action and unless you have the action, nothing will help to carry this scene. It will not be right, it will not be understandable. I shall take Chillingsworth by himself. In this action I shall take myself Chillingsworth. I am coming to the city, and I don't know anything about the events that have transpired during the past twelve years. I have not seen my wife in that time. I want to find out first where she is, how to find her. I don't know anything, but probably I am going and coming in the city and perfectly happy, in a perfectly good mood, and then the first sight, as Hawthorne insists in the novel, that meets my eyes, is my own wife standing on the scaffold. There is for me one part before I see her, when I come, perfectly sure, perfectly happy, longing to see someone, longing to rest, to find someone dear to me. I am in good health, there is someone, this most beloved creature. I want to speak to her, to embrace her, and I must say to myself, "Well, at one time you were happy." It is not an ordinary kind of happiness here. It is too eager, too strong, you would not have such a long pause in your life when you didn't see someone you wanted to see. In other fields, have you not had dreams? Have you not longed for something, not a woman? In your childhood and all your life, the dream about prairies, wild horses, and all the time, one work, America – something going on in the other half of the globe you wanted to join. Every summer you travelled but you were not in America. Then one day it happens that you are on the steamer and you know that in seven days you will be there and you look all the time forward, never once back and finally when you approach the shore, although it is night, you strain your eyes and try to make out what the lights are and what makes the glare over the city. You look through this and try to find something you can use for this situation. There is something.

Probably because there is nothing personal in it, nothing you would know but it is a long prepared dream, which, without any reason, was quite strong in you. The dream was lost the moment you set your foot on the ground, because you realized it was just the same. But the time before you went down to the pier, can you use that as this sort of happiness? Well, I can say to myself, probably yes, it is something of this kind. All right, so what will I do now? I will try to remember in my dreams every situation, every moment, every day, every thought, how I lived through them when this particular bit of my life happened. Through speaking to myself, through remembrance, maybe through looking at postcards, maybe through reading the description of the country, and so on, perfectly easy, the mood can be developed and brought back.

Now comes the next part, which is: shock. Instead of that which I expected to find, something terrible, something absolutely which could not come into my head, which I could not understand in this moment before I say anything. Now again it looks like nothing in life. Everything is lost to me. Well, not everything. Faith in human love, honor, and those mean a great deal to a man. Well, once before I had lost everything I had. It was not people, it was what you might call fortune. It was lost, lost. Was there a shock? Not so much, because it was quiet. You could not tell. You are trying to find in your life and you cannot, something that corresponds, but that for Chillingsworth, this was a tremendously important thing and you cannot find something, you cannot find it, and so you say, "I am trying to do it before you in a couple of minutes. Days can be spent looking for it. Someday maybe you find the substitute. Maybe, let us say, it would be the news of death of someone very dear to you, say, your mother. How can I apply it to this case? What was lost?"

Probably the things which are more or less important or significant were those lost to Chillingsworth in that moment. I will try to take it, and, again, through the remembrance of how it happened, through the circumstance of what was before and after, how I felt, how I may put my hat on when I got the wire, how I stood on the bridge and looked at the sea, how the next days passed, and so on. The feeling and a little bit of atmosphere is back to me again now. Through repeating this atmosphere day after day, I can reflect in myself something that will be pretty close to the feeling of this shock. Then maybe I am near to the words now. What did happen before the shock; the shock itself; now what happened after the shock? In the play, after the shock, the author says to me, "A long minute is spent when they can look into each other's eyes." So it is not that I got a shock and can run away, that I can be alone and can live through this shock. I have to carry it through and meet the eyes, the soul of the man who is guilty, who caused this shock to me. Again, it is a bit, and it is not a simple bit, because after the shock, it would probably be my inclination to yell or cry out, to say something, to ask something, but I cannot do it because the crowd is around and you don't want to throw yourself into the middle of the situation. Something else must be done. A tremendously strong situation between two people who know the mystery, the secret action of this bit. I would say that it is a tremendous soaking or draining through the eye – the whole person, dragging out his whole soul through the space of his two eyes. Can you find something of this sort?

Well maybe. Night. And between the one line of trenches and the other, three of us are sitting in a hole in the ground and you know your duty is to push a switch, to make an electrical connection when you hear a certain noise or certain things will happen in the line opposite you, which will mean that a gas attack is beginning. The situation is so tense that you are changed every two hours, two hours that are spent in fear because you know that you will be the first to know and the first in danger, the first who will be the victim of the situation and it is perfectly natural that you should not want to be. Two hours without any movement, any life but that of the ear and eye. Who you are is forgotten; where you are is forgotten; only now do you think of those two hours and even then you lose track of the passage of time, and you don't know whether it is an hour since you came or only fifteen minutes. For five minutes of one hour you know only the moment that you came and took the wires and you hold them like a human heart and you sit there, looking into the night, into the darkness and you listen and you soak in everything that is there from the darkness and afterwards, when nothing happened, you are like a dead fish, a squeezed lemon. All your strength is gone. Maybe this situation is not the same, because in the play it is a human being you love and here one you hate. Some sort of switching around may be necessary, but what you want is there. Soaking in, listening, will give you the way to meet the eyes of your wife, how to get the whole thing, how it is done.

Q: (If we ourselves have not had this same experience, could we do it? A: I am saying that everyone can find something in his own life he can use. When I cannot find something separately, I would try to make a mosaic from different pieces. The more the actor is experienced, the better it is, but every human being with a sharp mind has enough experience to do what most plays require, because they are written for human beings. True, the workman who works with his hands all his life cannot do Hamlet, because he does not do those things, but he can do the first or second Grave Digger. I cannot do Romeo. I would not have enough experience for it. A young man would have enough. My experience is past and gone and has become sort of tarnished. My example is not very good, but I as an example. I am showing you an example of a certain work.)

Q: (Why does it ruin the feeling to tell about it? Answer: This is human nature. I do not know why you can say many things to yourself but if you say them to other people you kill them. I don't know why it is so, but it is. It may be only another peculiarity of human nature which likes to keep things to itself. In life, the strongest, sharpest things are done in silence. If someone were to write a play in silence, probably it would be the greatest play in the world. When something happens you do not speak, it is done in silence.)

Q: (Can you use the same experience several times? Answer: Yes, if it is strong enough. Finally, you reach a certain maturity you will have twenty or twenty-five of these strong feelings and you will combine them and have something new again. Geniuses probably have many of these feelings.)

The third thing that would be necessary for me would be the moment I am looking at her. The next moment she passes, she runs away, and I stand alone and here, only here, starts the action but before the action starts I must make the decision to start it. Further, I would describe the bit as: I understand everything and now I must try to find out what it is. I must have something for my next steps. I am alone. There are only strange people around. No one knows me and I must not look suspicious because I must find out all about this thing. Hiding is something tremendously strong, significant, hidden but at the same time, you must speak about it without showing that you are interested, that you belong to it. She is the problem. The bit must be significant, a thing dear to you, but entirely hidden, entirely under cover. That means perfect self control, but self control is the result. You cannot play it unless you have to control something. Probably you will have to look for the thing you could not achieve in life and consider that you want to achieve them. Probably it will take you much to the side of the whole thing, but it may be the dream about a play, and I don't dare say a word about it. All the time I work on other plays, but I have this one underneath, this final play under cover, and I am not showing you I am interested. If this play is mentioned, I do not show you that I am interested. One thing, however may be all right for one, but for another it does not work. Each must have his own dream world, where he finds what he wants. The idea of Nihilism might be serious to you, a great thing. You speak about it and meet mockery from me and you can't stand it. All you can do is to show the result of your work, the already prepared bit of your art.

That something, the most important secret for you, the dream of your life, must be perfectly hidden, and you start to speak about it. Let us say my dream is to produce the play *Hamlet*. All my life, only *Hamlet*, and nothing else. Then I know that this certain man knows something about it. I don't want to say to him, "I want to know what you have," but I hide my thought and start to speak, being apparently uninterested. In this way, through repeating, you develop this feeling to such an extent it comes easy to you, and you can reflect it always when you want it.

Q: (Must you show the audience you are holding back something and exercising self control? A: I do not care about that. But I do care about going right, because if I take the lines I find that one says, "To the market place," and something else, but there is nothing about my being her husband.)

Q: (Then why must you make this mood? Answer: For myself. How else would I approach the moment when it would be necessary to learn? The people, if I did not do it would say, in the last moment he did not feel that before, it is not right. This must be done because the audience is like someone who stands behind the table in a card game and sees all the cards, while each of the players can see only his own.)

Q: (What is the connection between you in the play with Hester and your life connection with *Hamlet*? Answer: Those connections are the same for me. The big bit of atmosphere that I loved Hester, that she betrays me, that she is under this mark of shame, this all must be hidden, I cannot show it. This is the same as I think about *Hamlet*. It must be something very big, very dear, something I could not find right away, because it is very deep in me. Then I must learn to hide it. I will not then be empty. My exterior will be calm. First, I would look for those moments in my life when I had those things in me, moments when I was full of this idea and when I hid it and was calm outside.)

After this a man approaches me, and I pick him up as the man with whom I will speak and the action starts only then. If you will work honestly and prepare yourself in those three steps and then read your lines, you may not be a Duse, you may not be a Salvini, but every one will understand what you say, everyone will understand the atmosphere of the sentences and because you are honest you will attract the attention of every human soul. If you are talented you will receive much honor and many dollars. If you simply say this first sentence like a servant in the part, but in the right way, they cannot say it is not true.

With the words: If you will do all I told you and do it systematically, looking into yourself and then take the question, "Who is this woman?" you will realize immediately that it is not a simple question, like "What street is this?" or "What time is it?" Where can you get the quality of this question? It is awfully difficult unless you work in the way and come to the perfect understanding of how to say it, not mentally, but through your feelings. I simply prepare myself, create the feelings: then I ask the man about *Hamlet*. It is not then an empty space or a common saying.

Q: (Will this feeling that you establish at the beginning of the play last through the evening? Answer: You cannot keep those feelings unless they are very strong. There are those twenty-five things which you will keep, which are your reserve, but you will change them, combining one with the other. When you come to the performance you think only about the one: that you come as Chillingsworth and your long-distance mood is your love for Hester.)

Q: (Does this mood become mechanically associated with the situation? Answer: Yes, if you think about it a little at first.)

The actor as an actor must have a double sort of consciousness. Action as an action will be done and must be done quite unconsciously by you. Everything you get from your partner, from the situation, from the word is received unconsciously. When you play right you will be quite unconscious of any effort to play. You must not think, "How shall I say it," because Nature is more clever than you can be. Like Salvini, when he was asked how he built up Othello. The most interesting bit in his impersonation was when he was signing the papers and he says that once his hand shook and he broke the pen, and afterwards he always used that. Then only his eyes came out and looked at Iago. His feelings were built like that and he did not think how he said the sentence, but he said it perfectly calmly, you could not resist him. Then the sentence came out as unconscious action.

Don't think that this is all, but come to me and the company and check what I told you today, because maybe it is easy to understand because there is nothing complicated about it, but to do it yourself with a certain result, this is the whole thing and it does not come so easily. I have done one, two, three steps, and I am tired. That shows you that stuff like this must be worked out and it takes life and energy. To understand is simple; to do is more complicated.

3   Lesson 6

It seems to me that I shall have to speak once more and again try to make myself clear on a certain part of the method. From what I hear and a couple of letters that I have received from you, some minds do not seem to catch the point, and I do not think it is the fault of my English, of my words, or of the way I explain. It is probably something much deeper. For me the question is clear; you do not understand and I do not blame you, because it cannot be done in four, five, or even six months. You do not, however, understand the use and way of using the feelings.

I know this because some of you have said, for instance, that you knew everything that has been said to you. I don't deny that I say nothing new. I say what every actor who thinks about his work will tell you, something that you can find in the letters of Jefferson, Booth, Duse, and the other great actors. The difference is, once again, that to know and to understand is one thing and to use and apply is another. In the same way, I might tell you to make this table and explain how you should do it, but you yourself must be able to take the board, saw it right, cut it to the proper lengths, glue the pieces together, and so on. So you may say that you understand Memory of Feeling, and you may be able to make the table, but I don't think so, and to prove it, I am going to work with you a little bit, practically. What I am going to do is a sort of what I call a "One Minute Play," which is for the actor what the one-minute sketch is for the painter.

In these one-minute plays, I do not require from you exterior characterizations; I don't require literary quality in your words; I ask only the truth of your feelings. The way we usually work on these one-minute plays is for me to draw the situation – the way the thing is – then every actor asks himself as a character or as something which helps to clear the situation; you go and rehearse three or four times until it reaches a certain form.

I shall try to give you the situation. It is a passenger liner wrecked in the middle of the ocean. The boats are in the water already, and the crew is trying to keep order each in his turn, and the passengers are waiting to step into the life boats. Then comes a woman with a bundle like a child in her arms, running from one line to another, begging, asking people to let her in because she is out of turn. No one wants to do it, but finally another woman gives up her place, and the woman with the bundle goes down into the lifeboat, which goes away. Someone on deck says to the woman who gave up her place, "Did you think that was a child? It was a dog she was trying to save."

This is the situation. From the point of view of the actors, I want you to be what you are without any characterization, except for two actors whom I shall ask to do the woman with the dog and the one who discovers the thing. All the rest of you, your action is to find your place, to find your things, to take your place to wait until the crew will tell you, "Next – Next … " You try to make your turn come quicker than it is supposed to be, try to cheat. The spine is to get away from this place as soon as possible, and the long distance mood is to save your lives. This means that the situation is very tense. In small bits, you are free; you can do what you like, without characterization to disturb your minds, simply playing the things, doing the action I have told you about.

Now let us set the regisseur's beats: the first beat is: the play starts – every one is trying to find out where he belongs. We will have two beats and two lines. The first beat will be the panic scene where everyone tries to find out his place – from the wall, where it is painted on; from the crew; from his ticket. This is the first beat.

Gradually this beat comes to order, the lines are formed. After that the beat of impatience, when you wait your turn to go down into the boat. Beat of waiting. Let us say half of every line should step down and it happens that one personality expresses itself more strongly than the rest and starts simply to run from one line to the other, asking that they let her in the boat right away because she is at the end of the line. Everyone refuses. This is one long beat.

The next beat is when somebody says, "All right. I have nobody, take my place." This will be the fourth beat.

Then the fifth, the woman with the bundle enters the boat and everyone watches her with envy. In the next, someone realizes that the woman has not a child, but a dog and she tells it to everyone. "She cheated. It is not a child, but a dog – and she saved herself and the dog with her." Then everyone's reaction to the woman with the dog, as you feel toward her cheating, because in those big cases we feel it all together, not individually, not only the woman who was cheated, but everyone else is expressing what he feels toward her. And this is the end.

Now, let us repeat the order of the big beats. First: Panic – trying to find things; finally, it comes to a certain order. Second: Impatience – waiting; it takes time. Third: Woman breaks away and expresses herself more strongly than everyone else and tries to find someone a place. Everyone is resistant to her. Fourth: Somebody tells the woman, "I have nobody, I will do it." Woman goes down. Fifth: Somebody discovers it and says that the woman has a dog. Sixth: Reaction of everyone to the event.

I don't care about the business, only the general outline. One line is on one side, the other on another; one or two of the crew are standing about. Apply all you know about memory of feeling right away to this situation. Don't sit down and write a play, but try to remember yourself in such a situation – how you acted, how you felt, what you said. Then do it.

(Half the school proceeds to carry out the situation.)

Now, you see, here is the whole thing: what you have done is a pathological case. It is not art. It is a general nervousness. Anyone can do that, saying to himself, "I am desperate," and then go ahead with physical strength. Where are your souls? I don't see them. I see nerves, I hear screams. Where is the feeling built?

If I take myself, for instance, the first things I would say to myself – the first moment that the panic starts. I would not start from a scream, because that way, nothing is in the head our heart. The first thing I would try to find what the matter was. I would go and look myself, then I would have a moment when I realize that the boat is going down. In this moment I don't know what to do. This always happens when you are in a trap, when you don't know what to do. Then comes decision. It depends on who I am, what action I will choose. Then I will start to do the action. Then only I would find what I want to take with me, and there will be a time when I will think only of those things or that person whom I want to take with me, without thinking of my own escape – my own safety. I will think for a moment only to save this person or these things, and then again it will be action. Having found my place in the line, which, let us say, is sixth, I watch those in front stepping down, one by one. Why don't they move faster? Maybe I can go nearer. Everyone watches, but the hysteria does not start even yet, and it does not start in life until a man has nothing to do with himself – not before. All the time you can control yourself, and you then go on to the next problem. This means that you apply your imagination, your memory of feeling. You apply it as part of the whole thing. I don't know if I have made clear to you what I mean, but do you understand the difference between simply plunging into unconscious action and artistic building up?

(The other half of the class now goes through the same exercise.)

From this point, the next thing for you is your imagination. Maybe you say to yourself, "I will stay near the wall and be quiet." But this is the stage and what you do must be better and more expressive than in life. If you say to yourself, "I must rush and find my daughter," you must not rush and find your daughter three steps away. You build up the thing and when you find her, perhaps she is already in the life-boat. You see, your imagination gives you steps to build up you action, but the imagination has a right to exist only when the first line is perfectly prepared and you go from one problem to another. The first is most important. As we have it in *Scarlet Letter*, the words are a result of a tremendously important first bit which is without words and is even more important than the words themselves if the actor builds the situation. The words are only the result, but the moment when Dimmesdale does not know whether Hester will say he is the father of her child is the real moment. The words which will come later are less important.

This is the first beat, when you get the news and ask yourself what to do. When you do not do the first beat right, you cannot find yourself; you simply "sweep" without any ground under you. If, however, you will take the first beat perhaps a little heavy, like a big engine getting under way, but in the right direction, you will get the whole thing as it should be.

Another thing is the feelings: you cannot work with them if they are not trained, if they are not in as good form as a wrestler's or fighter's muscles. For that it is not necessary to work much, only five minutes a day, when you will walk along the street, in the subway, when you see someone here – in that moment when you will order yourself to apply your feeling and do it, then when you are called you will be ready – you can do anything.

Now I would like to have some questions as to what is not clear. What do you still not understand?

QUESTION: Does it not take more time than we have now to get the right mood?

ANSWER: These things do not require as much time as building a scene in a play. Here, if you get one second of the right thing it is all right. We can do dozens of them with any number of characterizations, any number of situations. You may do something with merely a spicy situation with a little theme. Situations as they are and when you will get a little of the right feeling transplanted into the situation you will be doing all that is necessary. The trouble with the actor is that he understands perfectly, and, after all, there is nothing that cannot be understood, but when it comes to creating for himself, he is lost unless he knows what to do with himself.

I would like next week to see you all in something which you have prepared for me, something not very important. I don't want any play but simple exercises. I will give you right away something else to do. This will begin Monday and every day at five o'clock. I would like to have groups of five or six come with what you prepared so that I may get acquainted with you in actual work. You may speak, but it would be better to have it all action so that I may know what you are doing, how you are applying your feelings and your bodies toward action. You will have twenty minutes.

Another thing – I would like to hear your voices, so if you will bring something learned by heart, you will recite it for me. It should be something not very long; ten or fifteen lines will be sufficient.

4   Lecture 7

I shall speak with you a little today about a subject which young people usually speak about very early. It is imagination in art, imagination in the theatre, in creative work. It is a very dangerous theme, because, after all, the imagination is something you cannot explain. You cannot teach it. It is not materialized. You can say, "My dreams are the most wonderful in the world," and I will agree with you perfectly, but you cannot say where they are. You cannot show them. The point is that we working in art cannot deal with imagination without any foundation or with imagination which is not deeply rooted in something which we can control perfectly.

That means, for instance, if I am simply a person of the average intelligence, I have read a few books, I have a couple of friends, I have seen a great deal, I have my dreams, my imagination. Have I a right already to use this imagination? My bold answer will be, "No," because to use this something you must have a practical habit, a practical craftsmanship to use one thing or another. When a person asks me if she can dance and I see she does not know how to use her hand, I say, "No." Her movements are good, but she can use her hand only as a windmill. The imagination is something that gives pain, that makes the artist suffer, because the nature of imagination makes it always better than every day life. That, too, is where it comes from, because the human soul is never satisfied; it seeks always for something better, and when it cannot find it around, it starts to look for something better in the imaginary world. All religions are based on this principle. What is art, if not creating a better life, a better world, perfecting what God has already created?

It is very difficult sometimes to say to the young soul, "Don't imagine anything." Sometimes it is a crime, because you may kill very good things, but for the benefit of the after work, it is necessary to say, "Don't imagine anything until you know what is real, what is imaginary."

And then do what you think is worthy to do in your imagination. One thing is certain: imagination deals always with a thing which did not exist before. Will you all agree on that point? It builds up out of the things which have exhausted; it goes up. It does not, for instance, take the same pipe which I have here; it dreams and builds another; otherwise it is wish or will. If I wish to have exactly the same one, it is wish, not imagination. If I wish to have a thousand of these same pipes it is human quality, but if I think how to make a better pipe, how to smoke it a better way, how the smoke comes out, that is imagination.

Does the imaginary world come from material things, or does humanity build its imaginary world without matter? This is a theme we could speak about for many hours, and it is the same question as who created the London fogs, Whistler? – or did the London fogs create Whistler? But that these questions exist shows that the imagination, after all, is not something abstract to the extreme. No, it is a thing which takes very material things from the world and shows them in such a way that everyone begins to notice. There is no doubt that the London fogs existed long before Whistler, but people did not care about them. Then he was born, and later he started to walk around London and paint pictures and he did a couple where he created imaginary fogs, and they are as much real now as the actual ones, and some people prefer them rather than the real ones.

All I am trying to do now is to make it clear that the imagination cannot appear unless you have a firm and concrete foundation for it. You will say, look at all the inventions. They did not exist before. A man simply started thinking and invented the radio. I don't think it was like that. Imagination, abstract dreaming always has roots in very material things, especially in art. Picasso draws crazy things which you may say never existed, but you analyze all his life, his works of art one after another, you will see that this man knows perfectly what the real hand is, that one bone must be joined to the others in such a way, that this one must be of a certain length and a certain thickness, that the muscles go in one direction and the skin has wrinkles which go in certain directions – he knows all this perfectly. When I was young, I had an argument once with futuristic people, and they showed that they knew more about classical poetry that I did, and it was not only necessary to be able to write a crazy line, but that you must know how to write like Petrarch or Dante before you could be a modernistic poet.

Going back to Picasso, you go back with him through all his life and you see how he was working hard in his youth, trying to get the Academy's prize and the Academy's support, and he studied very hard, probably so hard that he got disgusted with an art which is merely photographic, representing nature as it is, and then his mind burned to the creative side. He began to build on what Nature had already done. In what way? He picked out in his mind thousands of combinations of fingers and among them he found a certain few had a peculiar quality. From this he began to build what is called a crazy hand, long and tremendously expressive and having nothing to do with anatomy. Can you say that this sort of imagination has come merely from the air? No, because what I call business imagination, material imagination, builds from one real stage to another real stage, to three quarters real, to a little less real, and finally something which is a perfectly mathematical result of those four steps and looks to the outsider to be perfectly imaginary.

Question: From what you say, then, the difference between the Academy and Picasso is that one takes normality and the other abnormality?

Answer: No, the Academy has already certain fixed forms which the imaginary artist cannot use because he does not want them. He is not obliged to use a certain form; he goes where he wants to as he has a right. The Academician dreams exactly about this pipe here and will draw you thousands of them, but Picasso will not be satisfied. He will try to build three, four, five entirely imaginary pipes.

It is the same with paintings of Madonna and Child. If we would take simply the idea of a mother and her child, we would be free, but they take "madonna," which is Italian for "lady." It is not even Christ's mother, but interprets merely the Renaissance idea and picture of it. There was a painter named Hoffman who started to modernize the idea of Madonna and Child. He was caught by the poetry of the landscape and picking up a simple peasant girl, put a red cloak on her shoulders and put a landscape behind her with the child playing in a puddle. The mother bore a sorrowful look on her face. He caught the poetry of it and was probably the only one who was successful. Let us take him as an example, and again I will prove to you that his drawing was a very real one, although it gives you a full impression of the things it represents, but there are soft lines, tarnished colors, and tremendous eyes in his faces and bold lips. This is his style, and you would not say that you have seen such human beings, or that it is real, but you believe in it.

This face known in the art of painting as the special Hoffman face was the combination of the faces of his sisters, his wife, and his mother. He created his imaginary face with which he was in love all his life, with those three faces. I don't know the parts, but from one he took the nose, from another the eyes, and from the third the forehead, and he created his imaginary face, strong enough to convince everyone from absolutely real materialized things which existed. That was imagination, because he built something new. He did not use only the face of his sister, but loving them all, he looked for the unit where they would all be united, maybe psychologically or pathologically, but the line he worked on was the uniting these three in one. He has many pupils copying what he did, but they do not know, they do not understand the spiritual and creative quality of his work. If you will follow the history of art, you will find that the man with a great imagination, like Leonardo, created the type, and the others merely copy the form that he created, not building as he did.

The theatre is all imagination, and the value of the theatre is that imagination to such an extent that even when you create something you cannot touch it yourself, you cannot see it. It is dead the moment it is born. It may be the greatest power of the theatre that its creations die as they are born. It is easier in the movies, because it stays. In the theatre it goes away and the critic will be able to tell you only once. Because the theatre is much a matter of imagination, actors must be more careful than anybody else to be faithful to the imagination, not to use wrong and empty imaginations or unjustified imaginations, but to train and use only a real one. To give you a very simple example: There is a certain thing which has not yet been achieved by our friends the actors, but sometime we shall achieve it. The part of the Sea Woman is imaginary, because no one has seen one. Who has seen one, how she looks? You have fairy tales and you have pictures of mermaids. But the Sea Woman is not really yourself, and what will you do? Will you copy something that has already been done, something that already exists? That will not be real, creative art work. How should the actor seek to build up his imagination in such a case? By working with real things and searching in them for substitutes, looking in Nature for material and using his imagination for piecing, building, molding, creating, stretching out and in many other ways, but always by actually doing it. How?

I have never seen a Sea Woman. Fortunately, I was born near the sea and I know it, so it is easy for me to believe that something may exist in the sea. You will say that I am a poet to believe in that. But I have seen, and I do not believe it. Then I could say that you will have a hard time in the theatre. We must have some way to approach the things we want to use. When I say that I believe that something may exist in the sea, it is my imagination which comes from the sounds I have heard coming over the sea, from the sound of the rocks when the sea breaks over them, from the bits of foam that fly across the deck of a ship. When I speak about something I believe may exist in the sea, I am thinking about how green or blue the water looks at a great depth when it is so clear that it looks as if you could see right through the world to the other side.

These are little things which ferment in me and provoke me. Why can't they exist? In something that is closer to you? But I am perfectly open to the idea that the Sea Woman exists.

Then I have to materialize it. It is perfectly all right for me to smoke and dream, but I must come on the stage and do the Sea Woman, I must satisfy other people to the full price of two dollars. That is the trouble. Now the work begins. First of all, the foam, the waves, the sand, the seaweed, and fishes do not speak; and I must speak, for I have the words of my part. But all those things have a rhythm. Can I find a rhythm which will correspond with that of all those things I have told you about? I am sure it is possible with quiet, hard work. The author who wrote the play felt it and wrote a certain rhythm in the lines. You may read them, and they do not fit in what I think and see. Maybe you will look for something which is closer. Maybe a river or the mouth of a river where it meets the sea, where the rhythm is always whirling around. This may give you a certain way to speak the lines and may be perfectly beautiful and mathematical in the way it responds to the rhythm of a very real thing. From this it is but one more step for the technician to the dress which he puts on his performance. Sometimes he breaks the rhythm. Is it possible? Yes, because I have seen the water whirling around and suddenly a fish jumps out and falls back again, making a break in the surface. I walk along and suddenly I go out of the rhythm of the speech. Then I have marred the words, the sound, the idea, with the materialistic idea. What would you use? Only very real things. I have not used anything that does not exist. Then the movements. This is easier, because if you take any one fish you will find in him three thousand of Mordkin's lessons in one hour of his movements. Take, for instance, a fish with a complicated structure like the Japanese Fantail. Sometimes only one fin is moving. He looks at you and the other one starts to move. You can get along if you study realistically, not by saying, "O I am a golden fish." Watch how he moves, opens and closes his mouth, study him like a street cleaner studies garbage in a cynical way, because he takes all the dirty rags and old paper which goes through a certain process, and you receive nice, clean paper and write poetry on it. In art you must go deep and get your hands dirty, and when you are covered with it, then you can start to build your imagination. When the imagination plays with real things, it is like champagne. When it has not real things behind it, it is only like bubbles.

The next time, I shall go through characterization, because it will be clear for you to take characterization and work from these things.

You must be trained to take in and throw out. To use what you can and discard the rest. You may get your feeling of the sea from a reservoir or a river, any water that corresponds with you. Take in and try, throw out and keep, that is why all those exercises are important for the training in these things. You should not be sorry to try something, to throw it out if it is not right. The actor builds a long time but he does not yet understand how to sketch and try out before he adopts something. (The painter is not sorry to take his paper, draw a sketch, and throw it out if it is not right.) How does it come and what is it?

No, I am going to ask you a simple question. Is your disposition, your inside disposition, always even? Do you always feel good or sad, or does it change? It changes. Can you always trace the reason why it changes? Suppose you say, "I had a very bad dinner tonight," or, "Somebody told me I am a rotten actor," or you will have no vacation this year. Let us say from 99 to 100 cases, you can trace it. Now do you remember one case from 100 where you cannot remember why you are blue today, and the same thing concerns your being happy or cheerful? Sometimes you find $100 in the street, but sometimes you say, "Why am I happy?" You really do not know. You cannot trace it. Now, let me give you a hint. It's only because you don't know where to look and how to look that you don't know about this peculiar case without any reason being in you. The reason is a very definite one always. The reason is that your memory of feelings had registered a certain color of the sky or a certain smell of a breeze from the sea, but it is such a common thing that you didn't pay attention to it. Now let us say somebody spoke about that color of the sky, and let us say that something in the grocery smelled like the breeze from the sea, which arouses the registered feeling of happiness which was in you at that time and that feeling came back to you. And in spite of everything looking gloomy, the impulse came from the outside through your eyes and sense of smell and brought back the feeling which you had a week, a year, or five years ago, without your knowing wherever and how it came.

More, if you will trace the biography of the actor dead long ago, you will find that they did the same peculiar things which if you analyze, you will come to the conclusion that they were doing nothing else but fooling and playing around with memory of feelings. Here is a case

There was an American called Thomas [sic – Joseph] Jefferson, who, I assure you, knew nothing about psycho-analysis. In his contract agreement with other actors there was a peculiar point. "After six o'clock nobody talks to him." Now the actors thought, that's nothing, he pays money and we will sign. After six o'clock nobody had the right to open his mouth to him and nobody ever disturbed him. He would come to the theatre, wander around the stage, look at how the property man was bringing in the chairs, and nobody would notice him, and he would continue to wander. Then, at eight o'clock, the curtain would rise and Thomas [sic – Joseph] Jefferson, the great actor, would be created and he would start to play and he would be great. There is no doubt that he was a big talent, but when he took one or two hours to get acquainted with the sets where he played many times before, to look at them again – why? He wanted to bring the feelings back, the feelings of this success in that part; the feeling of his perfectly good acting in that part. I am not telling you that he wanted to bring the feelings which he had in life some time ago, or the feelings which actually helped him to create the feelings. For that I cannot find an explanation, except that he tried to recall and bring back all feelings connected with successful nights and successful acting with that part. So you see, unless you can prove that I am not right and Jefferson did not use it for the sake of getting a good start for his performance, unless you will prove this, you will have to realize that there is nothing impractical in it, that people use it all the time.

Memory of feeling is practical and sound for the actor and actress and is something that is used in every case of a good actor in different forms, though. To some people, it comes with difficulty, and they use it in their own way, by themselves in dressing rooms and they concentrate and some of them use it quite easily and naturally. Eleanora Duse had so much of it that she used it always in life. Her simple sincerity and simplicity in grief in dramatic situations, in sadness, was so close to her own life that she could not differentiate whether she was acting and whether it was life. In life, she was only quieter, but her voice and feelings were the same as on the stage. If she were to talk to you about flowers, that grief behind the smile would always be there. That tragic actress came into her from life. Her life was one big, tremendous drama. She was hit by that drama and carried it on with her to the stage. That was an overdone memory of feelings. She used the stage only for her feelings. Now, some actors underdo it, using technique only. Sarah Bernhardt did not use memory of feelings most of all. She used it only as a preparation, as a feeder to her imagination while preparing a part, but not using it while acting. She preferred to use technique. A person who is strong enough and has a good memory of feeling prefers to use technique. If you would ask Duse, "How will you act this part today?" she would say, "I don't know." But some people will tell you exactly to the point of how they are going to act.

If you understand, and I am sure you won't understand right now, that I am trying to put it as simply as I can. I don't want you to understand words only or just as a sort of theory. I want you to understand it as deeply with your soul and heart that in that particular moment where

I am telling you of memory of feelings, I am saving you twenty years of experience. It's a theory which comes from all big actors who work on the dramatic art of genius, but it happens that people forget about it. When I spoke to young people, one of the old actors, Otis Skinner, said, "It took me exactly 20 years to get what you are telling them now."

Where and how do we start our work on the memory of feeling? The first requirement is to register in yourself, take yourself under observation, be detectives of yourself and register every sort of a kind of mood or emotion which comes from nowhere, which you cannot use. Just register them. I bet from ten cases there will be one you will catch by its tail. Trace and find out in yourself an actual case where something came to you unknown and unreasonable and you did not know the reason and through your meditation and through your tracing you found out where it came from. It is very fascinating to trace these things. Have a book (don't show it to anybody), but write things down in shorthand because all that helps and two or three or four cases like that and you will know what it is.

How to bring back memory of feeling when you want it, bring it back, and make it just as you make the sound of the music, you can produce the feeling every time you want it.

(To be continued.)

5   Lesson 8

I want to talk to you about the most important and most difficult and precise part of the work of an actor. I want to talk to you about the source of where you get your feelings for the action on the stage. You know, and there is no use to repeat, that the main thing and the most important thing and the only vital thing on the stage is action. This is a very broad and wide definition, but after all, if you will analyze you will find that it is exactly as I say. It's action that counts. Even if you don't do a thing on the stage, the words themselves show you that you do something. You don't do. That means that you don't do a thing, and through denying the action you establish a new action, which is an action by itself.

Now, let us start from a thing which all of you know about and you experience it every moment in your life and it will be easy for you to analyze because you will have to do some little work by yourself. You will have to think by yourself and do some hard work by yourself, right now. Follow me, but don't take my words as gospel. Take them and immediately in your own brain – in your own work – verify them, and the result which you will get through verifying them will be a real one and different for each individual. You know that all human beings have something that is called memory. Now, what is it, and how you go after it, and how you get it, and what results it brings?

Well, how do you memorize a telephone number? It is very simple and very natural. Either you open the book, you look at the figures, and let us say the number is Endicott 3567. Then the first thing is that look and sort of photographic process when you get the landscape and our head is the camera. You get the landscape – Endicott 3567. You open your lenses, that's your eyes, and somewhere in the back of your mind is a film and Endicott 3567 is firmly registered on that film. Once and for ever it is registered. Now you will say that, "It is registered, but

I may forget." That is the question of your physical apparatus' not being exact and not being fit, and that's why you forget things. If you would be an ideal human being, once you see something you would never forget it. The animal sees something you would never forget it. The animal sees something once (true, he sees fewer things, just the things necessary for him) and he never forgets. This is the economy of registering things and the moment the animal sees it, it is there forever. Take, for instance, the trick which people who work with tigers and lions in circuses use. When they train them, they use hot spikes and when the tiger or lion tries to jump on the man, he touches that hot spike, gets burned and keeps away. After that, they never use the hot spikes, but paint the end red and then every lion and tiger knows what it means. They never touch it again, and they always remember that the red thing gives a pain. It is true that they don't have to remember so many telephone numbers, and that's why they remember things forever.

In the actual process of memory, the figure will be registered and with ideal conditions and under ideal circumstances, it should be remembered forever. Another proof that it is remembered forever is that very often in our dreams you recall things which you cannot recall in life. Haven't you witnessed things like that? You recall the wonderful landscape you have seen somewhere. You cannot remember the name, and suddenly, while sleeping, the name comes before you. And you know while you are sleeping that you have recalled that name, and when you wake you forget it again. What I am trying to establish is that the operations of outside life – whatever they are – are registered in the photographic camera which is your head.

Now, I have shown you how they are registered through the eyes. They can be registered through all five senses. For instance, through your ears you remember tunes, and if you are musical and your voice is coordinated pretty well with your ears, you can sing it. Very often you will find people whose voice is not coordinated with their ears – they can recall the tune but cannot repeat it. Now, a good musician who is trained, hearing the tune, can repeat that tune for days – months – years. We are not able to do that, but the operation itself is registered in a certain spot in our brains.

Through the sense of touch, you can remember less, because our sense of touch is not so developed as eyes and ears. If you will, for instance, take an example like this. You have all your dresses in the dark closet and there is no light. You want to pick out the certain dress you want. Don't you recognize it by the touch? That means that by the touch of that dress – silk or velvet, or even if you have two – you can distinguish it. That shows the thing is registered somewhere inside.

Now all those examples are very elementary and very simple, but you realize that you can enlarge them and can start with the telephone number, but you can go to the science of medicine, which embraces more than three, four, or five figures in the telephone, and you have all of them registered in the brain; and when necessary, you recall it. It is sort of a well organized post office, or good business office, where you get the order and deliver the order right away. Now that concerns just regular and common memory, which is connected with our five senses and serves everyday purposes. Now what is not clear in that statement, I would like you to tell me.

1.   You get the subjects for memory from the outside world.
2.   That they are registered, though you cannot make use of their registry, on account of your physical apparatus being over tired, or unfit, to do things; but, just the same, they are registered, and if you would know how, you can bring them back.
3.   And this is important. That the way you get that registry of the outside subject is the same way you usually recall it. What I mean is the telephone number which you got through your eyes, when you try to recall it, you will recall the book, the page, the street in which the thing happened, and through your eyes, you will get it back. The tune – if you got it through the ears – you will get back through the ears. Your voice, trying to produce sound, and your ear will listen, and you will strain your ear and try to hear it again as you heard it once, and you will get it through the hearing.
4.   Which is rather difficult to explain. It required always an effort which is mechanical effort which you are being compelled to use. In the case of the lion, the pain is the stimulant. The lion remembers he was hurt. He uses effort to remember and he does remember. In the case of human beings, you use certain effort to remember, or you don't register. You use the effort not to remember. I want to emphasize that even the slightest work of that kind requires a certain effort and training, but it is not a natural thing. With the human being, impulse comes from the brain – meditation – good behavior – ambition.

As far as I could, I called your attention to the things which you use every day and which you partly use on the stage, because you have to memorize and have to remember words. You have to remember not only your exercise movements, but your inside movements, where you have to remember where your muscle is, with certain stylized actions.

You use that memory in the same way you use it in life. In a case like this, the impulse will be your ambition of your love towards the theatre, art, or your devotion, but it is impulse and you use a certain effort. In Shakespeare you learn words through eyes, ears, or some people write them; that means they read them aloud, then while the read, they visualize; they write them; and all that is for the support of that power of memory. Some people are very lucky – they look it over once and they remember. Just the same, they do a certain amount of effort. Now you have to memorize on the stage with your common memory. Almost everything and always, but not quite always.

First of all: the order of the words.
Second: All your movements.
Third: You will have to memorize your outside characterization, how you look, how you hold your hands, voice, etc.
Fourth: You will have to memorize exteriorly a certain amount of physical energy which you have to spend for a performance.

That is something which you don't think about much and seldom find it in the actors, but it is coordination of the energies and the performance means very much. It gives harmony to the performance. If you play Ingebord in *At the Gate of the Kingdom*, it has a certain amount of physical energy, the way you move, etc. If you play Elina, the physical energy is much more than Ingebord.

But you see, as I said before, almost, not everything, and there is left now the very important part in acting, which are the emotions and feelings. Now where and how do we memorize them and where and how do we get them? It all comes from imagination. They are all imaginary and whereas some of you have very good imagination and they deal with unreal things. Art exists to make real things unreal. So if you use your imagination for the emotions and for feelings, you take something that does not exist and you try to make it real and that is where a mistake lies.

Not a single genius took the things which do not exist and made them real. They always took things which did exist and then shaped them in the life of art. Some of you take just general nervousness, anxiety, eagerness, and those feelings, being quite strong and easy to get in young souls, you mistake them for feelings which are required by the part. You have a part which you love, you are stirred up by the part to certain emotionalism, and you enter that stage. You try to reproduce your personal emotionalism. A combination of words and your emotion gives a thrilling result in acting. If you use emotionalism instead of emotion, it is like an empty shell – it explodes but does not hurt.

The actor must be absolutely normal and a healthy human being. You use your actual physical imperfectness of the state of your nerves as an emotion. For instance, you get excited on a tough monologue and you try to start with real tears, and then when you are through with the monologue, you still cry and tears are running, etc. Where is art? Your nerves are not in order – but there is no creation. If you give me a touchy subject, I will cry as a human being, but it has nothing to do with the art of the actor.

The product of your art is impartial, and you don't produce it with your own imperfection. The same things concern comedy. Sometimes you laugh because certain people are funny in life, and when they take something to perform you laugh at them because they are naturally funny, but there is no art. When you are not feeling funny, but you get the order and you make people smile and laugh – that's the art of an actor.

If you will not think for a moment that all that I have said right now, I am telling you for the sake of calling your attention to the fact that emotions and feelings should be just as set and under your control as everything else – as your gesture and behavior are under control. In the same way, your emotions, feelings, and nerves should be absolutely under control.

How can we remember feelings – the emotion? First of all, we don't have all of them in our experience. Shakespeare gives you 5,000 more emotions than you will ever experience in your life. How can we get them, to memorize and produce them for every purpose?

Now listen for a moment about the memory which is not common, but which exists just the same, and is called affective memory – memory of feelings – memory of emotions, etc. Now to use a uniform term, let us call it the simplest way: the memory of feelings. As it is commonly known, affective memory does not describe it in the same way, but memory of feelings is simple enough and is just what it is – memory of feelings. We almost don't use it in life. The memory of feelings is something that belongs to the people who work almost entirely in imaginary fields. The nearest example of every day men who use it is a public speaker or lawyer; and if you will trace all professionals who have to use a certain amount of creative power and imagination, you will find that consciously or unconsciously they have that memory of feeling pretty strongly developed and use it always when they have to make a new step. What is it, after all, this memory of feeling?

The structure of it is exactly the same as the structure of the common memory. Don't think it is something difficult – unnatural. It is exactly the same structure as the common memory. By that I mean that it comes through your five senses. It comes into existence through the same way as it was registered. It comes from the outside world and to get used to it and handle it you have to use a certain amount of energy, effort, which you have to train and have good strong will to get good results.

6 Lesson 9

Question: What is the difference between emotion and emotionalism?

Answer: When I say emotionalism, I mean something related to the affection – present, but which is moving without much reason. Emotion is something which comes and stays, the real thing, and a little bit unreal.

Question: How can you distinguish between the two in acting?

Answer: When you feel easy, when it isn't a hardship and you don't have to pull yourself, it's a real emotion. When you come to real tears without any effort, that's real emotion. When you pinch yourself and work hard and get one tear, that's emotionalism. It may move the audience. To chew the scenery is emotionalism, but to make it alive through acting is emotion.

To play Hamlet and take the skull and feel about it is emotionalism, but if you look seriously at it and get the feeling that that skull belonged to a friend of yours, you will get the real emotion. To get the feeling of sadness, think of a dead friend.

Yesterday I tried to make you understand that peculiar and uncommon memory which is the memory of feeling, without any exterior expression. You are just full of a certain feeling, and you are not required to play it or produce it, to act it again. If you can trace it in yourself, the feeling is like an echo, like a sound which was sung sometime before and comes now to you just as pure and crystal, but as a repetition, not artificial.

The next important question is how to develop this memory of feeling and common memory to such an extent that it will be and must be for an actor just as flexible and playable and practical as your common memory is. You understand that there is no use to know about it but to put it into practice. There is nothing that could aid but the same thing that is the same in every art, science, and trade; it's a technique and practice and training and nothing else. Don't think that you can get this by inspiration. The trouble with young people in art is that they think the art is a gift of God – art is toil of man. Don't worry that you will be called talented or geniuses. IF you will be called there's nothing you can do about it except prepare yourself and to build yourself up towards that position. Through the right understanding of what you are going after and through the right exercises, that peculiar and common memory, you will start – make the beginning of a tremendous experience which is absolutely necessary for the actor. There is no way to escape it. If one is to go unconsciously, like a man walking in darkness, working for twenty years and listen and fight in absolute darkness and try to build up intonation and then after sixteen or twenty years, or by accident, if you hit the part which is you yourself, you may catch it earlier. But that is an accident, and accident has nothing to do with art. There is no use to hunt for accidents.

Now suppose, as I asked you, you have found and traced down one, two, three cases of memory of feelings in yourself and you know how it feels to have that little thing when you recall some –

[Page of original is missing.]

Question: One step doesn't seem necessary. Supposing I know all the time that a blue sky makes me sad?

Answer: Suppose you do know – put yourself into the terms of a musician. He has eight notes and from these eight notes there are about 90,000 or 1,000,000 combinations. But he has only eight of them and he knows that "B" is "B" – but what he is looking for is the combination of that "B" with something else and then with something else, with the rest of them. The same thing with your feelings. You know it's a blue sky, but then it isn't the exact thing that you take and put into the part. You can use it over and over and it will be different in every case. For instance, playing Ophelia, your sadness will be a certain kind. That's why it is necessary to go through these steps, checking-up emotionally and mentally, experiences from life because you never know when you are going to use these notes.

How to characterize. Characterization to the actor is just like for the designer the kind of paper he puts his design on. The emotion or the spark which moves the audience is something which belongs to you. If you play any part – flapper or old woman – the emotion is yours and stays with you. It is your gold capital which stays in the bank, it is something that stays in you and you should not spend it.

Question: How can we remember all those different things when we have cues, etc., to think of?

Answer: After being technically developed, there won't be any difficulty to remember the business or physical characterization. It takes no effort if you are developed physically so that your muscles can remember the peculiar stage of your body of the business. We were trained very many times playing in crowds at the Moscow Art. We played year after year, every day, and rehearsing in the day time and we were used in the crowd and among 50 or 100 people; you would remember a certain cue that you would have to be in the middle of the stage, etc. It was sometimes much more complicated business than the leading parts which were quite simple and on account of that training which we got in our young days, it's nothing for me to remember the business of the whole crowd. It is just technique.

Question: What do you call inner characterization related to acting?

Answer: Example – Inner characterization of a stingy man, a miser. What is a miser? A man who has tremendous love towards a certain thing – gold. And who doesn't care about himself at all. A man who is very much on the lookout for danger. You decide that you have it for inner characterization. Now you go to your emotions and you look at a piece of gold, and you say, "It's a piece of tin, and I have to love and almost worship it." It doesn't exist – it isn't real – where will I get it? I go into my golden box (inside of you). What do I love? I will take a funny example. Suppose it's a cold watermelon on a warm day. When I was so thirsty last summer, I just wanted a drink, and suppose you didn't have a dime. You were almost ready to steal. Now the moment you start to think – watermelon – hot day – you will be full of your own emotion, which is similar to that stingy, greedy feeling of that money here. Now put it into action. Watermelon doesn't exist and gold doesn't exist. Maybe you would not feel that towards the real gold piece as you did feel towards the watermelon. Remember the next thing. Man doesn't care about himself. Doesn't care how he talks, dresses, and is indifferent. You can find cases where you were for a second like that. I was down and out but just the same I was always combed. Look on the outside and suddenly recall in Chicago at such and such a day, I saw a beggar in the streets and he just caught my attention with that absolute feeling of destruction around him, because the man was so neglectful about himself. You take the feeling – which you never experienced – from the outside through your eyes and you try exteriorly to copy that characterization – the dress will help you. Now the third thing is constant danger.

What is constant danger and constant suspicion? There is no doubt that you have experienced a strange noise in the night and you were looking for it and tried to sleep and then again it started. You can bring these things out like that. Now put together those three things and you have your characterization, using your own emotion. You have inner characterization, and if you will hold it and be suspicious of everybody and don't care how you look, you will be the miser. The outside is the easiest thing in the world – but how to handle every single muscle of your body? For an old miser, you will have to notice how the old man talks without teeth and how his jaws don't move fast enough. It's just control of the mouth and nothing else and then an old man cannot sit like this. (Demonstrates) He will have to do the same thing with a sort of stiffness. Suppose this miser is lame. Analyze the lameness and where? You decide it is hips. Then the whole thing that is left is to send an order and watch your hips and then you have the unconscious control of the hips.

But as you see, it looks simple and it looks easy if you take it piece by piece, but try to put it in the part and try to be simply alive and sincere and free with all those things? My answer is, it is just as simple as playing the piano, flute, etc. Somebody else said, to sing one uses beautifully proper notes, proper time, and proper place. It comes through training with constant repetition and perfection every time you do it. Now, when you are young you will develop in yourself a business-like attitude which is the most difficult thing in this country. You are tremendously business-like in business and amateurish in art. Art must be just as business-like as the production of automobiles. There is no genius. You must know that until I will be able to control my voice so that I don't think about it.

If they ask me, for instance, to be Romeo, I should reply, "Sorry, the age is gone; I can't do it." It's impossible for me, but – (Demonstrates) When Salvini, at the age of 61, came to Moscow, with grey whiskers, he was asked by old-timers who remembered him twenty years back, to play Romeo, and he said, "You are making fun of me. I have a little tummy, grey whiskers, and you ask me to play Romeo." But they were very persistent and said, "We want you to play only one performance." And finally, he felt so nice about it he said he would, but he wouldn't put any make-up on, or Romeo dress, but just some sort of a black robe and no wig. "I will be just as I am," he said. This man came on the stage in full performance, without any make-up, and at first, when he entered, you said, "Oh, what a pity, why is he doing it?" But in the third, fourth sentence, you forgot about his looks and only remembered the beautiful technique of the voice. He plays in it such a way that if you closed your eyes, you say, "What a young lion is talking." This impossible thing becomes possible on the stage.

For the young actor, there should be no limitation. "No, I cannot play that part." If you are young, only 30, you must be able to play every part. Through stage necessities for arranging the best, they may call on you and ask you to play another part instead of the juvenile. But it should not be because you cannot play it. If you are a craftsman, what difference does it make what kind of choice you make? A real shoemaker – like a real artist – can do everything.

You trace your feeling, you learn the reasons, and create mentally for yourself the same feelings. Start to file and check them up. Pick out more or less everything that looks to you of certain importance. Do not hesitate to put in funny things, because they can be very useful to you. Example: the mosquito. How am I going to feel murder? I always say, "How do you murder a mosquito?" Remember the mosquito and if you will file it in your heart, when it comes to a part, it will help. Don't hesitate if you feel like putting it down in writing, because that will increase tremendously your control of these things. And, again, good taste, quick brain, and with good effort, you can be successful and pick up anything you want. Put it down and start a business of your own, day after day, to collect feelings. When a certain time will pass, two weeks, you will have a little file of your own of those feelings. Go back and look at the first one. Say to yourself, "How can I bring back that feeling? Being alone, what is it – is it blue sky?" Don't think about the feeling, but the reason for that feeling. Blue sky, blue sky, blue color, form of the sky – and suddenly, the thought will start to work – what was it the first time? I was in the hills, I was sad already. You won't realize it, but the sadness will come. Now try to hold that sadness and say to yourself, "I am going to buy a newspaper, and come back home, and I will hold that feeling all the time; and even if I met on the street the most cheerful man, I will keep that sadness inside of me. I won't break it." *Don't*! Give yourself just two or three minutes, and when these few minutes expire, be cheerful. Work with yourself as though you were your own stage director. It will be difficult at the beginning. You will be funny when you want to be sad, and vice-versa. It matters not, but hunt. And afterwards, when playing parts, and you come to somebody like Jed Harris, Shubert, Reinhardt, you will see that if you worked by yourself, and if you know how to obey your orders, because your requirements will be much more difficult than the requirements from the outside.

So, after two weeks, go back to the forgotten feelings which you have filed, and try to re-establish them, but now by order. Go now into training, and every day go back a certain length of time and to your feelings through mental process.

You understand that you apply this to thousands of colors outside of happy and sad – stingy, jealous, generous, and thousands of colors. Every verb you can almost register as a certain emotion, as a certain feeling. Take almost every simple work, and you can find out when it was and when it happened to you. If you will go to that process of forgetting an established feeling, and re-establishing it again and forgetting it again, and if you repeat that three times, that means: suppose you find the blue sky once; you will recall it in two weeks (that's the second time), and then once again. I bet you will have it forever.

The thing is that some of you will be able to handle in two weeks twelve items, and some of you will be handle only three or four. Don't get discouraged. It takes a peculiar kind of brain for all those things, just like somebody may be easy with the figures, and somebody else not so fast.

Every one of us is interested in ourselves in the way of vanity – ambition. "I will be a good actress." But it takes time and quite a drive and strength, but after practicing through a year or fifteen months (it matters not if you play at that time or not), but if you will just practice like that, you will become to such an extent really histrionic that it will replace for you twenty years of experience. You will have the whole gamut in you, tremendous variety of feeling and all your own. That's the point. The trouble is that most of you repeat somebody else's feelings. That's the negative side of tradition. One good actor appears, John Barrymore, and then you have a generation of leading men trying to be John Barrymore, instead of knowing how to go after their own feelings and just taking the example of John Barrymore as one of a good kind of actor, whereas the way of the least resistance is strong: you all try to be John Barrymores, and that's repetition.

Look how a very capable man like Albert Caroll dropped down because he was always repeating somebody. He started very successfully in the *Grand Street Follies*, imitating John Barrymore, but now, only three years later, there is nothing left. Everything he is doing is John Barrymore. That shows you how repetition even unconsciously ruins one. Notice all other actors, look how they do it. For instance, Hartmann in *Danton* just gets the audience with his kind of acting and then turns around and winks at you. Don't copy him. Notice his faults, and if you pay attention to these things, you will grow in experience. Does the action of Hartmann's mean that he is not concentrating, just exhibiting? Or is it not exhibiting, but living through actually, but then as a good technician, just taking a rest for a second? As you know, every good speaker once in a while will tell you a joke, which gives you a rest. So, sometimes, certain actors use it as a diversion. Remember that it comes only with tremendous technique, when you will be able to put yourself into *Danton*. Don't try to do it right away.

Question: When you are acting and a person makes a break?

Answer: I know a very good remedy against it, but it takes tremendous will power. At the moment when the person breaks, if you will look at him with the eyes which say, "Don't be a damned fool," the person will just wilt. Control yourself and it takes a certain amount of technique to hold yourself. With a good technique, you cannot make me laugh. If I am not nervously exhausted, you cannot make me laugh, but at the same time there is nothing easier than to make myself laugh when I want to. It's just good technique.

Another good thing is to handle your emotions of acting well and one of the means is adjustment. You have to say a line. "Won't you please give me that book," and in that line your action is that you don't want to have anything to do with that person. You finish that relation and right before that line somebody will make you laugh and you feel you cannot stop, you've got to keep in laughing, use that immediately for adjustment. "Won't you please give me that book?" (with a laugh) Let it out like steam, or gas, into the automobile, because it will burst. Put it in another channel, but don't try to put a dam across, because it will go over. If you are strong enough in adjustments, you can always use the laugh towards the goal you want.

[Page of original is missing.]

... thing not through your brains, but through the inside. The important part of it is to find the reason for it. As I was telling you yesterday that because I put that dress on, I feel all right. Or because I meet that person which always makes me cheerful, and I saw her name or her picture, and that's why I got that feeling of cheerfulness. Or I smelled lilies-of-the-valley and something happened some time ago in connection with them which makes me sad. To run after the source is the first thing. Afterwards, when you will be trained enough, maybe you won't have to do that, you will be able to check up feelings just as you check up figures. You know enough about them and you remember the telephone number. You are trained enough in figures to recall them without recalling the source. But not so in the feelings. You will have to trace first in about 50 cases the reason or the source.

The next thing is after you do trace back one case like that and you know the reason for it is a blue sky, the moment you discover it and the moment you think about it for one or two minutes, it has registered in your brain, on the film the second time and it more or less fitted the pictures there already, but from unconscious it becomes conscious, because it goes through the brain by the order which comes from you. It registers through the order through your mentality.

Question: Why do you call it the second time?

Answer: You feel sad with no reason at all. You are hunting. "Why do I feel sad?" And you come to the conclusion, because I am looking at the blue sky, and the blue sky always makes me sad. And it was like that in the morning; and it did happen in the summer; and the moment the blue sky comes, I feel sad. When you realize what it is, that is what I call the second time. It was an unconscious thing, and it was necessary for you to see that blue sky and unconsciously it brought the sadness, and the moment you realize what it was and say blue sky, you reconstruct the situation for yourself, you build a little imaginary theatre for yourself where you bring the reason, which is in your soul to existence. That is the second time, when you say the words, blue sky.

Now suppose you said it and brought it a second time and forgot about it. The next time which may be a day, two, three or five days or a year, it makes no difference; as long as it went through your memory, it stays. You have a part and read about a woman standing in the room; everybody has gone and she is alone and doesn't feel cheerful at all. You think, where can I get that feeling of solitude and loneliness? And you open the golden book which is in your heart, and you say to yourself, "Blue Sky," and because it has registered inside you in your feelings and registered in your brains, it is something perfectly material. You can work with it. You can go into sadness naturally and without any pretense to be sad, because nature has given you that color. Nature has chosen you as the film for a certain picture and it stays there. With your soul you develop that picture and you file it in the filing box; and when necessary you open the file and you have it.

7   Lecture 10

What I want to tell you is how to apply what I spoke to you about last time to the actual performance. You have heard me tell you about the professional will, the will which the actor must have, which the sailor has, which anyone with a definite goal must have. It is something which makes you "want to do." This is just to remind you about it. And now you have before you a part, which is part of the play. You have the part, which is something which is your goal at present. Now this is an element, just as oxygen is an elemental part of the air and the air is much more important than the oxygen itself.

The action – that means doings, achievements – is the foundation of dramatic art. It is that which makes a performance. The actor is not only doing the things, he is acting. The word "acting" is strong – to act, not to play. Playing or performing is a wrong term. The term acting is very significant. Only the English language has the word "act"; others have "to perform," "to play," "to show," and I stress this – you must understand the performance as acting.

In the actual life, or in nature, which is the source of every art, whether old, modern, or stylized, are the roots of every art. In nature you will see that there is not a single moment when you do not act. If you will pay a little attention to yourself, watch yourself through the day, you will realize that every moment of your life you are acting. You get up early in the morning; you think what you will do throughout the day; you decide – you act. You wash yourself, you breakfast, etc. If you will go through your life, you will realize there is not a single moment when you do not act, even when you are tired and want to rest, you act. This is very important; please do not forget it.

When you see a good actor you will realize what he is doing, what he is thinking. Even if you see an actor who does not care about his partners, but simply talks to the audience, you will realize that he is explaining the word, the jokes; he is putting them across. He is acting

"100 percent," that is why he is successful. Acting is the foundation of the stage, the foundation of drama. This does not mean that I am for naturalism, for realism, or for the art of photography, but I do mean the words must be real.

Every one of you have experienced something probably that if you saw in pictures, you would not believe to exist. You see a character in real life and you say it would be impossible on the stage. But the stage exists for those "impossible things."

The word "acting" is very confusing. You imagine you must do something with your hands, your face, with a property. Let us give you a very simple example. You are thirsty and ask someone to give you a glass of water. You will ask in a certain way. Again, you are a designer and want a glass of water. Again, your relative has fainted, and you ask someone to give you a glass of water. Would you say that the action would be the same in all these circumstances? No. The words will be the same, the gesture might be the same; perhaps the intonation would be the same. But something else inside of you, that "acting" which I am talking about, will be very different in every case. This acting is what I care for. If you will develop yourself so that it will be clear as to that feeling inside, just as clear as you would know how to ask for a glass of water or a barrel of gasoline, this will be your technique. Now the intention – and attention – of the actor seems to be stressed on the intonation. Someone will tell you, you do not ask loud enough, or nervously enough, etc. What does that mean? I don't know. Nervousness is an action, just as much as anything else. I am not talking about a pathological case, but just simply natural human beings.

I tried to show you what brings action into your hearts by using that peculiar uncommon memory I spoke to you about, so that if you have in your part the action of asking someone to give you a glass of water for a fainting relative, or a glass of water to clean a strawberry stain on a white dress, you will get the right kind of acting. In developing memory of feeling, use even little things in such a way that it will be your very own. You can use anything in nature, you can use animals. From animals you can get the best, because they are so simple, so clean-cut. But a good beggar, for example, can be an actor when he is standing on the corner. He is cold 50 percent, but the other 50 percent is to impress the people that go by – to "touch" them. The place I would suggest to get memory of feeling would be the theatre – from actors. You may take the technique, the tricks, the outside things – "how to do" – but do not take the emotions, because they are artificially produced. Through the repetition of these, you will not develop anything of your very own. It would be like raising a hothouse plant; it would stop your own natural growth.

In real life, you go through it with small actions, one at a time – sometimes complicated, two or three at a time. Now go back to the stage. Every second you are on the stage, you have an action – something to do. Let us make further analysis. In life, you have the day distributed into certain parts. When you are home in the morning you have certain duties to fulfill, which finish when you are on the street. Then you make your walk as short or as long as you want; you do not want to mistake the streets. Perhaps you want to show off your new overcoat, if you have one. Then you enter your office, school, the stage, and another bit of action begins. These can be interrupted in certain parts, certain divisions. Now on the stage, there is exactly the same thing.

Let us talk about *Hamlet*. When you see him the first time, he is present at the big court ceremony. The new king makes his speech and Hamlet does not say a word, but he acts: he listens to that speech and makes a comparison between his dead father and the new ruler. Now look at a "ham" actor: because he is Hamlet he must be a sad prince. Actually, the more Hamlet is sad – the more he loves his father – the more he hates the king. He is young, full of energy; he will not be sad; he will be occupied with an important idea, and he will reason, but how? He gets the invitation to go to the university; he does not know how to act because he is so occupied with the idea to find out the truth about his father's death. Then everyone leaves the stage and he has the soliloquy; but unless he considers everything that the king says, how the king acts, and what is in his mind about his dead father, he cannot go into that soliloquy. He must understand what the "colors" are. What is before me? This will be one part before he opens his mouth, which is one action. Hamlet is human; his acting is very clear, very elemental.

In the first division is one kind of an act. With king, court, Laertes, and mother – he must watch them all. Shakespeare makes it clear he must watch them. In the last part of the act he is left alone, and the action changes and changes naturally. Then his friend enters, a very welcome friend, and tells him that his dead father, the man Hamlet is not concerned with, has been seen in a certain place. Now you see the action changed. He is saying right away, "I will be there tonight." Again action, a very clear one: to find out. "Is it so? My father – when? – at what hour?"

Take any play and find out one action after another action. (I mean a good play, by a good playwright.) The best judgment of the play would be to find out where is the action; not for the sake of the words, but for the sake of the action, that action must be put into words.

So now when you have your part in front of you, you would divide your part into separate actions – separate "beats." This has nothing to do with the scene, with the intonation. Sometimes the beat is between two or three lines of speech, but find out what is the main action on those particular lines. Why do people laugh? What is a joke? In that way you have all the part divided into actions.

In the first "beat" you may have "I want to defend myself." Then go back inside of you and look to find the color for defense. Once you remember when your mother spanked you, and you tried to defend yourself. You remember when a shell burst in the trenches; you remember when a burglar entered your room. Think them over. Only through this thinking will you develop your uncommon memory. When you have a strong experience, as in the case of war, or the provocation of the thought. You have the color for defense, and the actual making of the dialogue. When you start to say the words, you will not think of intonation, which is abnormal, but you will bring something that the feeling gives you. It is just as when you sing, you do not think of the note "B-flat," you do not have that thought in your brain.

So will the lines come spontaneously. They will have a springboard, presuming, of course, that your technique is developed and perfect, that you will not whisper your words, you will not lisp, and that your voice will be responsive to your change of feeling.

You now go to the next part: you try to find out if someone else is guilty. Again you will look into yourself. You will remember how you used to fight with the boys on the street, etc., and you will have the makings of the second part.

"No," you will say, "it will take a lifetime to go through a part such as Hamlet," but it will be much better than trying to remember the intonation. If you will go through it the right way the feeling helps the words and the words help the feeling. Furthermore, it is difficult to change the intonation; the feeling is always creative, not mechanical. From the bottom of yourself, with the love, with certain spiritual satisfaction, you can change the intonation much easier.

All I have told you about the bits, the sections of action, concerns only you, only the actor. You do not need to explain them to anyone. They are the source of your exposure for the part. Then comes something else. Let us go back to nature, back to yourself. You open your window in the morning, you breakfast, etc., but at the same time are you not also driving toward some goal? You want to be an actor, an engineer; you want to make money, etc. You always have in your life a certain goal. Let us take Edison, Rockefeller, Ford. Whatever Ford does is connected with the gasoline engine; whatever Edison does is connected with a new invention, etc. Now follow yourselves. Don't you have that same goal? Sometimes you change it. When you were twelve years old, you wanted to be a nurse; then you change your mind and want to be a playwright; then again, an actress. Sometimes you have the same goal from childhood.

Let us call this the spine or backbone. It is your wish. Suppose your aim is to be an actress. Don't you think that every one of your small actions will be influenced by that one big wish ... to become an actress. If you want to be a playwright, or a musician, you would probably do certain actions differently. If you are an architect you go along the streets and look at the houses; if you are an actor you look for characters, for types, etc. I am trying to show you how the actions are connected in life by one big one – one drive.

In the part there must be the same thing: the spine of acting in your part. What is it that makes you say the words, to go through the actions? What is it in Othello's part that drives him to the words he says? What colors his actions? It is simple to say that Othello is jealous, that Shylock is stingy. Is this right? Maybe not. These are cheap words and do not explain anything to you as an actor. Shylock is not stingy [and] cruel; he is insulted. Not only has he been insulted, but his whole race; he wants to prove to the rest of humanity that he has been insulted. Now how would an insulted man speak to his daughter? What drives him to say the words? All the time the actor will keep in mind the pride of a human being, who has made no mistakes, and who has been insulted.

With the drive toward certain actions you will never lose the feeling for the actions. Your part will always stay right, and in the construction of that part you will have small sections, elemental sections.

Now there is something that interferes: the literary theme. Take *Twelfth Night*. The professor would tell you that the theme is dealing with the gay court of Queen Elizabeth on the 6th of January, etc., etc. If you will start to think of all the literary words or everything that has ever been written about *Hamlet*, for example, you will never act. Stick to your business as an actor. If you are a scholar and under the influence of French literature, German Romanticism, etc., you will be lost if you say, "Now how am I going to act French literature," etc. By this I do not mean you must not read. No – read, engage in philosophical discussions, etc., but when you act, forget this.

8 Lecture 11

We are very grateful to you for your criticism of *Twelfth Night*. We have adopted a couple of your suggestions. I wondered why all of you did not give me criticisms. You must understand how we are building the whole institution, the life of this theatre, not only one performance, and the main way we work in the theatre, which is a collaborative way. That means that one must forget about himself, but remember well about the institution as a whole. I would like to you to spend the time while you are here not only in getting something in technique and atmosphere, but that you actually help to build the theatre, because, after all, the theatre is the very thing we all work and suffer and stand for, not personalities or individuals, but the big thing which is called the theatre. And so I would like to have anything you may have to say or suggest about *Twelfth Night*. Every criticism has been important, because they are honest and intelligent. They really correspond with the spirit of the whole thing.

I am sorry to come once a week, or else when you meet me and only to speak with you, not to work practically.

I would like to have you apply criticism that I tell you in words, because, although I got good criticism, I did not get one hint in the performance on the points of my two previous talks with you. For instance, one said that the beauty of the Shakespearean lines and words was not developed. Perfectly true, but if you knew how difficult it is to develop a Shakespearean line, that although it may be very eloquent, it may sound like an S.O.S., because it is so short and spicy. You cannot cut out or change a line, and it is not even the technique of speech which helps to say those lines in one way, but the spirit inside the actor. It is really concentration and problem; when the concentration corresponds exactly with the problem and with Shakespeare when he was writing the lines, you will have a full and perfect expression of the lines, whether they are very eloquent and long, or as short as an S.O.S.

It is not technique, for after all, it is very easy to learn the French manner of reciting, called sometimes the art of reciting verses. This art comes from the classical actors when the people were absorbed in the resurrection of classical moods and forms. Now all over the world, in all the other arts people start to look for a new way, something that will go away from the classical form, although keeping to the beauty, simplicity, and unity of that form. In all other arts but the stage, which is dead, this has been done, and as the first actor of the classical period, Talma, used to speak the lines, they are still spoken. Always and everywhere you can recognize the French actor, because he sticks to the dead form and applies his knowledge of how to say the lines and all his effort with such energy which is worthy of a better destination.

If you hear a stage-director who says, "You must say these lines in such a way that they go and up and then drop down," you must know that it is artificial and exterior, not from the inside, because if you have a problem so strong you cannot keep your mouth shut and you must shout of yourself, "My kingdom for a horse." If you build up with throaty, hoarse shouts, "My kingdom for a horse," it is artificial and you will not check; although it may appeal to the ear and eye it will not appeal to the soul, for after the last twenty-five years when many things have happened around in the world, we are much more sincere, and we want more the real thing, not a thing that is tarnished and renewed. We want more the real thing, a real, new thing ...

[Page of original is missing.]

... those three things tremendously strong. I am trying to correspond and transplant those three things into the world of the actor. Is this possible? Let me take *Twelfth Night* for example. I would like to say a few words, but first, do not think it is an easy and simple thing to apply to those things in dramatic art. It has been done in music and architecture and drawing, but not in the drama, because we stick to dead things. Do not be confused with literary ideas, because the art of literature is separate and has words, rhythm, spine, or direction and long-distance mood, but it is the art of literature. And we must find something else that will be the art of the theatre – that of the actor – which will possess those three attributes.

I will take *Twelfth Night*, and let us start not with the small problems, but with the most difficult part: the long-distance mood. Here you are. You have *Twelfth Night*. Forget about Shakespeare, that he is a classical writer; forget that it has been played by the greatest actors in the world, and remember that it was written for the purpose of celebrating Twelfth Night and was called *Twelfth Night, or What You Will*. Take only those two hints, and let us go ahead and try to establish the long-distance mood which should cover the whole thing. Let me remind you of Merrie Old England, and the jolly spirit, and the people who were not beset by war debts and the radio. They were perfectly free in the expression of that spirit. We are Anglo-Saxons and do not like to express these things. Whatever else, I have eyes, ears, and brains, and I know that merry spirit, and I have seen very self-controlled people when they were enjoying themselves and everything was as it should be. The merry spirit was the merry spirit. The form might have been different, but we are speaking about the happiest night in the year, when everyone was supposed to forget and forgive and to bother with nothing but his own enjoyment. For this reason *Twelfth Night* was written, and the spirit must be remembered by the actor whenever he plays it, because the play is called *Twelfth Night, or What You Will*, and you must keep the spirit and repeat the Twelfth Night of December whenever the audience calls upon you to do it.

I am repeating these things that you know to kill in you anything else outside of that thought, because this is the only way you can start to build what Shakespeare did in his own day. He started to build the spirit of *Twelfth Night*, crystallizing it in the form a play. Otherwise, if you approach the play you will find only faults in it and only your greatest respect for Mr. Shakespeare keeps you from saying, "Well, anyhow, he is a classic, but it is hard to believe the things he says." You must remember this on the stage and think that everything is all right and true as you do in carnival times. During *Twelfth Night* it is all right, and anything may happen. After all, he says, "What You Will."

You see immediately how your eyes open wide, and you can see everything possible and you do not need to pretend at all, and if you can establish this feeling in yourself you do not need to pretend that you do not recognize Viola and Sebastian, and that Viola does not recognize Sebastian, and you can believe that Olivia would push away the love of a nice young man and would fall in love in one second with Viola and afterwards, in another second ... not recognize him. But when you stand on a level with *Twelfth Night*, when everything is under the wing and guidance of the God of Old Merrie England, you will say, "Well, that is possible," and many other things are possible, too.

So you see how the long-distance mood carries throughout the play, how easy these things become familiar, how easy it looks, and how we will speak what we believe like children: "This is the castle, this is the King." And how we enjoy what we do with them.

Long-distance mood has nothing to do with history, only with the human spirit. If you take *Hamlet* and seek for a long-distance mood, do not think about history. (I have had the luck to work three times on *Hamlet*, and if I work two more, maybe I will understand something about it, and if you will take into consideration the fact that *Hamlet* is the ideal of truth of human beings, which are perfectly truthful and right into my knowledge in life or history, or anywhere, you will find that this is a collection of human souls in this play which are mirrors of human souls in life, and you do not need to apply history.) I am not trying to repeat what the Birmingham Players do when they play *Hamlet* in modern clothes, but am speaking merely of the mood. The human souls that you find in *Hamlet* are an ideal reflection of the whole world as concerns justice, injustice, love, hate, betrayal, and the theatre; *Hamlet* is for me a Bible. You cannot find another thing in the Bible which does not exist in the world. If I stage *Hamlet*, I take in the whole world. It took genius and a supernatural soul to embrace the whole world and put it in one play. I don't know when it starts and I don't think Mr. Darrow or Mr. Bryan know when it started, but it is there, and Shakespeare is the best proof that it really exists. If I look in *Hamlet* for the nearest thing to ourselves and our present situation, I can tell you exactly the scene. It is when *Hamlet* teaches the actors how to play. I cannot add more, and if you can embrace this whole monologue, it is everything that everyone in the world can say to you about acting, and nothing more can be invented. That is the whole trouble with it. You may think I am a very old-fashioned man who does not believe in progress, but there are certain things which are steady and firm, not only for our generation, but for our generation as part of the universe, and only the next epoch can bring something new. I know that after reading and trying to find out something else which could not be found in Hamlet's monologue on acting. I could not find it, and the Birmingham Players in their modern clothes are in the monologue perfectly; it is something that does not belong to history, literature, painting, or anything else, this long-distance mood, but it is the medium and instrument of the actor, his soul – and that only – which will give it to him.

If we took the historical side and tried to represent the Merrie England of the 16th century in *Twelfth Night*, it would be to you the most disgusting thing imaginable. I can give you such details as that it was quite a natural joke in those times when one was returning to his house late at night and making a noise, anyone might quite legitimately pour out the swill on his head. That was one thing, and another which you may not believe, although I assure you it has a basis in history, concerned the ladies and their knights. The knight was supposed to serve the lady who had given him her scarf with all his life, leaving her husband entirely out of the consideration and one way to spend time was to sit around some place and listen to the most beautiful poetry, while the ladies looked for those little jumping creatures in the knight's hair. This was a perfectly legitimate way to spend the time.

You know that the perfumes and spices were introduced because the people were afraid to take baths and the smell was terrible, so they brought in spices and perfumes to cover it up. We cannot repeat this historical side: we would be lost immediately. We must follow the human soul line, and it does not matter that they were looking in the knights' hair, but that they were enjoying the situation, and we have only to enjoy it with other means. The actor should play up to the humanity of today, not then. This is all the audience asks. If you wanted to present an archeological picture, then that would be all right. I do not know if anyone else but the professors and students of archeology would be interested in that sort of performance. The people of that time enjoyed Twelfth Night, and the point is that the date and tradition of Twelfth Night comes to our day and we know it was the merriest night in the year and all we have to do is repeat the most joyful and merry night in the year; and because we are actors, we must be able to repeat it every night. *Only well-written plays have those permanent things.*

Some playwrights consider, as some actors do, only the external side of the art of playwriting, and they write words that mean something only at the time they were written; but the eternal writers may have lived three hundred years ago, but their writing is a thing which can be transplanted anywhere, everywhere, and always, and it will go over because it will have the life of the human soul in it and that can be understood by all the people of all time. God and the idea of a God is enjoyed by cannibal and super-civilized person; and real art will be perfectly understandable everywhere and by everyone, no matter how sophisticated or how simple he is. It is like the air that one must have to live.

I have read many, many plays, but I am still looking for a good one, for most are all words and not action. Everything in *Twelfth Night*, *Two Gentlemen of Verona*, and other Shakespearean comedies belongs to the situation, with the characters, with the words and atmosphere. Every joke in most modern plays is only a joke for itself and would be a joke outside a play. Let us go on to the next thing, but remember always that this long-distance mood concerns, *in this case only the actor, not the playwright.*

It is what the actor must know: that he is on Broadway, not in the fields, and must watch for the police regulating the flow of traffic. In the fields, you may simply go along and dream, but on Broadway you must watch your step. You must know where your long-distance mood is and how to use it. In *Hamlet* it is the everyday life of humanity (not of the mediocre). Hamlet is perfect, and so are the Queen and Ophelia, and all the rest. They are the symbols of human creatures.

The next thing is the direction or the spine. This situation is very easy to confuse with the literary ideas of the play, but it should not be done. The literary ideas are one thing, and the actor's spine (call it direction, or what you will), is another, and it shows the actor what to do, just as the arrow of the compass points the way. Not what he should play, but what he should do, because the action is one thing which he is likely to live on the stage, and the actor must know every moment what he should do. Everything that you work in your problems must have action; it must have, "What I am doing," not "What am I saying," and your talent and your gift will prompt in the most perfect way how you must express this action. If you are talented, you will do it as a Bernhardt or a Duse; if you are not you will give an honest performance nevertheless, because you will actually be doing the things. People are not such fools that they cannot distinguish the real from the artificial – this playing with the voice and body only, which is a third-rate performance; and only because the audience is very kind do they attend all sorts of performances, but they really pay for one or two or three seconds in each performance when the actors really do. The more of these moments the performance has the better it will succeed. The success of *The Wild Duck* last season was that it was acted, not played. The actors were combined in such a way that the actors really did and the acting belonged to the action; they did not merely speak the words. You can find no more difficult author for acting, because he speaks only, and it takes a lot of trouble to find out what the acting is, and, because these actors thought about doing, they were successful. For this – the spine – is a little secret which will bring you such opportunities. First, it will show you what kind of adjustment you will have to apply to this play. Second, it will show you between what limits you will have to do your acting. Let us see if you can play Ibsen as Harold Hecht does Fabian, in a mocking way? You cannot do this is in Ibsen, because it would not be true. Third, in every situation it will make you safe from not doing anything on the stage. You speak or you do not speak – you express or you do not – you cannot be zero. You must do something, and if you are one of the two little pages among the attendants and you have nothing to say, you cannot do nothing, because you belong to the spine of the play, and your action will be that you know you are with the Duke, for him, that maybe a fight will start, and every moment you can feel with the action and the spine will show what sort of action may be applied.

How can we look for the spine? There is one condition: it must be simple and a verb; that is, you must find something that will prompt you to action, to the acting or doing. You will find thousands of stage directors and actors who can speak for hours, and finally the actor asks a very humble question: "But what am I supposed to do here? I know everything but what I am to do." What I am trying to do is to explain, to prompt the actor – not with literary or professor's words – to the exact job that he is to do. Looking for and finding the spine is probably more difficult that looking for the long-distance mood, because that can be found from the atmosphere and can be expressed in words, but the simple spine is very difficult. After many talks and much discussion we came to the conclusion that the spine of *Twelfth Night* could be expressed in such words as, "Playing with life," as you would play with a toy or a game. Everything in life prompts you to play with it. You do not take it seriously, but you play with it as a child plays with a doll, as a cat plays with balls of paper. You play seriously, but you do play. Here it was difficult not to be too serious and not to be too light-minded, because the audience must believe in the performance. The Duke plays with life. He must have love, although he has everything else. He says to himself, "Let us play with love for awhile," and he does. He says, "I want Olivia. Let me have music. It does not satisfy. I must have some friend go to her and tell her I cannot live without her. I am playing in lack of love." You smile when I burlesque the spirit of *Twelfth Night* because I do not say, "The Duke suffers from love," in which you would have a very stupid situation when the man suffers like a little girl, but only when you exaggerate and play with the situation, can you have a solution.

Take any character in *Twelfth Night*. Toby plays with life. Malvolio is a perfect character to play with, and Toby plays with him. Malvolio himself plays with the situation. It is hard to believe that the man did not know what was right or wrong, but this is the very reason why the play was written and they all play in life's situation with life.

I am jumping to *Hamlet*. You will ask me what is the spine of Hamlet, what will support me when I play Hamlet. I will tell you as far as I know. I am not in the character of Hamlet, and it takes a long time to find out, but I will give you a hint. It is seeking for the truth. Everyone seeks truth in this situation, and Hamlet is the first among them. He is seeking not for vengeance, but for truth, because vengeance will come afterwards, since nature abhors a vacuum and it does not like mean things not being revenged. The man who seeks only to kill Laertes when he plays Hamlet will be wrong. Even the second grave-digger gives him his point of view about truth. Everyone must know himself, must find the real situation, the real truthful atmosphere in his part and then you will have *Hamlet* coming on as an action, not as a play or performance, but as action. And the First Guard and Fortinbras and everyone is searching for the truth throughout the whole situation. But you see, you have the verb and something to keep you going on, to keep you busy all the time towards something that will really be the expression of the play. The literary ideas of the play are something that belong to the mental and psychological fields.

You may say of *Hamlet* that it expresses the restlessness of the human soul, that it expresses searching for justice, but these things are not very helpful to the actor while he is on the stage, because he has limited ground before him. Polonius, during his speech about the actors coming again thinks about the whole literary idea of the play, which is too large, and he must think, "I am searching for the truth in this situation." Here is an old man who says this is a crowd. He says it looks like a dog: "O it looks like a dog." He must have something to express. Whatever the literary idea of *Hamlet* may be, he will be lost as an actor's spine is like a recommendation for the very open-minded engineer or architect. The literary ideas are the engineer. The actor's spine is a recommendation, and by it he knows what he does every minute while the thing is being built.

Sometimes literary ideas and actor's spine are the same, but it is very seldom, and usually the least words you use for the actor's spine, the simpler you make the understanding, the better it is; but it must be done in such a way that it can be applied to any situation. It is not ideal, what I say about seeking for the truth and everyone in future years may be able to find a new way, a better way, but you see how helpful it is for the actor.

There is only one spine for the actor, for if I am seeking for the truth and you are also, your truth is different from mine, but we meet somewhere. If you are the King in *Hamlet* you are seeking for power which is truth for you, and you believe, "If I have power, if I have my brother's wife, if I send Hamlet away, it is the truth, because I am King and it is necessary." Hamlet knows that to everyone who listens to the King this is the right King and the right situation. You see how different the truth of the King is from that of Hamlet. When they meet, the catastrophe comes. Something secret, the highest truth for every one of the characters – this is the spine. I know that the spine has never cheated me, and if I play using the spine, I may play rotten, but I shall play right. The spine applies to everything, not only to your emotions. I am King.

I look for my own individual power and the spine which is prompting me toward the seeking of the truth is the very right situation, and it will prompt me what adjustment I should use. It will tell me I can lie when necessary; I can rave and roar and be brutal when necessary; and this Hamlet, who believes in supernatural justice, when he looks upon the praying King he is in a situation when he is near the truth and he says, "I will not kill him now when he is praying." If you can find the spine, everything can be smoothed out. The literary spine, however, uses the *reductio ad absurdum.*

When you are an actor and have to play the first or second grave digger you have the problem: "What is it for me?" To bring comedy relief? It seems very little, but if you have the actor's spine moving ahead, then you have a right to existence. I will ask that for the next time you will pick up a play, I don't care which, any one you know and try to think, and tell me the literary spine, the long-distance mood, and the actor's spine. If you take any play and read it over, it will really give you pleasure to find the material thing you can start work with.

The last thing is the steps of the walking man from A to B, which is really the easiest ones. How simple the life of a man is when he knows perfectly what is the goal of his action. All he has to do during the day. The boy in school knows that from nine to ten he has arithmetic; from ten to eleven, something else; and after you graduate from school, you think, "How quickly I am through that period of eight years." The people who do not know what to do in life are so because they have no problem. They wake up in the morning and do not know what is the next thing for them to do. In the play which is the very essence of life and very strongly concentrated, you cannot be without the most perfect knowledge of what your next step is as action, not as words. You start your play, let us say, with early morning, and you are preparing the room for your brother who has been away a couple of years and is now expected to return home. The first scene is that you are preparing the room for him, so if I were to play, the first thing I should try to establish would be this action. I would not care what was spoken. From the regisseur's point of view, I would consider it. Another man, the play-wright, says these are the best words for the situation. They are speaking about the brother. "He likes these cigarettes, so I shall put it on the table. He does not like this book, so I will put it away." The ideas and words come from the author, the situations and the actor make the play. The playwright usually builds his scene and thinks only about the words and he has the two sisters sitting down, doing nothing but speaking about the brother who is to return. The audience does not want merely to hear, but to see and to hear. The whole secret is to consider every situation. If you like a book you may consider only the words, but for the stage consider the poor actor who must really do something. You must consider his doing, his action.

So the question comes to the steps and beats of the small problems. When I was young I had quite a distance to walk to school from home, which was terrible when the weather was cold or bad, but I knew I must go and be on time, so one day, walking in a very gloomy mood, I threw my lunch box ahead of me about twenty yards, and I realized that to pick it up I walked with great joy. I threw it ahead again and I did not notice how I got to school.

I want to establish, let us say, a performance, and this is the goal, the spine, but now what are the problems? The problem is to pick up one man and to convince him to act this part, to do all these bits which when taken together fill out everyday life. They are the steps which lead to the end. One day I had milk in my bottle when I went to school, and when I opened it it had turned to butter from being thrown ahead. My teacher told me if I liked those tricks I should throw my books ahead of me, but I told him I was afraid I would run the other way.

The simplicity and the necessity for the beats in life should be seen from this and especially those in dramatic art. You know that in amateur performances you learn your lines by heart, but that on the opening night you are like a diver in cold water and you just go ahead. You must think when you are on the stage and know, for instance, that your first problem is to listen to the music and analyze the value of it for yourself; this is the first problem, outside of everything else. Then it is possible that you may pretend to be a beautiful, sick Duke, but as a human being you will listen and analyze the music and say as a human being with real feeling: "If music be the food of love, play on." And you will again listen. You will have your problem done, acted, and there is no human being in the world who will resist acting, but 99 percent will resist playing. At the sight of a young creature, perhaps not very strong in technique – not very strong in actor's personality, but strong in that which everyone can do, in listening to the music, no one will be able to resist. This is the whole foundation of dramatic art.

Résumé: When you have a play, first find out what is the air or atmosphere, or long-distance mood of the whole thing. Next, you must find out what is the acting line, the spine which will save you in every moment when you have nothing to say; and third, you must know in every moment what is the little problem, the beat that you are going on to. Afterwards, I shall tell you how the stage director has his own beats, the ensemble have theirs, but this is for next time or later. All you need to know now is that before you do any one of them, remember and know those three things, and in every play you read or see, try to apply your judgment and come to me with the results and together we may find something important which will be good to those who are seeking the truth in the theatre.

Notes on Acting with Maria Ouspenskaya

Editor's note: Boleslavsky's work would not have developed and been disseminated as it was without his collaboration with Maria Ouspenskaya (1876–1949). While Boleslavsky, as director of the American Laboratory Theatre, set the curriculum and articulated the fundamental elements of the training, Ouspenskaya seems to have been very nearly as important as Boleslavsky as a studio teacher. Her contribution to the spreading of basic Stanislavskian principles through her teaching of a number of generations of actors has generally been underrepresented, no doubt in part because she never wrote about her work. However, the following four essays were published in late 1954 to early 1955 under the title "Notes on Acting with Maria Ouspenskaya" in *American Repertory Theater: The Art Magazine*, the monthly newsletter of the long-since-disbanded American Repertory Theater in Hollywood, California. Compiled and edited by Harriet Pratt, one of Ouspenskaya's assistants, these notes are one of the few remaining detailed descriptions of Ouspenskaya's thinking about acting and of her work with actors, based on her work with Stanislavsky and in collaboration with Boleslavsky. The following reproduces the original documents with only minor typographical corrections for ease of reading.

1   October 1954

Introduction

For more than twenty-five years Maria Ouspenskaya was part of the American theater. To her school in New York, and later in Hollywood, came those students who desired to learn acting. They found much more: they learned how to develop themselves for any of the arts. Many are now actors; some sculptors, writers, painters, designers, puppeteers; theater managers, teachers, technicians and producers for stage, radio, television and films. Former students often say "she taught me so much about living," and "it was Ouspenskaya who taught me how to create."

Madame Ouspenskaya closed her own school in 1942; visitors were never permitted in the classes. It took time to absorb her training and be able to use it. On meeting her, people often asked, "What is your system for acting?" I have heard her reply: "I do not call it a system – but it takes me two years to teach my students. How can I tell you in five minutes?" We allowed class visitors with her reluctant permission, when she was teaching for the American Repertory Theater; they usually jotted down a few sentences and the basis of the teaching was completely overlooked. With her usual good humor, Ouspenskaya would say: "Well, I wonder how much they would understand from one class lecture with Professor Einstein?"

There seem to be as many different ideas of what Stanislavsky and Ouspenskaya were teaching as there are people who are certain that they alone know. The idea of sincerity in acting as accepted by Americans in the amateur and college theater makes everything so easy – anyone can do it. But Ouspenskaya put it this way: "Sincerity may be all right if you want to do your acting in a shoe box, but in my classes you are learning what is necessary for the professional stage."

While the Ouspenskaya acting classes were working on specific problems, notes were made of her personal comments. It seems only fair that some of them should be printed. Maria Ouspenskaya died in 1949 at the age of 62.

These "Notes" were compiled by Miss Harriett Pratt, one of Madame Ouspenskaya's assistants. Financial assistance in publication has been given by Mr. Hilmar Sallee, Director.

H.I.S.

I

In the world of the theater that I have known in my lifetime, there have been ceaseless workers establishing a technique of acting. Stanislavsky's methods came into being through the analysis of those moments when the actor was in inspiration – when he was giving his best.

Every good actor learns the same things – how to see the ocean on the brick wall of a stage, how to smell fresh apple blossoms from a tree made of muslin and fish glue, how to create emotion and so forth – every good actor comes finally to the same results.

As to talent, no one can add to it or take away from it. Talent is an agreement between the individual and God. God gave you talent – but you must develop your instrument. All of us here work together because, with love for the theater, we want to help to give you technique. I never show you *how* to do a thing – I want you to do it in your own way – but I sometimes show you how *not* to do it. That works wonders. We are trying to wake up your imagination and curiosity.

On the day when acting becomes more to you than self, you will stride ahead.

Work like a slave on flexibility of body, voice and speech; create different characters. Do not always be yourself. Do not get upset when you try and are not successful. Face all these things with one hundred per cent concentration, and you will use even sleeping hours to get your subconscious mind to work for you – it will help and you will wake up with better understanding. You must begin to understand with all your being – not just with the tip of your tongue and a newspaper mind.

It will be very difficult for a while. We want you to choose your own material. Try and find many different interpretations for each part.

You must go through certain sufferings for growth. We will understand because that happens with all creation. Artistic creation, or any creation, cannot be done by using the line of least resistance. When a mother is delivering a baby there is great suffering, but afterwards there is terrific joy. Do not be afraid to struggle. Trust yourselves. Only when you can trust yourself and are strong enough will this work be useful to you. Struggle until you have a moment of truth, and then, when you have grasped that moment, nothing can stop you. We will learn truth in acting. That truth which we are trying to convey to you will never be forgotten.

Learn to accept divine inspiration – exhilaration. You all choke joy. Accept things more easily, do not just do factory work. Otherwise your performances will not be inspired or inspiring. They will just be – nice! They must be better than everyday life. We must treat our art as something special, something festive. Do not bring your home life and your party life and your outside relationships to the theater; they should not be here. Any place of your art must be secured from everyday life and galoshes. Move your minds and your souls to higher planes.

You are artists. That means that you can never be satisfied with what is done today and you must always aim higher for tomorrow. Our life is made by the law of moving on. All of you have your gifts. Take care of them. It will be sinful if you do not use all your efforts and intuition to develop these gifts.

I want you to understand that you will greatly profit and economize your time by not allowing yourselves to wonder and question and use the path of least resistance. My aim is to give you knowledge so that you will go ahead in the right way. That idea of "getting experience" before you are prepared is so wrong. You will crystallize your faults and nothing else.

Do not stop working because of my disillusioning you; hate me, but go ahead. Understand that I am not picking on you. If I feel you are not suited to theater, I will have a private talk with you, tell you "God bless you," and wish you the best in life. Real kindness is not soft.

When you do a scene or exercise, we teachers are your audience. Please do not watch for our reactions while you are "on stage." We are here. Be right for yourself – concentrate on what you are doing. Win us by doing rightly. When a moment is right, we are looking for it with all our eyes and ears and hearts. For us it is like candy.

There is one thing we do not accept – "I can't." Do you want to do it, or don't you want to do it? If you want to, it will take time, but you will do it.

Do not write this down. No pens and pencils in this class. *Remember* it, and write it down at home – if you must write. Then your notes will not be literary. They will be what you really know.

Please do not try to explain to others what we are doing until you yourselves understand what we are doing. Then by all means go and spread these ideas. Some people say that I am teaching you how to be purple envelopes and bottles of milk. This kind of talk is ridicule. I do not mind for myself, but it keeps away those who might be helped.

II

No one can add to or take away from talent. But the instrument *can* and *must* be trained and trained. The stage arts are most difficult. Other arts have an instrument with which to work: the painter has brushes and canvas, the sculptor has chisel and granite, the musician has a violin. But we actors have only ourselves. We are the instrument *and* the artist. Our instrument is made up of voice, body and speech. It is difficult to get crystallization of material knowing that you are the instrument and the artist. Some actors think that they do not have to develop and perfect their instruments. This attitude is passing, thank God. The life of the theater is moving towards normal, right results.

I am frank and honest. I think it is criminal not to see and tell what is wrong with young actors.

Start to realize that no matter what beautiful things you feel, and how rightly you feel them, you cannot express them unless you train your instruments. Jascha Heifetz not only practices, but also takes care of his violin. We have to take care of ourselves as violin and violinist, instrument and artist together. Take time and perseverance to perfect your instrument, and then your instrument will express your feelings.

The human instrument is very rich. You must learn to use it in all its combinations. If you are capable of producing the psychological and emotional part of a character, be thankful that you have that ability. But it is not everything, and you cannot fool that audience – they will know if you are lacking in your professional technique.

As Stanislavsky said, when the public pays $3.30 to $5.50 for a seat, you have no right to make them strain to understand your words. You may have a perfect conception of the part, but if your body and speech are not controlled and flexible, the public will see only your mistakes and miss what is right.

You cannot progress unless your instrument is worked on every day. You need more than just a special time to do this work. Be conscious of it all the time. Practice constantly. Buy potatoes with proper breath support.

You cannot stand still in anything. You go forward or you slide backward.

No matter how clear your thought, how deep your emotion, it will never shine through a body as twisted as a fish hook.

Find comfortable positions on stage. When the actors are uncomfortable, the public is ten times more uncomfortable. Very seldom do you see beautiful "sitting down" on stage.

Find how to move elegantly, or you can never do drawing room comedy. So often you feel people on stage do not belong in their clothes. Find out for yourself what people do with their bodies to be elegant. Only you can do it. To find and crystallize this refinement will not come easily. It means loving work and repetition all through your life.

We cannot change our features, but we can learn to command them. If in real life you are upset, bored and temperamental, you get downward muscles of the face and wrinkles in the forehead. When you are acting, this tenseness shuts out the natural reflection of what is going on inside.

Do not hide yourself behind mannerisms. Let your face relax. Trust what is coming through.

Become conscious of unconscious mannerisms and quit them.

Gestures should emphasize something that comes from within.

Learn economy of gesture. If you emphasize everything with shoulders and eyebrows, the audience will be hypnotized with your movement and lose your character, your emotion – everything.

When I entered theater school, being nervous, ambitious and shy, my movements were tiresome. I tried to stress everything. Then I had a teacher who said, "Economy of gesture!" He said that my hands were a windmill, and my face was constant lightning. I had the part of a gossipy mother. He put me in an uncomfortable chair and let me find the way to sit still for a whole act of a Russian classical comedy, in which I did most of the talking. Throughout the whole act he allowed me to do only one gesture. That taught me.

Avoid unnecessary gesticulating. Gesture *when it has meaning* is as important as the words.

People are always afraid of using artificial speech, but only the *process* of learning is artificial. Be very conscious – even self-conscious – about your speech, and get rid of local dialects. We have to perfect our speech – but never worry that you will lose your local speech. When you need your dialect speech for a part, you can go back to it easily. Correcting speech does not kill your personality. You must start to love good speech, control of voice, and breath support, enough to work for them. Rightness in the emotional and mental concept of the part are not enough if your faults in speech stand out.

Do not allow your stage emotion to choke your speech into inarticulate mumbling. In life, the stronger the emotion, the stronger the desire is to get it across to the other person. You try to be very clear in what you say and how you say it. We see so often on stage actors whose emotion makes their speech inaudible instead of clarifying it. Dropping your voice and muttering is not true simplicity – it is the line of least resistance.

If you force your voice it will crack. The only way to overcome noise, echo, and distance, is clear articulation and breath support. Otherwise you have vocal strain instead of more support. Sometimes when we were touring in Russia we had to play in opera theaters. Each time we came to a new theater, we were taught to come into the theater alone in the morning, before the rough rehearsal, to try out our voices. When you are doing a show in a new place try this: see if you are filling the space. If you discover the conditions of the place, and how much volume is needed, then you are the master. When you have to shout, whisper, or die on that stage, you will still be heard.

There is a feeling you have when you *know* you are heard – when you know it is right.

When it comes to the performance you will fill the house adequately without losing the simplicity of your performance.

Usually, when the curtain goes up, the audience is still not settled. Therefore, the first sentences of a play require extra voice and articulation to win the audience. You must have special energy for the beginning of a play.

2   November 1954

Introduction

When Richard Boleslavsky, Alexander Koiransky and Maria Ouspenskaya first taught theater in this country, many people received conflicting ideas. Some thought they heard the words "effective memory" instead of "affective memory;" the pronounciation of the word "bits" sounded to American ears like "beats" and this set up a whole school of thought based on rhythms in a play. It should also be stated that the well-known purple envelope, vase, inkwell and what-not, publicized as belonging to the training given by Ouspenskaya, were never used in the acting classes. These objects do not offer anything of purpose for the unfolding of talent or expressive means. Their insistence that the actor must have something for himself to share before he can communicate anything to an audience goes hand in hand with their demand that he develop his individual technique for expression through control of body, voice and emotion.

H.I.S.

(This is a continuation of the "Notes" beginning in the October 1954 issue which included Parts I and II.)

III

On stage you must have three pairs of eyes and ears – you must be quicker than in life. On stage you will be amazed how difficult ordinary things are: to learn to establish the five sense realities for theater use we have to start at the beginning again almost like babies.

Affective memory must be developed. For instance, in a play you must carry a pail of milk across a stream. An artist will paint the stones on canvas, but you must create the rocks and the stream. You must change for yourself what is given you on stage from the make-believe thing to the real thing. Unless our memory of real things is there, we have so many other problems on stage that these little details will get in the way.

In the theater many events happen off stage. The audience knows about them only through the actors – these events will seem only as real to the audience as they are to the actors. On the screen also the actor never sees or hears off stage happenings – they are dubbed in later.

You alone have to bring the illusion to the public. If you know how to do this, you are armed for any occasion.

For example, when I worked in the motion picture, "The Mortal Storm" there were very few shots with real snow; the rest were done with a powder in the studio. Powder snow will seem false to the audience unless through your senses you know what real snow is, and feel it.

If you do not use your five senses, the public will know, even through your voice on the radio: if you do not quickly experience – cold, for instance – your voice does not respond. The public will immediately sense that you are talking about cold, not really experiencing it. You have had the experience in life, and when you come to the stage you must remember how it felt, and re-create this feeling.

You must work on the five sense realities until they become second nature to you. If you try to learn to establish the five senses at rehearsals and performances, it will be too late. You will be remembering to remember, and you will not be free to create character, emotion or action.

Until you come next door to perfection in the five sense exercises in class, it will be boresome work. When you come near to perfection it will become so fascinating that you will not be able to stop.

Sometimes it is difficult to combine your mind, which is intelligent and understands, with your instrument, which expresses. You must be able to bring a *living human being* on stage who feels, sees, and hears. Then every line of the playwright will come as a result of something that you yourself touch, smell, taste, see, or hear and your emotional reaction to it. Go patiently after the five senses as a musician goes patiently after scales. I do not know why people think acting is an easy thing that can be done without practice.

The only worry I will allow you is about not working every tiny bit of the day. Whether you are weak or strong, I do not know and do not care. True, or not true, is all that matters. Remember that you are human beings, and that all things are possible for you.

Have you started to taste the pleasure of getting precision? When you taste it once, you will start to have joy, and from that moment on, no one will be able to stop you. It may come first through one sense or another, consciously or unconsciously.

Our art should be pleasure but not labor.

Unless the actor re-creates and believes in the scenery, that scenery will look false to the audience even in a motion picture that has been shot on actual location.

Try to get the feeling of a place. Often a place has a mood and when you get that mood, it will affect your performance.

Do exercises. Try, for instance, in a cold, semi-dark room to bring warm sunshine. On stage if lights are used to bring sunshine, and you do not bring warmth, the lights will remain only lights. It is up to the actor to create the whole universe about him.

Whatever emotion is within you is the same whether the setting is a drugstore, a streetcar, or a park; but when you speak the *way* you say it depends on the place. What is in the heart of the character will be the same wherever he is. But the time of day or night will affect him and his way of saying it. Stage hands or carpenters *set* the stage, but to *establish* that place and bring life to it is up to the actors. The actors must establish the real place for themselves, whether there is a most elaborate set, or merely the barest suggestion of one.

From your position on stage you may see the electrician and the stage manager quarrelling in the wings; but the playwright asks that the audience must feel that you see the ocean.

The movies use process shots, which are very clear for the public but not for the actor who never sees them until the movie is released. You as an actor must be able to bring the reality of all five senses at the moment they are requested by the director.

Unfortunately, on stage most actors' hands are like skeleton hands. Your fingertips should be antennae. Your hands and back can bring more expression than words. Make a habit of investigating through touch and remembering the feel of a particular object, its weight, its surface texture, its temperature, its size, how your hand fits around it.

Learn to observe. In life observation is subconscious. The actor must learn to be conscious of how things affect him.

Hearing is one more difficulty of our art. If an off stage sound is produced on a phonograph the actor usually hears it for the first time at dress rehearsal. On the screen the actor has the same problems. For instance, I heard the actual boat whistle in "Love Affair" only when I saw the picture, five months later. In movies, many times we must see and hear things by affective memory. We must create these things for the audience. It is the same on the stage. And also in radio you prepare a show without sounds. So affective memory of listening is a great help to us. Some of you are likely to use your eyes for listening instead of your ears. To me, this is like tasting the seasoning with your elbow.

Do plenty of exercises ordering yourself to hear all the horns you can catch, or heavy cars, or dogs barking, and so on.

I once knew an actor who was almost completely deaf. He learned to hear within himself, and the audience never suspected that he could not really hear.

At the beginning of your work, do not do any characterization that will lead you away from the five senses. *Really* see, instead of *acting* seeing. *Don't act, do.*

In life, observe distances for seeing. Seeing must be one hundred per cent accurate. The audience sees what is not shown, through us.

Always give yourselves time to react to what you see. Stanislavsky said, kill a person first with your eyes, then with the dagger. You can do more with your eyes than with words.

On stage when you avoid your partner's eyes, there is little chance for inner talk from person to person. Strong desire and belief make your eyes penetrating, expectant, waiting.

If you wear glasses, do special work with sight. When you take your glasses off, you are likely to use your eyes only as you actually see. Get a special memory of what your eyes do *with* glasses, and use that when you are without them. See through your eyes even without glasses. This is difficult but possible.

Do exercises at home for seeing. Look at a picture. Put it aside. Recall the details you saw in that picture. Look at it again. Look again the next day and see what you missed. Do this for a week. Look at your room in the morning, too. You will be surprised that, living in your room for years, you did not really know it.

Another exercise: look at a picture in a book and then "project" it on the wall, establishing the frame and the picture. Do not just remember it, really "see" it. When you can project a picture with one hundred per cent belief, you will have the thrill of an artist-painter, even though you never handled a brush. When your concentration is a little bit tired, do something else, or you will begin to mentally remember the picture instead of really seeing it.

In movies much of the time actors have to see and hear things that are not really there – things that you must establish. In "Love Affair," watching the departure of my grandson, I was given a handkerchief on a stick to watch for his going down the hill. Movies do this even more than the stage. Without this five sense approach, you are lost. In radio, if you do not visualize everything, the public hears only lines; but the public becomes excited if the actor visualizes.

For stage use be conscious of what you eat in real life. An exercise: get sugar, quinine, and salt, and find where on the tongue the taste first starts its reaction.

Almost never on stage are you given the same food that your lines indicate you are eating.

Become conscious now at mealtime, and find out what it means to use utensils, and to taste, smell, and handle. In my own research for the Maharani in "The Rains Came" I had Indians teach me how to eat with the fingers, and then I went home and practiced. They also taught me how to drape, wear and move in a sari.

IV

The difference between real emotion and emoting is that real emotion must have a source *within you*. It is another thing when you disturb only the periphery of your nerves. It is easy to emote, but the audience will not be affected. When the actor is external, it is embarrassing and meaningless.

Nervous tension is neither art nor life, but a wrong conception of creating a part. It is embarrassing because it is insincere, and does not have real justification of thought, and elements of character. When you play a character, *you* disappear. When you are on stage you have no right to feel as *you* would feel. When playing parts you must lose all shame. You must make a fool out of yourself many times.

Nothing is ever lost. If you long for certain emotions in a part and cannot achieve them, your subconscious will remember and work it out for you. Later, the emotions will appear in another part when you least expect them. If you work on a part, and fail to achieve what you set out to do, the work is not lost. It will be used later.

In the class some of you hide your natural feelings and then act out what you think they should be. If some emotion comes to you, do not choke it. Open up. Become for a while a complete fool, do not be afraid. For a while some of you may have to overdo. It will give you the courage and strength to open up. I invite you in this class for a couple of weeks to become complete fools.

Trust your emotions and believe in them. Then we, the audience, will share them with you. This cannot be understood by the mind alone. Some of you are still trying to act your emotions out externally. Forget about acting completely. Before you have that flash of understanding when your whole being will feel what emotion is, your trouble-maker (conscious mind) will make you suffer. As long as you approach emotion in a literary way, that "understanding" will not come to you.

Do not be afraid of your emotions. Do not force yourself to bring what you do not have. But let happen what is inside of you.

Do not worry about what your face and body are *showing*, just feel it. If you feel it, the audience has a sixth sense, and understands. *How* the truth is expressed is not your business. Your business is to believe and enjoy. The audience magnifies both true and false emotion. You cannot convince them by just words, only by actually experiencing something within yourself. Do not worry – if you have real, true emotion, with an aim, even your back will express it.

When you punch emotion, it dies. When you force, emotion disappears and only muscular action remains.

If you use external means, not letting your reaction to the situation create the results, you will sound superficial. Never be tense for emotion; muscular tensity always chokes emotion.

3   December 1954

(The following is a continuation of Part IV of the "Notes" which appear in the November 1954 issue with Part III. Parts I and II are printed in the issue of October 1954.)

IV

It is a most difficult thing to explain the difference between emotion and hysterics. When you produce hysterics it is dangerous for the nerves and is not pleasant for the public. It hits the audiences as weakness. When you become hysterical, you choke breath support. Everything is tight. Instead of relaxing and making room for real emotion, your voice is choked and starts to break. Sentences and words become meaningless. *Only through relaxation can we produce enormous emotions for acting.*

Do not worry about over-acting; if you believe in your emotion, and it is sincere, it is never "too much." But if you are trying only to convince the public it will be too much.

Do not try to give more emotion than you actually have. If you force, it is as if you began to pull the leg of a baby to make it grow faster.

Maybe you are so reserved in life that nothing touches you. Then break that reserve. With it you cannot be actors.

Do not be afraid of using your hearts. Glycerine tears and empty hearts are not accepted any more for theater. You will not find hearts for a performance if you are an amateur looking for compliments. Be professional in your approach and find satisfaction in your own joy of creation.

Do not look for your tears in your handkerchief. Using a handkerchief with dry eyes spoils everything. Do not *try* to produce tears. Allow yourself in emotional scenes to get all the emotion you can, and then restrain. Have the emotion, and fight it, and then it will grow. Do not rely on the old externals, wiping away the tear that is not there. It is not necessary to cry externally if there is feeling inside. All that is needed is to have that little germ of emotion. Do it for yourself, believe in it, have artistic joy.

You can get softness or warmth only from within. Do not "act" soft. Recall moments in your own life when you have been soft. You have been soft plenty of times for you are a human being. Recall those moments; exercise them as gymnastics. We have to exercise our emotions.

Have the separation between life and acting. Your personal current emotion is always unpleasant and embarrassing to the audience. You can become pathological on stage if you bring today's feeling. To use your own emotions of the present on stage is comparable to appearing naked. No matter how closely your present emotions coincide with the part, you must not use them. Learn to recall from your childhood: there, in your past, are the most beautiful sources for acting. If you have to play a love scene, do not take your present love. Go to a past love. Recollect things which are already past and half forgotten, and refresh them and use them now.

How much past experience do you need? A small germ can expand and expand to produce a great emotion. Killing a mosquito can be expanded for the killing of Desdemona. Water flowers expanding from a dry small particle to a colorful pattern are an example of this. You must expand the germs yourself. We can lead you, and show you how, but the expansion is your own problem.

You do not have to go, in your life, and do – God knows what! We are born with every reaction. For example, you must lose a loved one on stage, and never did in life. Losing a pet as a child is enough to translate and use on stage. Beware of pathological states. Keep your mind cool, your heart warm. You are an artist using material needed for a specific part, truly channeling emotion.

We have to develop an artistic memory that becomes second nature. Stanislavsky said, when you approach a part and look for sources, there should not be any shame whatsoever. If you play a character who is ashamed, Stanislavsky said, use anything to get the feeling of shame – even if you must remember when you were a child and wet your pants.

When you need to find a mood for an important place in the play, try to find a time in your own past when you felt the mood which is needed. The audience are not thought readers, they will not know what memory you are using. You as actors have to start to search, look for, and store moods. Stanislavsky said even at the grave of a very dear person, some-where inside, you will observe and remember your emotion. Maybe you would be ashamed to tell what memory you use to get a mood. You do not have to tell – but use it. And even if you give a hundred performances of the play, the emotion will always be there.

Find your own secret – find what makes you warm and calm and wise – healthy and cheerful. These things are your own secrets, nobody can prompt you. Feel within your own heart and radiate the feeling. Find the sources and sustain them.

Remember, *never recall the mood itself.* Recall all the circumstances surrounding it, and the mood will come.

Never start with the feeling – that is a result. Recall the day in detail – use your five senses. Recall where you were, whom you met, what you did, how you were dressed. Go after details, and the mood will come. Find the embryo of a mood. That is all you need. Through action it will be developed.

There are three psychological steps. Unhappy, catastrophic moments or important happenings do not penetrate all at once. Your mind realizes, then you do. You are, in acting, apt to come to results too quickly. The *process*, not the *result*, is what holds the audience.

Here is the process.

1. I see but I do not understand.
2. I understand but do not believe.
3. I believe fully and experience and digest it.

Do not come on stage empty. Before you enter, you must have an off stage bit. Every good musician before playing takes time to play a few scales, or to warm up his voice. The actor thinks that is not necessary. But you cannot go on stage unprepared.

A play is part of a certain life – there should be an infinite continuation of the life of the characters. Life on stage does not begin with your entrance.

As a character, do not carry pre-conceived ideas of what will happen in the play. As an actor, of course you know what is going to happen. But as a character things must happen to you for the first time. Do not play results.

If you go after causes, results will be unexpected and original. If you go after results, they will be like a "rubber stamp" – always the same. The public is not interested in printed words. They could read the play at home. They want to see words come as a result of what is happening within the actor.

We depend on literary words so much that we forget that we have rich expressive means which should work before the lines come.

We depend on the lines too much, and frequently the lines are cold and intellectual only.

The audience senses it and goes to sleep if the actor plays on the surface of the lines. You have to hold your audience with something under the lines and between the lines. If you act on the surface you can play until the trumpet sounds and you will not be interesting and the audience will sleep.

Each part is a chain of changing moods. *Do not anticipate the end* of the play. Actors have no right to let the audience guess that there is going to be a tragic moment later on. It is a most dangerous thing for actors to play the first act in the mood of the dramatic climax which does not come until the third act. The audience knows what is going to happen then and loses interest and the actors exhaust the mood and the play becomes empty.

In every performance, do not forget the necessity of checking on your surroundings, including living things. Your partner may give much more or much less than he did last night – observe and use this. If your partner is stronger or weaker than usual, you have to respond and adjust. Being a human being, one cannot produce the same moments *every* night. Unless you are really listening to your partner there is no harmony between you. You will be answering as you made up your mind to answer, instead of responding to what your partner gives you, and there will be as many stages as there are people on it. Do not think "should I be this or that?" Give spontaneously. Change yourself through listening to others. If you really listen to the person speaking you may not say a word and yet be most interesting to the public. When your partner does not bring enough strength, intensify your own strength and unconsciously your partner will be lifted. On the other hand, if you are weak and your partner is strong, take strength from him and use it.

Our work is ensemble work. We must work together to create.

All acting is give and take.

Listen, get receipts, then answer. Talk to, rather than at, the other characters.

The connection between you and your partner should be strong that it will be radiated to your audience. That is why the Moscow Art Theater could do plays in Russian for European and American audiences and be understood.

Become curious about what new things your partner will bring to you each night. When there is curiosity there is energy.

Your salvation is to make the other character more important than yourself. Always be more interested in your partner than yourself. Stop acting and thinking about yourself. Notice what your partner is giving you, and respond. Respond and share – and from that connection is born. Otherwise you will react in the same way even to a new partner. That happens only in very bad ham acting. With connection you will no longer be nervous. You should remember how your partner felt, not how you felt.

If your reaction to your partner's sentence is ready before your partner speaks, you do not know how to listen. Learn to listen and you will learn how to answer.

Be preoccupied not with yourself but with the action of the scene. Make your action eventful and purposeful, then it will be alive and flexible. It is dangerous to be literary, to have the action only in your mind. It must be all through you, otherwise you will be unable to adjust and change quickly. Do not use action straight – it never will work. If it is just straight and stretched, it dies. It must be continually fed with imagination and emotion.

In every play, as in life, there is a leading action and counter-action.

Example: "Escape Me Never" by Margaret Kennedy

MADAME: Bob, what is your action in this scene?

B: To get my ballet produced.

MADAME: That is the story, not the action. What do you really want to get?

B: I want to meet Fenella.

MADAME: That is your action. When you have one goal, one big strong action, your play will not fall in pieces. Now Mary, as Gemma, what is your goal, or action?

M: To save myself and my baby and my husband.

MADAME: No, think carefully. What is your goal?

M: My goal is to keep my man.

MADAME: That is your action.

When you approach a character, do a few scenes for yourself about how the character would do several simple things in life. Then the character will be easier for you to understand and do.

In creating the background of a character, do not just write it out – being literary will not help you. Experience it. You must experience the biography of your character in your imagination before it will help you. When you walk on the stage, you must bring the character from the day of his birth to the present. Every play should be a continuation of life. The play takes only bits of lives, but the characters have full lives. Do not drop out of your character at the last line, or before your exit. When the scene is ended, the life of the character goes on. You do not have to remember the background you have created for your character while you are playing the part. Your subconscious mind will take care of that.

Find the key for your character – sometimes it will not be until the end of the play. Sometimes it will be in something another character says about you. Sometimes finding one moment will give you a whole characterization. This takes time and patience.

Find your way to what you feel in your character. For example: I am the character. Father spanked me when I was too old, and now when he comes into the room I resent him.

Absorb all your past, as a character, and then your reactions will come spontaneously, and everything will be there for you to call upon.

If you want to create three characters on sex appeal, and then be forgotten, all right. But if you approach a part with the idea that "I am the character," you can go on creating new characters and never become dull to your audience. Be ninety-nine per cent the character, and one per cent the actor's mind directing from the background.

Stanislavsky said that even a genius can get only once in his lifetime a part which corresponds exactly with him. With other parts he also has to work at the five senses and at characterization.

4   January 1955

(This is the fourth issue containing the "Notes"; the other portions were printed in the magazines of October, November and December, 1954.)

In choosing the essential qualities for your character, choose for *yourself* playing that character. In all characters there is an essential quality which is your own. You do not have to work on that one. But when one of your qualities is wrong for the character, consciously work to get it out. As for those qualities which come very easily to you yourselves, either do not emphasize them at all, or choose a quality which will reduce your natural quality.

Simplify the character as much as you can. The ideal is to find one word that will create the character for you. Do not analyze the essential qualities too much. You will become too intellectual and complicated and you will fail to bring out the really important qualities.

It is one thing to analyze and create the character in your mind, and another to think of yourself as that character. Remember, when you portray a character, you as a personality disappear. Find things foreign to you that are right for the character. Do not use previous characterizations, or personal mannerisms.

Do not follow the line of least resistance. You must take out your every day behavior and posture, and build a person of another background and environment. Find the specific for each part. Even when you play a character who is scatterbrained, you must have accuracy. Precision on the stage is very thrilling; on stage we cannot act "about," "approximately," or "supposed to be."

Just mood and sincerity are not enough. Through contemplation find details. Do not seek details in rehearsal – that is too late. The place and technical things are uppermost then and fine details are gone. Yes, occasionally a bright thought comes in rehearsal, but that is luck, not a usual practice.

Think through your whole being, not just your mind. Then try out your idea for the character. See if it is possible. If it is not, reject it and try again.

Always find specific things, but never imitate a specific person. You may take some things from many people, but you probably will not take them exactly. Be sure it is not imitation. It is dangerous to have only one person in view. Through observation of people you will learn a great deal – walks, manner of expression of emotion, and so forth. But make it the character and divorce it from the person.

Learn to think "in the mind" of the character, and experience his thoughts and feelings. Try to find the bodies of your characters, so that if you had to run to a fire, you would run as your character.

Do not depend on your first impression or first opinion of the character. Where we find the character we can never say – sometimes in the background, sometimes in the last act, sometimes after the play is over. To get sources, constantly return to the play and re-read it.

Never allow yourself as a character to pity yourself as a character unless you are playing an insignificant nobody. The audience is disgusted with self pity. You must have strong characters, not a quarter teaspoon of sugar in a gallon of water.

Remember, there has never been in the universe a person without a heart somewhere in him. Unless you love your character, it will be a caricature. We have to find love, even when the character is laughable. We have to find heart in a grimace. In a villain we have to find heart. We always have to find something in the character a little above everyday life. If you are playing a villain, ask yourself, why did he become a villain? We have to find sympathy for this period of his life. Also, there is always a soft spot in every heart. In a villain, find all the white spots possible, then the black will stand out.

Do not allow the characterization to overpower the human being. First be human, then be the character.

It is a little difficult to explain, but the artist should offer himself to his creation. The character is more important than the artist. Do not just exhibit *yourself*. You must find concentration to allow you to be an artist and present a character. Remember this: Our art is difficult because we are both instrument and artist. Do not become bored perfecting your instrument and learning your "scales." Be ceaseless perfectionists. Apply everything you learn to your twenty-four hour a day lives. Hear the speech of others for your own sakes. Do not criticize them, but check on yourselves.

When you have a part, live it twenty-four hours a day. It must always be in the back of your mind, whether you are buying cigarettes, or making coffee, or having an hilarious time.

Your work in the five senses will aid in your observation of others, and help to make you a very sensitive actor, on and off stage. You will change and adjust quickly and rightly to people and happenings on stage. Right now you are blind. You have to learn to see the world and people.

Observation will help you learn that there are no types. Do not stare at people – just observe them and try to guess their background, temperament and mood. There is not a minute I do not learn. I am supposed to be your teacher, but do you know how much I learn from every one of you?

If you observe, you will remember, though not consciously. Do not take an inventory. If a part comes with that quality, you will remember, though you will not know when or why or where you saw it. It is the method of working that counts not whether your guesses about people are "right."

As an exercise, try for a while to sense how each person feels before you say hello to him.

Never, never, never imitate anyone else's performance – even a genius. The future theater belongs to you. You must do it in your own way.

When you learn a dance, you have to do it accurately and mechanically at first. But even when you learn the steps to the finest detail it will not yet be a dance. Only when it becomes *your own* is it a dance.

Learn to develop fully whatever ideas come.

We must go after the depth of human beings. The whole world has to be nothing except the moment which is living within you.

Do not depend solely on mentality. There is something higher than that. In the play itself, Stanislavsky said, when you have finished a bit and fulfilled it right, then as an artist, for one moment stop to enjoy it – and that moment will inspire you to another bit. You cannot create anything without joy. Use your sense of humor or you will not be creative.

After moments of real creation, when you give a great deal, you will become empty for a little while and feel despair. You will feel you have failed. You will not be satisfied – but the purgatory of struggle has to be loved. With me, I love the process of making the part, but after opening night I am invariably in despair.

When the emptiness is filled, you start to enjoy yourself. You receive a compliment or a good criticism. The second performance you enjoy, but it will be rotten, because you already feel on the clouds and do not do your part intuitively and creatively.

I never leave myself in peace when I am acting. In "Cricket on the Hearth" I had three sentences and was always on the stage. They started to accuse me of playing for the gallery. I said I was not. Finally I asked an actor to come and see the show. It was about the two hundredth performance. He came and said I loved the part so much that something new came each time, and the public reacted each time. The audience finally stopped seeing the story and just watched me. He said, go home and review what you are doing, and only do one third as much, but always different, and always sincere. *Creativeness must always be within the psychology of the scene.*

To be drawn to something is a very powerful impulse. Find one part of your role you are drawn to – and then fulfill it.

Instead of creating a character from within some actors use certain emotions on the surface. They disturb their nerves on the periphery. They can get hysterical but they cannot create. Every character is themselves. They demonstrate everything. Remember, inside you there is a terribly rich thing. Do not take only one or two elements. Stanislavsky used to say if music has only seven notes and composers have never exhausted the combinations, think what human beings can do with ninety-six notes! The actor's tragedy is to get a combination of two or three notes, and be satisfied. Say to yourself, I want to get those ninety-six notes – all those varieties of thoughts and emotions.

Who am I, where am I, what am I doing? Always answer these three questions. Some actors go unconsciously in the line of least resistance, depending on and hoping for inspiration. Inspiration will be your dearest guest when you answer these three questions.

With love, perfection, and beauty, undoubtedly joy will be the result. Do not be afraid to make mistakes; it is the only way to perfect yourself. I want you to start to cultivate this attitude. I am not preaching. I am trying little by little to put you into the mood which we call the creative mood. Without a sense of tingling before you go on stage, you will not get anything but a literary result.

I want you to learn to believe that you can do what you want to do. If you feel tired, concentrate for a couple of minutes, and then face fascinating work toward perfection. In this way we can have energy, health and the creative mood whenever we really want it.

Never be satisfied with yourself. Enjoy your achievement for a moment, and then go on. But do not reopen a wound and irritate it; do not constantly analyze and criticize yourself. To do this is as if you planted a plant, and just as it started to grow you picked it up, studied the roots, and then replanted it. If you continued to do this, the plant would die.

Never try to judge yourself. Sometimes Stanislavsky would come from the stage all excited, saying, "Oh, tonight was good!" And Nemirovitch-Danchenko would come from the theater and say to Stanislavsky,

"What was the matter with you tonight?" So you see the actor cannot always tell.

You have no right to allow yourself to criticize your performance *as you give it* and feel it is low and dull. It is as much a crime as killing a child. Your responsibility is to give your best to the public – the best of which you are capable at the moment. Criticize and weep after the performance, but do not be an individual on stage. It is not your business to criticize yourself as to whether you are doing your part right or wrong. In working on it, establish the place, the other characters, your character, and what your character gives or gets. Let your artistic being establish these things, bring them to life, and get your answer to "did I do it?" from the reaction of your public.

In every play there will be moments when you are dissatisfied. People who are satisfied and allow themselves to float on their laurels are finished. I hope you will always have those moments of despair. It is a good, healthy sign, and you will progress.

How can you sell yourself if you do not trust yourself? Quite a majority of you frighten yourselves. It is a very nice, humble approach. Humbleness is part of real talent. But being just plain scared and hiding in dark corners is wrong.

Stage Energy – If you do not have joy in attacking your problems, you will never conquer them. If you have joy, your emotions will be on a higher level, and your imagination will be more active. Did you ever see a racehorse before a race? That is what an actor should have before a performance. Try to find, individually, what will make you like a horse before a race. Start to get artistic energy, which is the power to cut off the outside, the past – everything. Have even more inner energy than you need, and then condense it. The audience wants to feel that the actor has "more" to offer. You have to come to the stage as actors with good amounts of inner energy. That fire, foundation, and backbone must be developed. The stage should be better than life. If we just photograph life, it is realism for realism's sake, and nobody will be interested. The audience will start to think they know more about it than the actors. Exercise the inner instrument all the time to jump above everyday life. Learn to get into an exciting state of mind and heart. It will make all the difference in the world in your performances for you and for the audience. Even when the actor feels low, a moment of recollection of an exciting moment will bring a different state of being. Sources will also minimize nervousness. Go to your childhood and store a couple of experiences when you were excited and use them before each scene. If, in a theater, you cannot cover the fourth row, you will start to yell and bring out all your mistakes of speech and voice. You have to have enough inner energy to get hold of and keep the audience. For a small room, you have to have the power and hold it back. Unless you find that professional feeling, you will be weak, shrilling, and shrieking – and not understood. For motion pictures, radio and television perhaps you will not have an audience at time of performance. You must train yourselves so that even two stagehands constitute an audience. Your inner feelings must be there one hundred per cent, but they must not be pushed. You do not need to change anything if your art is created rightly – only adjust to the medium.

Sense of Humor – You all need the actor's sense of humor working to heighten your performances beyond the every day normal level. There is a difference between lack of seriousness and sense of humor. The more you do with joy and humor, the more you will bring to your public. Do not be constantly upset about the world. You cannot foresee an earthquake! Take my suggestion, and take the slightest cobweb of an excuse to be gay. As I used to say when I started to speak English: "Be happy and snappy!"

American Repertory Theater